*Culture and
Customs of
Somalia*

The principal cities of Somalia and Somaliland.

Culture and Customs of Somalia

Mohamed Diriye Abdullahi

Culture and Customs of Africa
Toyin Falola, Series Editor

GREENWOOD PRESS
Westport, Connecticut • London

Library of Congress Cataloging-in-Publication Data

Abdullahi, Mohamed Diriye.
    Culture and customs of Somalia / Mohamed Diriye Abdullahi.
        p. cm.—(Culture and customs of Africa, ISSN 1530–8367)
    Includes bibliographical references and index.
    ISBN 0–313–31333–4 (alk. paper)
    1. Ethnology—Somalia.   2. Somalia—Social life and customs.   I. Title.   II. Series.
  GN650.S65 A34   2001
   306'.096773—dc21   2001016169

British Library Cataloguing in Publication Data is available.

Library of Congress Catalog Card Number: 2001016169
ISBN: 0–313–31333–4
ISSN: 1530–8367

First published in 2001

Greenwood Press, 88 Post Road West, Westport, CT 06881
An imprint of Greenwood Publishing Group, Inc.
www.greenwood.com

Printed in the United States of America

∞™

The paper used in this book complies with the
Permanent Paper Standard issued by the National
Information Standards Organization (Z39.48–1984).

10 9 8 7 6 5 4 3 2 1
Every reasonable effort has been made to trace the owners of copyright materials in this book,
but in some instances this has proven impossible. The editor and publisher will be glad to
receive information leading to more complete acknowledgments in subsequent printings of
the book and in the meantime extend their apologies for any omissions.

In memory of my beloved sister Shamis Diriye Abdullahi
and her husband Col. Jama Hussein (Jama Yare)

Contents

Illustrations

Series Foreword

AFRICA is a vast continent, the second largest, after Asia. It is four times the size of the United States, excluding Alaska. It is the cradle of human civilization. A diverse continent, Africa has more than fifty countries with a population of over 700 million people who speak over 1,000 languages. Ecological and cultural differences vary from one region to another. As an old continent, Africa is one of the richest in culture and customs, and its contributions to world civilization are impressive indeed.

Africans regard culture as essential to their lives and future development. Culture embodies their philosophy, worldview, behavior patterns, arts, and institutions. The books in this series intend to capture the comprehensiveness of African culture and customs, dwelling on such important aspects as religion, worldview, literature, media, art, housing, architecture, cuisine, traditional dress, gender, marriage, family, lifestyles, social customs, music, and dance.

The uses and definitions of "culture" vary, reflecting its prestigious association with civilization and social status, its restriction to attitude and behavior, its globalization, and the debates surrounding issues of tradition, modernity, and postmodernity. The participating authors have chosen a comprehensive meaning of culture while not ignoring the alternative uses of the term.

Each volume in the series focuses on a single country, and the format is uniform. The first chapter presents a historical overview, in addition to information on geography, economy, and politics. Each volume then proceeds to examine the various aspects of culture and customs. The series highlights

the mechanisms for the transmission of tradition and culture across generations: the significance of orality, traditions, kinship rites, and family property
distribution; the rise of print culture; and the impact of educational institutions. The series also explores the intersections between local, regional,
national, and global bases for identity and social relations. While the volumes
are organized nationally, they pay attention to ethnicity and language groups
and the links between Africa and the wider world.

The books in the series capture the elements of continuity and change in
culture and customs. Custom is not represented as static or as a museum
artifact, but as a dynamic phenomenon. Furthermore, the authors recognize
the current challenges to traditional wisdom, which include gender relations;
the negotiation of local identities in relation to the state; the significance of
struggles for power at national and local levels and their impact on cultural
traditions and community-based forms of authority; and the tensions between agrarian and industrial/manufacturing/oil-based economic modes of
production.

Africa is a continent of great changes, instigated mainly by Africans but
also through influences from other continents. The rise of youth culture, the
penetration of the global media, and the challenges to generational stability
are some of the components of modern changes explored in the series. The
ways in which traditional (non-Western and nonimitative) African cultural
forms continue to survive and thrive, that is, how they have taken advantage
of the market system to enhance their influence and reproductions also receive attention.

Through the books in this series, readers can see their own cultures in a
different perspective, understand the habits of Africans, and educate themselves about the customs and cultures of other countries and people. The
hope is that the readers will come to respect the cultures of others and see
them not as inferior or superior to theirs, but merely as different. Africa has
always been important to Europe and the United States, essentially as a source
of labor, raw materials, and markets. Blacks are in Europe and the Americas
as part of the African diaspora, a migration that took place primarily due to
the slave trade. Recent African migrants increasingly swell their number and
visibility. It is important to understand the history of the diaspora and the
newer migrants, as well as the roots of the culture and customs of the places
from where they come. It is equally important to understand others in order
to be able to interact successfully in a world that keeps shrinking. The accessible nature of the books in this series will contribute to this understanding
and enhance the quality of human interaction in a new millennium.

Toyin Falola
The University of Texas at Austin

Acknowledgments

I EXPRESS thanks to all the people who helped in one way or the other during the writing of this book. It is simply impossible to list everyone to whom I turned to with a particular question or two; however, I thank especially the poet and playwright Mohamed Ibrahim (Hadrawi) for answering my questions about his works; I thank also engineer Mohamed Hassan for contacting him on my behalf and recording the answers.

In addition, I would like to thank my own mother, Osob Ali Hussein, whom I had not seen for sixteen years, for welcoming me back home, and for helping with the collection of traditional material art such as the wooden spoons and milk vessels whose pictures are presented in this book. Last but not least is my niece, Fowsiya Jama, who helped with collecting material art. Any errors are, of course, mine and, I might add, unintentional.

Chronology

Fourteenth century B.C.	Egyptian expedition to Punt.
Second century B.C.	Judaism arrives in the Horn.
First–seventh centuries A.D.	Axum Empire spanning the Horn of Africa and southern Arabia. Arrival of Christianity in the Horn.
First century A.D.	The unknown Greek author of the *Periplus* gives a description of the coastal towns.
c. A.D. 570	Birth of Prophet Mohamed in Arabia. Defeat of the Axumites, "the Owners of the Elephants" in the Koran. Decline of the Axum Empire. Arrival of Islam.
c. tenth–seventeenth centuries A.D.	Rise of the Ifat sultanate, later known as Adal, with Zeilah, on the northern coast, as main urban center.
c. fourteenth century	Massive Somali migrations to the south.
1331	Ibn Battuta, the famous Arab traveler, visits the port cities of Zeilah in the north and Mogadishu in the south.

1415	Negus Yeshaq, king of the Highland Copts, invades Ifat and kills the Muslim ruler Sa'ad ad-Din. First written record of the word Somali.
1499–1518	Portuguese expeditions attack coastal towns.
1530s	Imam Ahmed Gurey (the left-handed), with his Somali armies, defeats the Copts (Amharas-Tigreans) and unifies the lowland and highland areas (later-day Ethiopia, Somalia, Eritrea, and Djibouti). The Portuguese come to the aid of the Copts.
1800–1870	European travelers scout out the region for colonial occupation. Richard Burton, an Englishman disguised as an Arab, arrives in Zeilah in 1854 and reaches the Muslim city-state of Harar in the interior.
1884	Berlin Conference. Major European powers carve up Africa among themselves.
1896	The battle of Adowa. Menelik, founder of modern Ethiopia, defeats the Italian forces and checks the Italian aspiration to occupy all of the Horn.
1880–1900	Division of Somali-inhabited areas into spheres of British, Italian, French, and Ethiopian Influence.
1900–1920	The "Sword and Fire" years of Mohamed Abdulle Hassan (the Mad Mullah), a Somali from the hinterland. Terrible atrocities committed by the Mad Mullah's forces in the northern hinterland.
1921	Defeat of the forces of the Mad Mullah and the start of a return to normalcy in the northern hinterland.
1930s and 1940s	The Awakening of the "Somali nation" in its modern conception. The start of political and social organizations.
1935	Fascist Italy occupies Ethiopia, creating the Italian East Africa comprising Eritrea, Somalia, and Ethiopia.
1940	Fascist Italy invades British Somaliland putting most Somali-inhabited territories under Italian flag, with the exception of northern Kenya, under the British and Djibouti, held by Vichy France.

1941	The Italians lose the battle of the Horn and their possessions to the British. For the first time in modern history, all Somali lands come under one authority with the exception of Somali areas in Djibouti.
1947	Formation of Somali Youth League (SYL), the major political party that led the South to independence.
1951	Formation of Somali National League (SNL), the major political party that led the North to independence.
1960	June 26: Independence for British Somaliland. July 1: Independence for Italian Somalia. July 1: Somaliland and Somalia amalgamate as the Somali Republic with Mogadishu as capital.
1961	Attempted coup in the North (Somaliland) by young officers fails to take Somaliland out of the union with Somalia.
1964	First war with Ethiopia over the question of frontiers.
1967	Policy of Détente in the Horn. Abdirashid Ali Sharmarke, president, and Mohamed Ibrahim Egal initiate a policy of easing tensions with neighboring Kenya and Ethiopia over the question of their Somali-speaking regions.
1969	October 15: President Sharmarke assassinated. October 21 : military coup without bloodshed launches General Siad Barre's dictatorship.
1971	The writing of the Somali language in the Latin script.
1977	Second War with Ethiopia.
1981	Foundation of the Somali National Movement (SNM) by Isaaq dissidents to fight the regime in the North (Somaliland).
1982	Twenty doctors, businessmen, and civil servants arrested in Hargeisa for daring to organize a self-help scheme to improve the sanitary conditions and services at Hargeisa's major hospital. Students riot and are shot dead by the security forces in Hargeisa.

1982–87	Government terror and popular insurgency intensify in the North.
1988	In May, the forces of the SNM stage major attacks in the North briefly capturing the main towns of Hargeisa and Burao. The regime counter-attacks turning northern towns and villages into rubble and forcing the civilian Isaaq population to flee into neighboring Ethiopia.
1989	The USC (United Somali Congress), representing the Hawiye of the central regions and Mogadishu, was formed and insurgency against the regime moves from countryside into Mogadishu.
1991	January 27: Siad Barre ousted after twenty-one years in power. Members of the USC, Mogadishu section, hastily name Ali Mahdi as president of Somalia but he is rejected by the other movements that fought the regime. Chaos and fighting spread all over the South. May 18: Northern conference delegates abrogate the union with Somalia and declare the restoration of the sovereignty of Somaliland, signaling the end of the Somali Republic.
1992	Terrible famine specially in the south-central region around the city of Baidoa, dubbed "the City of Death." Operation Restore Hope launched by the United States with participants from around the globe, with the aim of securing the delivery of food and aid to the famished populations of southern Somalia.
1993	May: The United Nations takes over the operations of the international intervention in Somalia under the name of UNOSOM (United Nations Somalia Mission). October 3: Fierce fighting between Aydid supporters and the Rangers of the U.S. Army's contingent to UNOSOM leaves eighteen American soldiers and hundreds of Somalis dead.
1995	End of UNOSOM and the international intervention in Somalia. General Aydid captures Baidoa from the Rahanwein and brings an end to their regional administration.

1998	Puntland Regional State of Somalia established in Garoowe under the urging of the members of Majeerteen subclan with the aim of a regional administration in their immediate area.
1999	Second regional administration set up in Baidoa by members of the Rahanwein community after liberating their area from the occupying Aydid militia with help from the Ethiopian army.
2000	President Guelleh of Djibouti sponsors a series of talks between invited personalities, including many high-ranking officials from the Barre regime, leading to a highly contested nomination of yet another president, Abdiqassim Salat Hassan. Mr. Hassan, a former interior minister in the Barre dictatorship, is rejected by all the regional administrations and all the armed factions, including those in Mogadishu.
2001	May 31: Voters in Somaliland overwhelmingly endorse a constitution which states Somaliland is an independent country.

Note on Spelling of Somali Names and Words

The transcription of Somali proper names usually varies between different authors; however, it is not difficult to recognize the persons or places that are being referred to. For example, different authors might write down the same name as Sharmarke or Shermarke. As for Somali words, these are given as they appear in Somali Latin orthography, except in cases where that would distort the approximate pronunciation of the Somali word. In such cases, an anglicized version is given. For example, the pharyngeal-voiced fricative, noted by the letter "c" in the Somali orthography, is marked with a superscript "c"; the pronunciation of this sound can be approximated as an "a" sound with a slight retching sound. The pharyngeal-voiceless fricative, noted by the letter "x" in the Somali orthography, has been replaced by the letter "h"; English speakers might pronounce it, roughly, as the English "h." Additionally, the two letters "dh" represent a sound (a voiced retroflex stop) that might be approximated as the sound "d" in "day"; the letter "q" represents a sound that might be approximated as a "k." Finally, the two letters "kh" represent an uvular sound equivalent to that found in Scottish "loch."

1

Introduction

GEOGRAPHY

IN THE BEGINNING was the land, which has been called many things: Punt, Land of the Barbaroi, Terra Aromatica (Land of Aromatic Plants), Regio Cinnamafore (Land of the Cinnamon), Land of Milk and Myrrh, Land of the Somalis. The northern coasts on the Red Sea and the Gulf of Aden and the adjacent mountains are the ancestral home of the Somalis. This area was known as Punt (The Land of the Gods) to the ancient Egyptians, as the land of the Barbaroi to the Greeks, and as Regio Cinnamafore to the Romans who thought the Somali coasts produced cinnamon.[1]

Later in the nineteenth century, the whole peninsular section of northeast Africa, the projecting region that gave rise to the name of the "Horn of Africa" would be known as the Somali Peninsula. The Somali Republic, formed in 1960 from the former British Somaliland (the North) and the former Italian Somalia (the South), is situated in the Somali Peninsula. It is the Somali Republic, now in disarray, which is popularly known as Somalia.

TOPOGRAPHY

In the northern regions, facing the Gulf of Aden, the topography of the land consists of three zones. These are the coastal *Guban*, the mountainous *Golis*, and the high plateau *Haud*.

The Guban is a low-lying stretch of country about twenty to thirty-five miles in length that is crossed by numerous dry riverbeds, known as *tog*, that become swift torrents when they carry the runoff water of the Golis mountains. It also has ridges and knolls in some places. Its name means "the burnt," in allusion to its desert environment, searing heat, and sandstorms. However, even if it is generally dry and has sand dunes in some places, it has grass and shrubs in other areas, which afford excellent grazing to sheep and goats, especially when it rains.

During the hot season (June–September), Guban temperatures are high during the day and are accompanied by hot winds; traveling on foot is not advised therefore in daytime. The local people move to higher ground when that is possible to the extent that the population of the coastal towns is sometimes at half the usual during that time of the year. In hot weather, the locals say that snakes never come out during the day and hunt only under the rays of the moon.

Traditionally, nomads used to move their stock from the Guban to the slopes of the Golis in a familiar pattern of transhumance. But this is being modified by permanent settlements on higher grounds, leaving less land for transhumance between coast and mountain. The Guban is not just a slice of desert terrain below the mountains; it has the most ancient towns and places of habitation in the entire region. Zeilah, Berbera, Bulahar, and Bosaso are just some of the ancient ports that dot the Guban coastline and that had been visited by sailors, travelers, and merchants as far back as the time of ancient Egypt. Guban beaches, practically unknown to international tourism, are also fabulous, and with their hot sands they are said to cure one of rheumatism in just one day.

As one travels inward from the coastal Guban, the land steeply rises as one scales the mountains. Modern roads follow the caravan routes of old along the mountain passes. Because of the abrupt ascent, the road to the mountains can be at places precipitous. The most spectacular pass is the Sheikh pass, a serpentine route sometimes hewn straight out of the mountain flank. The Sheikh pass lies on the Berbera-Burao tarmac road and proceeds through the mountain town of Sheikh. The northern mountains top at places at altitudes of almost 8,000 feet above sea level. The highest peak is Mount Surat. The width of this zone varies; its widest parts are in the west and far east, and with the center having the shortest width. Borame, Hargeisa, Erigabo, and Sheikh are the only major towns situated in the mountains.

The *Oogo* is a small strip with varying lengths that forms the first southern descent of the mountains and at places the table top of the mountains. However, it is ecologically a part of the mountain region. It means "the top" in Somali.

The Haud plateau is the zone that slowly descends in a north to south direction; it extends from below the city of Hargeisa in the west to as far south as the plains of central Somalia and the Somali region of Ethiopia. Haud is the Somali word meaning "a country of thickets and grassy plains." This zone forms the best rangelands for the pastoralists and supports the largest number of livestock; it is livestock from this region that forms the bulk of Somali livestock exports to Arabian markets on the other side of the sea.

South of the northern regions, the landscape consists of mostly flat plains, as the Ethiopian high plateau slowly smooths to sea level. However, there are outcrops that occasionally break the monotony of the land, such as the Bur Hakabo rock, which resembles the famous Ayers rock of Australia. This zone has Somalia's only two permanent rivers, the Juba and the Shebelle, both rising in the Ethiopian highlands. The Juba reaches the sea near the city of Kismayu, while the Shebelle finishes its course in sand dunes, a few miles away from the Indian Ocean.

CLIMATE

The southern tip of the land of the Somalis straddles the equator. But the Somalis do not live in a lush tropical country but in a dry land where humidity is not a factor except along the southern coastal areas.

In the interior depending on the elevation, day and night temperatures can vary considerably, and the unwary traveler might be exposed to uncomfortably cool nights in the mountains or to cool drafts blowing over the prairies and scrublands. On the higher summits of the Golis, such as where the city of Hargeisa is situated, sometimes rain with hailstones, known as *dhagahyaale* (rain with stones), falls, injuring people and destroying crops such as corn. In July 1999, for example, one such hail storm hit the small town of Arabsiyo to the west of Hargeisa, damaging homes and crops, and leaving in its wake large blocks of ice on the ground that took two days to melt.

Somalis divide the weather into four main seasons: *gu, haggaa, dayr,* and *jiilaal*. Gu and dayr are the wet seasons while haggaa and jiilaal are the dry seasons, although coastal areas might get some light showers during the haggaa, known exactly as *haggaayo* (haggaa rains).

The gu season might be called "the long rains"; it starts in March or April and tapers off in June, and in a good year in July. It is the season that both the land and the people await and pray for; if missed, the consequences are disastrous for both agriculturist and pastoralist, that is for the majority of the population. If the long rains come in plenty, the gray scrublands and yellow prairies become lush green; water is plentiful again for both man and beast; the voice of the frog is heard again and the people rejoice—it is a *barwaaqo* (prosperous year). The word barwaaqo itself is deeply rooted in the ancient culture and religion of the Cushitic people of northeastern Africa, of whom Somalis form part. It is composed of *bar* (raindrop) and *waaqo* (the ancient Cushitic god) whose abode is the sky. The rains are therefore *Waaqo's* raindrops and Somalis wish each other *bashbash iyo barwaaqo* (plenty of prosperity and splashing) from *bashbash*, an onomatopoeia for the sound made while splashing in water, and barwaaqo (god's raindrops). This shows the close relationship between water and human life in a dry country where water graphically equates with life.

The gu rains are usually accompanied by thunderstorms and strong gusts that precede rainfall. During this time unpaved country roads can become unsuitable for motor vehicles, especially in areas where the soil is prone to water-logging such as in riverine regions. The numerous dry rivers also become torrents at this time of year, and, depending on the width of the river, some have a current swift enough to upturn a six-ton vehicle. Large-scale flooding might also occur in riverine areas, especially if it rains a lot in the Ethiopian plateau, which feeds the Somali river systems.

The haggaa (short dry season) runs through July, August, and September. This is the hottest time of the year anywhere. Temperatures can vary from 80°F (43°C) on the southern coastal areas to around 100°F (48°C) along the northern maritime zone. This is the time of the southwest monsoon; it brings slight showers to the southern coastal areas; however, in other areas, it is a dry wind that blows sand. The Guban zone is hot and windy at this time of year, when the *Kharif* wind drives sandstorms during the day that have the strength to loosen the tethers of a tent.

The dayr (short rains) season runs from October through December. The dayr rains are usually heaviest in the immediate vicinity of the Golis mountains. If the dayr rains fall heavily and are widespread, pastoralists look forward to the dry season without apprehension.

The long dry season, jiilaal, runs from around the middle of December to March or April. This is the season that both pastoralists and cultivators fear. It corresponds to the dry winds of the northwest monsoon. However, the sun being away in the Southern Hemisphere, temperatures are not high. In fact, they are at their lowest. This is the cool season in the northern highlands. Everywhere water levels drop dangerously low, and vegetation, except in areas of permanent water, is reduced to a drab gray scenery. The Guban receives light showers knowns as *hays*. If the rains do not come in May or April, the country is said in the grip of an *abaar*, the dreaded drought. Livestock prices are low at this time of year, as the herds become gaunt. People start praying for rain, sometimes holding public praying ceremonies—*roobdoon* (supplication for rain)—especially if the jiilaal seems to persist.

In time, the jiilaal is followed by the long rains again; just before the onset of the rains, there is a short period of intense heat lasting about a month known as *kaliil.* Thus ends the cycle of seasons in the lands of the Somalis.

Rainfall varies from zone to zone. The Guban might be said to receive less than ten inches; generally, the Golis receives the most rain. However, rainfall can differ from year to year; for example, 1998, due to the El Niño weather phenomenon, a warming of the Pacific waters, there were unusually high levels of rainfall and vast areas of the south riverine were flooded. The two rivers, Juba and Shebelle, overflowed their banks and temporarily formed an inland lake where there had been human habitation and fields. Crocodiles, hippopotamuses, and snakes were reported to be vying with humans for the little ground still above water in some places. A year later, 1999 was mostly a drought year with dire consequences in the South, while rain storms inflicted heavy damages to some areas in the Golis in August and October, especially around the northern capital, Hargeisa.

VEGETATION

The land of the Somalis is usually portrayed as a desert. True, there are desert patches with rolling sand dunes and little vegetation. But such places are usually confined to the coastal areas. Inland, the vegetation is that of a dry land but not that of a true desert. The coastal areas have little vegetation, although because of the togs that carry rainwater from higher ground, thickets are sometimes found near the sea. In the lower ranges, and especially at their western and eastern extremities, there is little or no vegetation on the mountains. However, at around 4,000 feet in elevation, the mountains have a good cover of short grasses, acacia woodlands, and flowering aloes. Sometimes the lower banks of mountain togs and gorges have dense thickets of trees, grass, and climbing plants.

On the highest peaks in the central Golis, there is still a remnant of the ancient cedar forests (the cedar of Lebanon); the best standing forest of this type is the one at Daalo mountain, near the town of Erigabo. It is a reserve now. The cedar tree itself is known as *dayib* in Somali.

The mountains, after rains, are a sight not to be missed; everywhere small rivulets and cascades of water are to be seen and all the plants and trees bring forth flowers. The African violet is one of the many small flowering shrubs that dot the higher slopes of the mountains at such times of the year.

The Haud zone has undulating grasses in its plains (*ban*) and clumps of acacia trees in thicket country (*gaaroodi*). This can be said to be savanna or veld country. In the old days, the gaaroodi country used to have a lot of tall acacia trees—so much so that a saying developed: *gaaroodow geel maaragtey*? (oh thicket country, have you seen my camels?), which the Somali say when something is indistinguishable from its surroundings. This saying alludes to the fact that from a distance the legs of grazing camels in gaaroodi country look like tree trunks; it is the equivalent of the English saying "not to see the wood for the trees."

In the areas between the two rivers, *jiq* (thick bush), an impenetrable country of thorn bushes and tall grass is found, in addition to open plains and spaces devoid of vegetation. Clumps of trees and bushes, known as *gosha*, also occur on the banks of the Juba and the Shebelle Rivers, and is especially true of the banks of the Juba. There are also seasonal swamps in the river areas that dry up during periods of prolonged droughts. The gosha country is infested with tsetse flies and other biting insects such as mosquitoes so nomads avoid encampment near rivers. Somalis have known for a long time that mosquitoes carry a feverish disease, a fact that Richard Burton, an English traveler arriving in the land of Somalis in the nineteenth century attributed to a superstition, the link between malaria and the mosquitoes being then unknown in Europe.[2]

No discussion of the vegetation of the Somali peninsula can be complete without a mention of the shrubs that produce frankincense and myrrh, products that brought fame and wealth to the northern coasts of the Somali peninsula for thousands of years. The trees, two species of the boswellia tree (*Boswellia frereanna* and *Boswellia carteri*) and one of the commiphora (*Commiphora myrrha*), grow in the eastern and central mountains of the Golis. The trees also occur, although to a considerably less extent, on the Arabian side of the Gulf of Aden.[3] The aromatic trees grow on high mountain slopes out of the rocky ground. The young trees supply the most valuable gum, while the older ones produce a clear, glutinous fluid that resembles coral varnish.

Frankincense and myrrh were very important and expensive products in the ancient world. They were the perfumes of the ancient civilizations and religions. They also had important medicinal uses, as part of the pharmacology of the ancient peoples; myrrh, especially, had a status of being a panacea for many illnesses. The medicinal values of myrrh are not unfounded, and a recent study showed that Somali myrrh as used in Somali traditional medicine has antibacterial as well as antidiarrheal effects.[4] Today's use is, however, largely limited to making incense, used a lot in the Muslim world, and to manufacturing pastilles.

In the fifteenth century B.C. Queen Hatshepsut of Egypt sent a commercial expedition to Punt to fetch the precious substances. The Greeks and Romans in turn were much interested in getting these resinous products. Herodotus, the Greek author known as the Father of History, states in his *Histories* that frankincense was important in both ancient Egypt as well as in ancient Persia and Assyria. He says that an amount of two and one-half tons was offered every year to Bel, the Babylonian god, on the great altar of Bel's temple in Babylon.[5] He also points out that the frankincense producing region was about two month's journey in a southerly direction from Egypt, an indication that corresponds to the northern Somali coasts. We also learn from Herodotus that incense was called *ledanon* by the Arabians—the Greeks thought all incense came from Arabia—incidentally, that name is still recognizable in Somali as *luubaan,* a generic name for incense.

To obtain incense sap, a deep, longitudinal incision is made in the trunk of the tree with a sharp instrument called a *mangaf.* When the milk-like sap comes out, it is left on the trunk and is exposed to the air for a few days until it hardens into yellowish "tears." The workers return several days later to collect the now clear globules and to make new incisions. The harvest season runs from May to about the middle of the short rains. Working in the hillside aromatic groves is not an easy task, yet laborers usually are without ladders or climbing equipment, thus, accidents that happen on the slopes are often fatal. The groves themselves belong to hereditary owners, members of the clans in the area who pass them from father to son.

THE PEOPLE

The population figures for the Somali Republic have never been uniform. However, a figure of about ten million at the present time is reasonable. Too often, the people have been represented as homogeneous—the ideal nation-state. The central government actively promoted the idea that the Somali Republic was the most homogeneous nation in Africa and one of the few in the world. That view was further spread by scholars both Somali and non-Somali.[6] It is true that Somalia in terms of ethnic or linguistic diversity was far from being like the Congo, the Soviet Union, and even neighboring Ethiopia. However, behind Somalia's shroud of homogeneity are a number of ethnic groups and cultures different from those of the majority Somalis, after whom the country took its name.

The word *Somali* itself today refers to any inhabitant of Somalia; it also refers to any person of ethnic Somali origin in the Horn or elsewhere. But "it seems that the ethnic name Somali has been extended . . . in much the same way as the various inhabitants of the British Isles are known to foreigners as 'English.' "[7] No agreed-upon etymology exists for the word itself. One possible source is the mythical father, Samale, whose supposed descendants form the majority of the population. Other popular unscientific etymologies include *soo maal,* which means "go and milk," heard, as the story says, by some foreigners who were visiting the land. Hence, the people became known by that name. However, the source might as well have been *salama,* which means "became a Muslim," since Somali identity is intertwined with Islam.

The Somalis

The Somalis are a people of a predominantly pastoralist culture, even if their ancient cities have maritime traditions spanning several millennia. The original Somali homeland was along the coasts of the Gulf of Aden and the Red Sea areas; it is there among the hot coasts and the cool mountains that oral history places the ancestral homes of the clans. This is true even for clans such as the Abgal, whose members are found today residing in southern Somalia, around Mogadishu, and in the Benadir hinterland. According to legend, the founder of the Abgal clan, itself a subclan of the larger Hawiye clan, lies buried at Abdal, near the northern port of Berbera. The northern regions therefore hold a significant spiritual and cultural significance for all Somalis.

Somalis speak one language, Somali, and are not confined to Somalia or Somaliland alone but also inhabit parts of Djibouti, Ethiopia, and Kenya. They are culturally homogenous with few variations. However, Somalis divide themselves into numerous clans and clan confederations. The largest clan confederations are the Hawiye, the Darod, the Isaaq, and the Dir. The Isaaq predominate in the northern regions, the Darod, the eastern parts of the north and the central regions, and the Hawiye, parts of the central regions and parts of the Benadir farther south; the Dir are found in the extreme north and in parts of the south.

Clan confederations are historically the result of political groupings, several minor clans banding into a large clan for a pragmatic reason. However, over time, Somali clan historiographies, much like the noble lineages of Europe, have become convoluted, as the genealogies were embellished with saints and noble ancestors. At the same time, the clan became associated with notions of common ancestry, perhaps as a result of Islam; later, the colonial practice of giving salaries to chiefs also helped to institutionalize what was a minimal associative system into a more reified one. The result is that rivalries between the clans, which in the old days used to involve minor vendettas between close neighbors in the countryside, in the fashion of the legendary Hatfields and McCoys of U.S. lore, have become politicized under the hands of political leaders who are jockeying for positions of defending their own interests.

The Sab (Maay, Tunni, Dabare, Garre, and Jiido)

The largest minority in Somalia is the related group of peoples referred to as the Sab, who live in southwestern Somalia in the riverine area. "Strictly, the word 'Somali' does not apply to the Sab, who say themselves that they are 'Sab,' and are so described and distinguished by the 'Somali.' . . . The Sab stand opposed to the Somali."[8] Sometimes the Sab are called the Digil and the Mirifle, after their (political) clan confederations, and sometimes they are simply called the Rahanwein.[9] The Sab are thought to be descended from an admixture of migrating Somalis, Oromo substrate populations who had preceded the arrival of Somalis in the area and pre-Cushitic Bantu villagers, and even more ancient hunter-gatherers of the area. The Oromo, also known in the literature as the Galla, are a group of people who belong, like the Somalis, to the Cushitic-speaking peoples of northeast Africa.[10] They live mostly in neighboring Ethiopia.

The origins of the word Sab are obscure. It has been, however, linked to Sabo, an Oromo clan, the Boran, which contributed strongly to the ancestry of the Sab in Somalia.[11] Linguistically, the Sab groups consist of five linguistico-ethnic groups; the Maay (or Maay-Maay), the largest and dominant group, while the other smaller groups are comprised of the Jiido, the Dabare, the Tunni, and the Garre. It is in the language more than anything else that the Oromo connection is evident among the Sab groups. Their languages lack, just like the Oromo dialects, the sounds from the pharynx, which are characteristic of Somali.

The Maay number about a million while the four other groups are much smaller; perhaps each of the groups Jiido, Dabare, Tunni, and Garre, do not have a population of more than 50,000. Under the traditional clan politics these smaller groups formed a political confederation, the Digil, to counterweight the Maay-speaking clans of the Mirifle confederation. The Sab practice agriculture, especially of the rain-fed type, more than the Somalis proper.

The Benadiri

Benadiri inhabit the southern coastal region of Benadir, which historically corresponds to Mogadishu, and then southward down the coast. The Benadiri were part of the coastal Swahili peoples and city-states that stretched along the East African coast before the Portuguese and later the British modified the commercial relations between the Indian Ocean and Gulf basin countries. Their ethnic origins are eclectic and include coastal Bantus, Persian and Arab immigrants, and without doubt people of Cushitic origin such as Somalis. The Benadiri speak a Somali dialect known as coastal Somali or Benadiri, born out of the situation of contact between Somali and Maay speakers on one hand and Swahili speakers on the other.

The Bantu Groups

The Bantu groups, also known variously as *Wagosha* or as the *Gosha* (the people of marshes) in reference to the location of their villages near the lush river banks, are rather scattered groups in southern Somalia. Their farming communities and villages are strung along the Juba and Shebelle Rivers upward to the sources of these two rivers in Ethiopia. Before the invasion of the nomadic Somali and Oromo, their oral traditions told of a legendary kingdom known as Shungwaya that had control of the riverine areas and the adjacent coastal zones. In some areas, they are known by the name of *Baarfuul* (the palm people) as they are the only people that know how to plant and care for the palm trees in Somalia. Some of them have migrated to urban towns in the Benadir and to other southern towns where they tend to reside in one quarter. Thus in Mogadishu, the Waaberi quarter is associated with them, even if other groups reside in it. In urban centers, they tend to work as carpenters, mechanics, plumbers, electricians, or masons. They speak either the Somali dialect of the Benadiris or the Maay language of the Rahanwein, depending on the location of their community.

Only one small community, Mushunguli, still speaks a Bantu language that is not a Swahili dialect. The Mushunguli are mostly rural folk and tend to be very close-knit and reserved probably because of the language barrier.

The Eyle, the Hunter-Gatherers

In ancient times, hunter-gatherer societies held sway over much of southern Somalia. Things changed when the Bantu peoples migrating northward reached southern Somalia.[12] Later, the Cushitic Oromo and Somali, migrating southward, would overrun everyone else. As a result most of the hunter-gatherer societies disappeared by absorption. Today's little known Eyle are remnants of that bushman population.

Eyle in Somali means "dog owners." The Eyle use dogs in their hunting forays; by contrast, the Somali and Sab nomads neither hunt nor own dogs—they despise hunters and consider dogs as dirty creatures whose contact the Muslim must avoid at any price. Physically, the Eyle have a slightly yellowish complexion and slightly slanted eyes. In the 1960s and 1970s, they inhabited some hunting and farming communities in the plains to the south of Baidoa. However, their communities have been constantly in decline since the 1960s due to assimilation with the Sab and Bantu agricultural communities or through migration to large towns such as Mogadishu where they found employment as butchers. Moreover, the civil war has scattered those few communities they had, and it would be difficult to reconstitute their former settlements.

The Swahili-Speakers

There are two small ethnic groups that still speak Swahili (Bantu) dialects in the Benadir region. These are the Barawani, also known as the Amarani, and the Bajuni. Their origins like those of the Benadiri are from diverse groups such as coastal Bantu, the hunter-gatherer societies of southern Somalia such as the Eyle, and later additions such as Arab, Persian, and Cushitic immigrants. The Barawani live chiefly in the city of Barawe or Brava.

The Bajuni are perhaps the smallest minority, numbering around 10,000 in the 1970s. Some authors have thought they have some resemblances to Indonesians because of their physical features.[13] Instead of an outside factor, however, whatever Asiatic resemblances they may exhibit are probably due to the absorption of large numbers of the bushmanoid hunter-gatherers of the region than anything else. By tradition, they are seafarers and fishers. Their habitat is the tiny Bajuni islands off Kismayu and, on the coast, the town of Kismayu and the villages around it. In recent years, some migrated to Kenya, where they have joined the Bajunis of Kenya in Mombasa and other coastal towns.

HISTORY

Early theories mostly speculated on a view called the Hamitic myth under which the Somalis were characterized, by virtue of not closely corresponding to a standardized image of the African, as being relatively newcomers to Africa whose ancestors crossed over from Asia and mixed with the former inhabitants. This was a view that was based on the nineteenth-century European view of inhabitants of African as a monolithic group; any variation between African groups was then to be explained in terms of external migrations. By the same token, the great Egyptian civilization was to be lopped off from African history and African contributions by virtue of some early Egyptians not corresponding closely to the standardized image of the African. Today serious scholars recognize the wider cultural unity of the peoples of Africa as well as the localized variations in its populations from north to south, all as part of the African mosaic.

One of the more recent theories about Somali history is provided by Herbert Lewis, an anthropologist, and E.R. Turton, a historian.[14] They base their theories solely on the strength of the "theory of migration" postulated by the linguist Isidore Dyen, which might be summarized as: if a certain region has more dialects than another region where similar dialects are spoken then the first region is the original homeland of the group that speaks related dialects.[15] Lewis and Turton, noticing more linguistic variety in southern Somalia, therefore theorized that early ancestors of the Somalis lived around Lake Turkana in northern Kenya and southern Ethiopia where they were supposedly living until well into the beginning of the first millennium.

However, Dyen's theory is not a physical law, and when applied to linguistic diversity in Italy, for example, it would wrongly predict that the Romans originated from the border area between Italy and France, since there is much more linguistic diversity in that zone, and then spread out toward Rome and central Italy, whereas in fact the opposite is true and is known from recorded history. Additionally, as far as linguistic diversity in southern Somalia is concerned, Lewis and Turton were laboring under the assumption that Maay, Jiido, Garre, Tunni, and Dabare are all dialects of the Somali language. In fact, they are not Somali dialects but are separate though related languages, whose main characteristics, moreover, in sound and syntax show them to have much in common with the Oromo language; this is not surprising since it is well known that Oromo speakers were in the southern areas well before the Somalis arrived. Despite such serious limitations, Lewis's and Turton's theories have caught on and have been subsequently well quoted in recent works. As for the relative lack of diversity of the Somali language proper, it is due to the intermingling of pastoralists, to constant trade, to itinerant clergy and their students, and to history, such as epochal times when Somalis had to unify their ranks in the face of Christian groups such as the

Amhara-Tigreans or in the face of the Galla (the Oromo), who had in the old days mostly ancestral faiths.[16]

Even if Herbert Lewis presents no other evidence, except Dyen's theory, itself an intuitive postulation incapable of explaining all forms of linguistic diversity, he affirms, "At the moment we have no written evidence nor oral traditions to support this view, but neither, I submit, have we any evidence seriously to question it."[17] To the contrary, Somali oral history as well as that of related groups such as those of the Oromo and even of the Bantu groups in Kenya provide abundant material about the general direction of Somali movements. The version of southbound migration sketched by another scholar is more accurate in that it is corroborated by both Somali oral history and accounts from early travelers.[18]

The Somalis were still migrating southward in search of greener pastures when the British arrived in Kenya and put a stop to the Somali advance on what became British East Africa. One historian tells us that "the British government in Kenya halted the Somali migrations at the Tana River in 1910, and the point beyond which Somalis could not pass came to be known as the 'Somali line.' "[19] Without that edict, Somalis would have been today probably south of Kilimanjaro and in Tanzania.

Ancient visitors to the Red Sea areas and to the Gulf of Aden systematically give descriptions of peoples whose modes of livelihood, government, culture, and even physical appearance agree with those of coastal Cushites such as Somalis and Afars. Medieval Arabs knew today's Somalis as the Berbers, a name still borne by the port city of Berbera in the north. Medieval Arabs also traded with peoples farther south than Somalis in what became the Swahili city-states, but they knew the inhabitants of these areas as the Zenj. The word Berber is itself related to the older word Barbaroi, which is used in the document *Periplus Maris Erythraie* (The Periplus of the Red Sea), a document written in Greek in the middle of the first century A.D.[20] This document indicates that the Barbaroi, meaning the inhabitants of northern Somali coasts, were trading with the inhabitants of Arabia before Islam; they were also trading with Egypt, then under the Romans. The document then lists some articles of commerce in the land of the Barbaroi such as frankincense; it also gives the names of some of the ports of the Barbaroi such as Avalites, doubtless today's Zeilah.

Other than the fact that the Barbaroi were able sailors and traversed the Red Sea and the Gulf of Aden themselves for commercial purposes, what is more interesting is the comment on their mode of government. The author of the *Periplus* wrote that the Barbaroi were without a central government, with each port city an independent political entity; they were, he wrote, an unruly people. From that description, it is certain that the author was writing about the ancestors of today's Somalis and other coastal Cushites. In fact, the mostly nomadic peoples of northeast Africa have been for most of their history without a king or feudal lord. The Englishman and explorer Richard Burton, arriving some 1,900 years on the same coasts after the *Periplus* was written, found, in 1854, the same organizational mode among the Somalis and described them as "a fierce and turbulent race of republicans."[21]

However, more ancient glimpses of these "republican" inhabitants of the coasts than those recorded by the *Periplus* exist. For example, Herodotus wrote that the Ethiopians, meaning the peoples immediately south of Egypt, on the Red Sea coasts ate a lot of meat and drank a lot of milk; we learn also that they had little esteem for those who ate the fruits of the soil.[22] These cultural traits are still mostly applicable even today to Somalis and their Afar neighbors. In contrast, their cousins, the Oromo, have adopted, for the most part, an agriculture-based mode of life after having mixed with non-Cushite agriculturists in the southwest of today's Ethiopia and in the south of today's Somalia.

However, we can go further than the Greco-Roman times for information about the early inhabitants of the northern coasts. In the fifteenth century B.C. Egyptian Queen Hatshepsut sent a commercial expedition to Punt to get supplies of the precious myrrh and frankincense, so indispensable to their religion.[23] The expedition arrived in what is today's northern coast, where the best frankincense in the world grows not far from the sea. Ancient Egyptians knew the difference between true frankincense and the varieties found much nearer their home in certain parts of the Sudan. After the return of the expedition, the queen had engraved the account of the event on murals at Deir el-Bahri near Luxor in the Valley of the Kings. What can be learned from the history of that voyage is that the Egyptians depicted themselves as arriving in the land of another brotherly people and that, during the course of their stay, they lived in the homes of the Puntites. We also learn from the murals that the people depicted, whether they were Egyptians or Puntites, looked alike, as far as physical appearance, clothing styles, pigmentation, and hairstyles were concerned.[24] We can say those depicted resemble the Cushites such as Somalis still living on the same coasts.

What is more, whether it is by reason of a common linguistic origin or by reason of cultural influence, the Somali language has many terms that have an equivalent term in the religion of ancient Egyptians, which the Lewis–Turton hypotheses would not be able to explain since, according to their theories, Somalis were around Lake Turkana and far away from the

Red Sea and the Gulf of Aden as recently as the dawn of the second millennium. An example of these words is the word *neter* for diverse divinities in Egyptian religion; the Somali equivalent is *nidar*, the righter of wrongs. Somalis say: *Nibar baa ku heli* (The Nidar will find and punish you). The Egyptian word of spirit (*ba*) has the Somali equivalent of *bah* (soul, courage). Somalis say: *bahdii baa laga saaray* (His essence and soul have been taken out from him; he has no more courage). There is also an equivalent for the Egyptian moon diety *ayah* in the Somali *dayah* (moon). Additionally, the *huur* bird (the marabou, a large black stork), the herald of death in Somali mythology, is akin to the Egyptian bird, *Horus*, depicted as the divinity of death.

The facts as we know them, either from historico-cultural sources or from the accounts of ancient, classical, or medieval travelers, tell us that the ancestors of today's Somalis were in fairly stable existence for millennia in their northern homeland, following their herds of sheep and goats back and forth between mountain and coast in a pattern that still continues today.

In the end, increasing population and the need to find pasture for their livestock were the initial causes for the southward migration of Cushites; it might be said the direction of the migration was dictated by the sea barrier in the northern direction. Also, in the case of Somalis, their adoption of Islam incited them to propagate the faith. The mode of migration of Somalis was not a hapzard one, in fact Somali nomads sent exploratory expeditions (*sahan*) before breaking camp so that the *maato* (women and children) as well as *hoolo* (livestock) would not be exposed to danger from lack of water, pasture, or peace. Only when the sahan were back and brought news of desirable pastures would the camp be broken. If therefore, Somalis were in northern Kenya any time before the nineteenth century, then they would have headed straight for the verdant lands of Kenya and Tanzania. It is highly improbable that they would have migrated northward in the direction of drier land.

Briefly the period from 1000 to 1900 witnessed a continual expansion of Somalis from their original coastal homeland downward to Kenya. In the west, Somali expansion was hindered by the Christian kingdoms, which themselves were expanding east, west, and south and constantly jostling with the Somalis, as the proponents of another missionary religion in the region.

As the Somalis advanced from their northern homeland, they clashed with the Oromo who had preceded them in that direction. In the riverine areas of southern Somalia, they found diverse populations consisting of Galla pastoralists and agropastoralists, agricultural Bantu populations who had stayed behind after the Oromo advance, leftovers from still older populations such as the hunter-gatherer Eyle, and, in the coastal areas, the Swahili peoples of the Benadir, all living by then in a fairly stable accommodation long after the Oromo attacks had ceased in the region. By the fourteenth century, the Ajuuraan Somali clan had moved into the riverine areas and had established a hereditary dynasty, thereby controlling the flow of trade between the coastal cities of the Benadir and the southwestern hinterland.[25]

Meanwhile, in the southwestern direction Somalis clashed with the Christian Amhara-Tigreans and the largely pagan Gallas. From the twelfth to the sixteenth centuries wars tinged with religious fervor raged between Muslim Somalis and the Christian Amhara-Tigreans. The period between the tenth and the sixteenth centuries brought the development of important Muslim sultanates such as Ifat, later called Adal, based in the port city of Zeilah. In 1331, Ibn Battuta, the Arab traveler, visited the port cities of Zeilah in the north and Mogadishu in the south.

If the era between the tenth and sixteenth centuries was an era of development for coastal cities and city-states, it was also an era of turbulence and religious antagonisms. Information from the Crusades—the series of wars fought from the late eleventh through the thirteenth centuries, in which European kings and warriors set out to gain control of the land in which Jesus had lived, the Holy Land, from the hands of Muslims—were filtering down to the Horn of Africa and feeding local conflicts between Muslims and Christians. To the Somalis, the crusaders would be known as the Faranji (the Franks), a word which to this day denotes a European.

THE WAR OF 128 YEARS (1415–1543)

The increasing populations and prosperity of Muslim sultanates, especially of Ifat, led to renewed confrontations with the highland Christian Amhara-Tigreans. The history of the most tumultuous confrontations roughly corresponds with the start of the depredations of Negus Yeshaq, king of the Christians, and ends with the death of Imam Ahmed Guray, the leader of the Somalis; that era was a period of rampaging armies and continuous wars between the Christian highlanders and Muslim lowlanders. In 1415, Negus (King) Yeshaq, qualifying the Muslims as "enemies of the Lord," invaded Ifat, defeated the Muslim armies, sacked Zeilah, burnt its mosques, and killed its ruler Sa'ad ad-Din on the island off Zeilah that would ever after bear his name. Yeshaq compelled the Muslims to pay a tribute and had a victory song composed for him in which we find the first written record of the word Somali. But the story would not end there; Sa'ad ad-Din's sons would reorganize Muslim forces and one of his sons, Jamal ad-Din, would chase Yeshaq into the confines of the Blue Nile, burning in revenge Christian churches and cities.[26] However, the war was inconclusive for either group and it would only be in the 1530s when the next major battles would take place.

In the 1530s, the Somalis, who were fragmented in their political organization as they had always been, rallied under the Imam Ahmed Gurey (the left-hand), known as Gragne to the Amhara-Tigreans. He unified the Muslims, obtained some muskets from Turkish sources, which were the most advanced weapons at the time, and conquered the Christian highlands. He practically took possession of their land "save a few hill forts."[27] But the Portuguese—who like other Europeans held the legend of the kingdom of the Prester John, a Christian kingdom, which, if only it could be contacted, would come to the aid of the Christian Europe against the Muslim Turks—came around the Cape of Good Hope in southern Africa, sailed up to the Red Sea, and arrived just in time to shore up the defeated forces of the Christian king. Imam Ahmed Gurey would die from a battle wound received from the Portuguese-Coptic forces, and the Somalis who were yearning to go back to their lowland homes fell back. The history of this turbulent period has been captured in writing by the Somali chronicler of the time, Shihad Ad-Din, in his *Futuh Al-Habash*, which is one of the important documents of the history of the Horn.

The Christian-Muslim wars eased after the middle of the sixteenth century, largely because of the devastation that both groups had wrought upon each other. However, another religio-ethnic group, worshiping mostly an ancestral divinity or the *Waaqo*, the Gallas (Oromos) moved against both Muslim and Christian. Galla depredations of the time were described as a "scourge" that afflicted both the Christian Amhara-Tigreans and the Muslim Somalis. Somalis were pushed back toward the sea on the northern front, with the Galla penetrating sometimes as far as the sea. These far-flung Galla attacks were possible because of the use of the horse, which the Galla had earlier acquired from the Somalis.[28] However, the Somalis would recover from the Galla invasions and the Portuguese attacks on their coastal cities in the mid-seventeenth century to attempt to drive out the Galla from their northern territories and consolidate their southern possessions.

In the south, because of the increasing migrations of Somalis, the area became Somalized and coastal cities such as Mogadishu, Merca, and Barawa, which were traditionally part of the Swahili world, became more and more Somali in dialect and culture. In the interior to the west of the Benadir coastal strip, the populations that remained from the Galla, for all of them had not been pushed out by the southward driving Somalis, and Somali migrants, incorporated into their tribes through the traditional method of adoption of new arrivals, gave rise to the present Digil and Mirifle confederations—the

Sab.[29] Toward the end the nineteenth century, the Somalis crossed the Tana River in what is now northern Kenya.

The Decline of the City-States

As soon as they came into the Indian Ocean and the Red Sea, the Portuguese started harassing the coastal cities. Unable to take the cities by force, they would then content themselves with bombarding them from their ships and making brief sallies for loot; thus in 1499 Mogadishu was bombarded by Vasco Da Gama; in 1507, Barawe (Brava) was sacked by Trista da Cuita; Zeilah was burned in 1517, and Berbera sacked in 1518. By the eighteenth century the glory of the city-states was mostly gone. Both Zeilah in the north and Mogadishu in the south were a pale shadow of themselves; the effect of Portuguese plunder and new trade patterns, set by the arrival of the Europeans in the East and in the Indian Ocean, had caused a downward spiral in growth and trade.

The former glories of Zeilah and Mogadishu have been handed to us by travelers through the centuries. In the sixteenth century (circa 1517–18) Duarte Barbosa, a Portuguese, said of Mogadishu: "It has a king over it, and is a place of great trade in merchandise. Ships come there from the kingdom of Cambay [India] and from Aden with stuffs of all kinds, and with spices. And they carry away from there much gold, ivory, beeswax, and other things upon which they make a profit. In this town there is plenty of meat, wheat, barley, and horses, and much fruit; it is a very rich place."[30]

The Arab traveler Ibn Battuta visited in 1331 both Zeilah and Mogadishu. He described Zeilah as "a large town with an important market," where a lot of fish are landed and many camels slaughtered for meat, evidently to feed a large urban population.[31] After a sea voyage of fifteen days, Ibn Battuta arrived in Mogadishu where he found the inhabitants also slaughtered many camels for meat. He also mentioned that its merchants were wealthy and exported locally manufactured clothing to Egypt and other places.

The decline of Mogadishu was such that the Omanis of Zanzibar started exercising a nominal suzerainty over the Benadir in the nineteenth century. As for Zeilah, when Richard Burton, arriving aboard a Somali sailboat from Aden, visited it in 1854, he found it barely able to assert any control beyond its walls; its governor, Sharmarke Mohamed, nominally tied to the Ottoman Empire, through their Mukha representative, was still dreaming, according to him, despite his advanced age, of carving out a new state by conquering the rebellious Somalis. It was never to be and in 1875, the Egyptians, under the then khedive (viceroy), Ismail Pasha, who was having his own dreams of creating an empire of his own in northeast Africa, occupied, with British encouragement, both Zeilah and Berbera and then went inland to colonize the independent city-state of Harar.

The Egyptians evacuated their Somali possessions in 1885, unable to sustain their occupation financially. Emperor Menelik, the founder of modern Ethiopia, then attacked Harar in 1887, defeated its Muslim inhabitants, and placed Ras Makonen, the father of would-be emperor, Haile Selassie, as governor of Harar. Realizing the significance of his victory over Harar, seat of Iman Ahmed Guray, the conqueror of the Christian highlands in the sixteenth century, Menelik was to declare: "This is not a Muslim country, as everyone knows."[32]

The Partition of the Somali Lands

The last two decades of the nineteenth century were ones of uncertainty for Somalis; Europeans were actively reconnoitering their areas—explorers such as Richard Burton and G. Revoil had visited their lands; rumors of the Faranji (the Franks) coming to Christianize them and to take their lands were rife. Their traditional political and religious rivals, the Amhara-Tigreans, freshly armed by the Europeans, their coreligionists, were venturing out of their mountain redoubts for the first time since the sixteenth century and expanding their control to traditional Muslim areas.

In the end, the Somali populations would be partitioned in the late nineteenth century between three European countries and the Amhara-Tigrean kingdom of Menelik. The three European countries were Great Britain, which got the northern regions; Italy, which got the southern regions; and France, which got a portion of the extreme north, subsequently known as French Somali Coast, and which would become part of the present state of Djibouti.

British interests on the northern Somali coast as well as the Yemeni coast were motivated by their strategic plan for their more valuable colony of India, especially after the opening of the Suez Canal in 1869. Aden in Yemen was to be a coaling station for ships en route to India and a garrison city for the troops guarding it. In turn, the Somali coast was to be the feeder of the troops in mutton, and so it had to be added to the British dominions, in order, as the British Lord Curzon stated, "to safeguard the food supply of Aden, just as the Roman Protectorate was extended over Egypt to safeguard the corn-supply of Rome."[33] Aden, of course, had prior commercial relations with the northern coast before the arrival of the British. But the British sought to strengthen these ties as both their garrison and the population of

Aden were totally dependent on shipments from the northern coasts for meat.[34]

To secure the northern coast from its European competitors, which were scouring the area after the opening of the Suez, Britain signed treaties of protection with the northern clans between 1884 and 1888. This was the beginning of the British Protectorate of Somaliland. However, in the early years, the British presence was a nominal one consisting of political residents in the main ports such as Zeilah, Berbera, and Bulahar whose responsibility was limited to ensuring the flow of maritime shipments. At that time, the protectorate was actually governed through the British colonial government in India. The Indian connection continued for fourteen years after which Britain became more involved in Somaliland due to the war in the Sudan.

The British administration in the north has been characterized as one of indirect administration, since the Somali traditional system of politics was included in the ways the country was run; the *qadi* judicial system as well as the functions of clan chiefs, the *akils*, were recognized and even strengthened. The British rule was not therefore felt in the north as too harsh or too alien. However, the reason for British magnanimity in the north might be dismissed as benign noninvolvement in the affairs of a country that had neither gold mines nor verdant lands suitable for European settlement such as the green lands of East Africa or Southern Africa.

While the British were establishing themselves on the northern coast, modern Ethiopia was taking shape under the guns of the *naftanya* (Menelik's riflemen). The Europeans gave supplies of modern weapons to Menelik, while denying them to the Somalis; more important, Menelik, recognized as a head of a Christian state, could buy weapons from European merchants whereas the Somalis could not.[35] The Somalis saw the whole affair as Christians helping other Christians. Be that as it may, Menelik's hordes, without pay or provisions, were now well armed and raiding Somali pastoralists and expropriating livestock far away from their mountainous country.

With increasing European maneuvers on their shores and Amhara plunder in the rear, Somalis were caught in a spiral over which they had no control. The Europeans stood to profit from the Amhara menace they had created in their quest for protectorate agreements. No doubt the Somalis were utterly confused, bewildered, and powerless. Somali sentiments of the time had been caught admirably well by the poet Farah Nur:

> The British, the Amhara and the Italians are conniving
> The country is snatched, divided by whosoever is strong
> The country is sold without our knowledge!

Somali reactions to these events included both defiance and a call for a *jihad* (struggle) as well as acceptance of European hegemony, and even Amhara hegemony; in 1891, Col. Swayne, a British officer, for example, found members of the Somali Bartire clan acting as "cat's paw" for the Amharas; armed by the Amhara with rifles, they were requisitioning cattle from other Somali clans such as the Habar Awal and the Ogaden for the Amhara garrison at Jigjiga.[36] The Somalis among whom Swayne traveled pleaded with him by saying: "We are not allowed to import firearms, the only effective weapons against the Abyssinians [Amharas]; and we ask the British, who have occupied our ports, either to protect us, or to allow us to import guns with which we can protect ourselves."[37] As a result of Amhara depredations, Swayne found everywhere he traveled Somalis pleading to be placed under British protection; even the riverine cultivators at Imey, now in Ethiopia, of non-Somali origin but of Muslim faith, were pleading to be placed under British protection, and when Swayne did not sign the paper of allegiance, one of the councillors of chief Gabba Oboho cried, "Ah, it is as we feared, you English have sold us to Amhara."[38]

Among those who called for a jihad was notably a man by the name of Mohamed Abdulle Hassan (the Mad Mullah). His appeals got him in the beginning a large number of followers from the Somali clans. However, despite his rhetoric of pushing the invaders to the sea, his massacres of thousands of innocent Somalis, including women and children, and his camel-rustling activities spoke louder than his words, and he was in the end abandoned by the seaward clans. He was still, however, for many years able to keep a band of coerced followers from the more hinterland clans, notably members from his father's clan, the Ogaden, and from his mother's, the Dhulbahante. His activities paralyzed movement and trade in the hinterland and brought his followers head to head with British forces. In fact, the British, who as long as trade kept going had no interest in venturing much into the hinterland, were obliged to mount expeditionary forces far into the interior to capture the sanguinary *mullah*, who by then had acquired a mythical fame of being invincible—legend had it that he had sold his soul to the *'aasho badhi*, a desert lizard believed to be the abode of the devil, in exchange for invincibility.

Mohamed Abdulle Hassan was also a poet of keen finesse and did not spare any words to exhort his followers with poetry while at the time painting his Somali adversaries as "infidels" whose massacre would earn paradise for his followers. His contemporary and fellow poet, Ali Jama Haabiil, engaging him in poetic duel answered him in the now the famous line: *Nimaan mu-umunimo kugu dhaqayn muslinimo khaas ah, gaal maxasta kuu dhowra ood magansataa dhaama* (An infidel who will not hurt your weak and will protect you is better than someone who will not govern in a just and Muslim way). He would be routed in 1921 when the British organized a force among the Somalis who were fed up with his banditry and massacres; but once more the elusive mullah got away to die in exile among the Oromo.

Ironically, instead of defending the Muslim faith, his massacres left so many children orphans that priests from a Catholic mission were picking up roving and dying kids from the desert. By the succor afforded them, they became the first Christian Somalis in several centuries. The Mad Mullah's orphans would give rise to several Christian Somali families, some of whom would become household names; they include the Mariano family of the Habar Jelo Issaq, and the Siyad of the Dhulbahante Darod.

Other British colonial possessions in Somali areas included the most southerly Somali habitation, which became part of British East Africa and later part of Kenya. That territory was labeled NFD (the Northern Frontier District) and placed under a special administration with the aim of checking Somali advances in the area. The British organized a referendum in 1962 to ascertain the wishes of Somalis in that region before Kenya gained its independence; 83 percent of Somalis expressed a wish to join the Somali Republic rather than stay in Kenya. However, higher imperatives of the British, who were threatened with an expulsion of their farmers from an independent Kenya by the leaders of Kenyan independence, meant that the wishes of the Somalis of the NFD were conveniently disregarded.[39] After independence, Kenya renamed the Somali area the Northern Province and fought Somali independence guerrillas for a decade after the departure of the British. Today, NFD, as the Somalis still call it, endures as the least developed of Somali territories, as the containment of Islam and Somalis undertaken by the British has been succeeded by neglect and outright discrimination in independent Kenya.

France and the French Somali Coast

In 1862, France got the port of Obock in Afar country, then it extended its protectorate over a spit of a country inhabited by Somalis on the coast, after Britain cheated it out of the main city and port, Zeilah. This small coastal colony was first mistakenly called French Somali Coast, since, at the time, it contained mostly Afars; but Afars are not Somalis, although they share with the Somalis common ethnic origins and a common religion in Islam, as well as a common history of feuding with the Christian highlanders.

Today, the Republic of Djibouti resulting from that French colonization is about half Somali in population.

Romanente: In the Manner of the Romans

Romanente (in the manner of the Romans) read the milestones on the first main road built by the Italians in their Somali colony. The Italians were latecomers to the game of colony making in Africa, as Italy itself was constituted as an independent entity in 1861, but they invoked ancient Roman glories to inspire them. The Italians went looking for their "place in the sun" (as if the heat of southern Italy was not enough), as was the fashion of the times among European powers. Unlike the British, who in the early years made no tangible attempt at administering the land and whose residents on the coast let the Somalis go about their business without hindrance, the Italians were more aggressive and soon got involved in the local commerce.

These direct contacts increased the number of incidents between the Italians and the local populations. On October 11, 1893, the Italian flag was hoisted in Merca for the first time. A Somali attacked and killed an Italian soldier, who in turn was shot by the Italians.[40] In 1895, an Ethiopian force reached the vicinity of Lugh, increasing Somali suspicions of an Ethiopian takeover of the area. In 1895, the Italians established an outpost at Lugh in the far southwest, under the guise of protecting the Somalis from the ever-expanding Amhara-Tigrean empire of Ethiopia. In 1895, Captain Cecchi, a proponent of Italian assertiveness in the Somali peninsula, set out from the coast, in an attempt to increase Italian influence, toward the interior, but his forces were defeated by the warriors of the Biyomaal clan at a place called Lafole "the place of bones" in the vicinity of Afgoye. The captain, thirteen Italians, and their *askaris* (locally recruited troops) perished.[41] This event set back active Italian penetration for a while in the south.[42] In 1907, two thousand Somalis attacked an Italian regiment at Turunley; the attackers, from the Biyomaal clan, were defeated and sustained high casualties—several hundred died.[43] In 1908, with calls for a forceful occupation mounting, Italian troops were sent to the hinterland. The town of Mererey, which had attracted resistors from the coastal towns, was destroyed and more than seventy fighters of the local Hintire clan perished.[44]

In a more northern direction, the Italians had placed in 1899 a protectorate under the sultan of the Majeerteen clan, and also over Ali Yusuf, warlord, adventurer, and sailor, who had established himself in Obbia; an Italian consul general based in Aden had responsibility over those northern areas.

In 1908, the southern coastal area of the Benadir and the northern Italian protectorates were unified. In the more northern regions, Italian penetration was even more nominal than that of the southern areas, and Italian expeditionary forces had to be sent in several times. However, Somalis were disorganized, unlike the highland Christians who had been united by the strongman tactics of Menelik; therefore, despite their spirited resistance and calls for a jihad, Italian administration was firmly established by 1927 in all regions, with Mogadishu as the capital.

Italian colonial endeavors were also helped by the British, who were afraid of competition from the Germans, whom the British considered more potent contenders. As one Somali said, the British were practicing the Somali proverb that says "give your stick to someone from whom you can repossess."[45] The British facilitated Italian occupation of the central regions. In addition, in 1924, Britain ceded the Jubaland province, in the extreme south, to Italy.

THE RISE OF MODERN SOMALI NATIONALISM

While Somalis had always been aware of being part of one ethnic group unified notably by one language and one religion, historically, they had rallied more on the basis of religious identity rather than nationalist identity. In their brief moments of great cohesion, Somalis had come together as Muslims instead of as Somalis. City-states, sultanates, and independent clans were the normal mode of Somali government since time immemorial. The advent of modern Somali nationalism and its centralist state are therefore a tributary of the nationalist ideals and the concept of the nation-state that started to take shape in nineteenth-century Europe. Somalis had always been seafarers and travelers, and with the opening of the Suez, they were working and traveling in Europe and even as far as Australia. They came back with the feelings of a need for a state for their nation. Colonial experience also, even if it divided up Somali territories, brought together the disorganized clans, sultanates, and city-states under a single administration and indirectly helped foster Somali nationalism.

Some writers start the Somali struggle for nationhood with the so-called Dervish disturbances, instigated by Mohamed Abdulle Hassan (the Mad Mullah). However, Mohamed Abdulle Hassan had no grasp of the wider implications of Somali nationhood in the order of nations; his movement and rhetoric as well as his many bloody battles were parochial in nature and involved large-scale looting of camels, exacerbation of clan antagonism, and massacres of innocent Somalis in unprecedented numbers; in fact, the one other Somali who equals him in wanton destruction and massacres is General

Siad Barre. Mohamed Abdulle Hassan's other endeavors were also about local events such as the competition between *sufi* (religious) orders or expressions of some historical antipathies between Muslims and Christians.

Conscious and thoughtful Somali nationalist movements started in the 1930s in urban settings. No single person can be called the father or mother of Somali nationalism. There certainly had been a number of individuals in the movement, such as Farah Omar (1864–1948), a man who, like Mahatma Gandhi of India, sought change in a peaceful way by writing and petitioning British authorities.[46] The Somali poets and composers who produced a large repertoire of nationalist literature in the 1940s and 1950s had indisputably the largest role in Somali nationalist consciousness.

Early Somali discussions coalesced, as is only natural, into the formation of political and social groups. We witness the first such organizations in the north, where the British colonial regime was politically more tolerant than the fascist Italian regime in the south, which was advocating separation of the races and had no tolerance for the political emancipation movements of the colonized. Somali nationalist sentiments crystallized particularly after the end of World War II, as happened in many nations under colonial regimes. Somalis had fought and died in Africa, Asia, and Europe for the Allies. They had also fought on the losing side with the Italians in Ethiopia. These events brought them even more in contact with the outside world and the other peoples aspiring for liberty from colonialism.

In the north, the Somali National Society was formed in 1935. This organization later evolved into the SNL (Somali National League).[47] This would be the main northern political organization until independence from Britain. In the south, after the defeat of fascist Italy, its colony was placed under British military administration. It was during this period that the SYC (Somali Youth Club) was formed in 1943 under the encouragement of British officers who did not like the powerful pro-Italian lobby in Mogadishu. There was a sizable number of Italians and pro-Italian locals in urban southern centers at that time who were clamoring for a return to an Italian colonial status. The SYC changed its name to SYL (Somali Youth League) in 1947. The SYL dominated southern politics until independence from the Italian trusteeship period and it continued its hegemony after the amalgamation of north and south into the Somali Republic.

While the Somalis had no history of a single central administration, they had territorial contiguity, a widely diffused language, one religion, and of course a single ethnic origin, for the most part. The various minorities in the south were also warm to nationalist aspirations since the word Somali was acquiring wider meaning than the people to whom it referred in the past. The unification of the Somali territories naturally became a burning question—the Somalis wanted one administration over their heads. In particular, the return of Somali-speaking territories such as NFD that went to Kenya and the Somali areas that fell to Menelik's Ethiopian empire were sought in a movement that would be known as "Somali irredentism," which would lead to disputes with both Kenya and Ethiopia. The sentiment of restitution applied also to the French colony of Somaliland, only partially Somali in ethnic composition.

In 1946, British foreign secretary Ernest Bevin pleaded for the unification of all Somali lands under one administration. He was vetoed by the three other members of the Four Power Commission, comprising the victors of World War II (United States, Great Britain, France, and Russia), and charged to decide the future of former Italian possessions in Africa after the war. Russia suspected Britain of expanding its colonial possessions in northeast Africa. The commission traveled to the south in 1948 and had audiences with the populations of the region. The pro-Italian lobby did an intense campaign for thirty years of trusteeship under Italy; however, the commission granted only ten years of trusteeship.

In the north, nationalist sentiments focused on the transfer of the Haud and Reserved Areas in 1954 to Emperor Haile Selassie's Ethiopia. This Somali-inhabited area served as the main grazing land for the clans in British Somaliland. The Somalis of the north felt a sense of immense betrayal and hastened to send the British home. With poets rallying them at every point, northern Somalis went through paroxysms of nationalism that took them to independence and to a hasty amalgamation with their fellow Somalis in the south in 1960. On June 26, 1960, the SNL, the majority party, headed by Mohamed Ibrahim Egal, led British Somaliland to independence. But the resulting State of Somaliland was short-lived; on July 1, it combined with Somalia, on the same day the Italian colony gained its independence. In the British paper, the *Herald*, it was called "The Colony That Rejected Freedom"[48] and the name stuck.

THE FORMATION OF THE SOMALI REPUBLIC

The amalgamation of the north and the south was the result of a nationalist fever in the north; the southerners were not much interested in a union; this was specially true of the southern leadership who were afraid to lose their prominence. The northerners flew to Mogadishu, the southern capital, a few days before the "precipitate union," and were housed in a hotel.[49] The southerners deliberated alone for a day about what their conditions would be for the union with the north. Finally they summoned the northerners in the middle of the night and presented them with a set of options that all started with the word *hal*, a word which means "one" in southern Somali dialect but which meant a "she-camel" in the northern dialect and had to be explained to some of the northern delegates. The southerners rattled off five conditions: "The president is one, and it is going to be ours; the prime minister is one, and it is going to be ours; the capital is one, and it is going to be ours; the currency is one, and it is going to be ours; the flag is one, and it is going to be ours."[50] The southerners thought they had raised the stakes so unpalatably high that the northerners would not be able be to swallow their conditions. But the northerners knowing the nationalist fervor in the north duly accepted the southern proposition.

"The unification effort, however, fell short of the legal requirements mandated by domestic and international law."[51] The new state, the Somali Republic, would have "nothing more than the recognition of other states to testify to the existence of Somalia as a unified state."[52] Despite the union, the new country was functioning in all reality as two countries under one flag: there were two administrative systems, two monetary systems, two customs and taxation systems, two official languages, and two educational systems. With faraway Mogadishu calling the shots and Italian the language of the government, the northern population soon felt a sentiment of "marry in haste and repent in leisure." Within a year, in June 1961, the north voted, in a referendum, against the constitution of the new republic. The main northern party called for a boycott of the referendum; voting did take place but the result was still a negative vote in the north. The south voted overwhelmingly for the constitution. In an effort to declare a massive yes vote, southerners not only reported a yes vote higher than the estimated population for their region but also declared a small village called Wanla Weyn in the vicinity of Mogadishu to have registered a yes vote higher than the 100,000 ballots cast in the entire north![53] This not only gave northerners a new term for southerners—Wanla Weyn—but it also made them suspicious of the political culture of southerners.[54] No other referendum was held for the constitution even if it was not approved by the north.

THE CHAOTIC DEMOCRATIC YEARS

In the first years of the Somali Republic, northerners had no influence on the government and felt politically marginalized. In the newly formed National Army, things were no better; under the Italian Trusteeship administration, the south had only police contingents but no standing army.

However, just before the union, the police officers of the south, themselves products of the semiliterate colonial force, gave themselves, with the full knowledge of their political bosses, generous promotions in rank with the express aim of "outranking" the northerners. In the north, the British had a territorial army of 2,000 men whose junior officers were graduates of distinguished British military academies such as Sandhurst and Mons. These young officers now fell under the command of the old *carabinieri* (police) officers such as Siad Barre. The northern officers were outraged and staged a coup to sever ties with the south. However, the coup, poorly organized, failed as noncommissioned officers did not follow their orders. The officers were arrested but could not be sentenced in a court. The judge decided to acquit them "on the basis that, in the absence of an Act of Union, the court had no jurisdiction over Somaliland."[55] Relations between the north and south continued to simmer.

In May 1962, Egal, the man who took the north into union despite his personal misgivings, allied himself with some southern opposition leaders in a new political formation, the SNC (Somali National Congress). Egal, unlike many of his northern countrymen, understood the workings of southern politics, which were articulated around clan politics and clan balancing mainly between the Hawiye president, Aden Abdulle Osman, and his Majeerteen-Darod prime minister. The challenge was to wrest power from the SYL and its alliance of clans through a more diverse grouping. When the first national postindependence elections were held in 1964, the SNC coalition of northerners and southerners did not win the election, but it narrowed the SYL seats to 54 out of 123; the SNC won 22 seats, the Digil-Mirifle party (the HDMS) won nine seats, and the SDU 15 seats. More than anything else, the election proved that the SYL, the governing party, could be beaten. But instead of preparing for the next elections, Egal shrewdly realized the significance of the American adage: If you cannot beat them, join them. He joined the SYL and was instrumental in getting Abdirashid Ali Sharmarke elected in 1967 as the second president of the Republic by corralling the northern deputies against the incumbent Aden Abdulle Osman, the man who had presented the five conditions of the union to the northerners. As a result, Egal, now in the SYL, was invited by President Sharmarke to form the next government. The Republic had thus its first northern premier.

Gradually, the integration of the two regions improved and northerners felt less alienated in the union mainly for three reasons: (1) the crossed political alliances such as the SNC or Egal's entry into the SYL inner circle; (2) the increasing use of English in the south as a result of the internationalization of that language; and (3) increased commerce between north and south and investments in the south by northern businesspeople who built the highest buildings in Mogadishu.

While fears of north-south breakup evaporated, Somali politics became a game of clan parties, as politicians sought to mobilize members of their clan instead of seeking election solely on a debated platform. Party formation was a front to getting elected, and it did not reflect any ideological convictions or any specific visions. The number of registered parties thus arose phenomenally. The small one-man parties were meant to dissolve as soon as the election was over by joining the SYL. In the last free elections held in the country in 1969, 68 parties and more than 1,000 candidates representing the intricate set of clans and subclans of the Somali clan mosaic contested the elections. The SYL again won the elections, amid sharp accusations of electoral improprieties, through the use of public resources and slush funds.

Inevitably, the general public became disillusioned with the machinations of the politicians, who while electioneering would promise to bring in development projects to their districts but who would be seen soon after catering first to their personal needs. Little surprise then that one politician was dubbed *bad-ma'aaneeye* (he who sweetens the sea), as he was fond of hyperbole while fishing for votes. Perhaps more than ever before, the legislative elections of 1969 were a mess of disorder and irregularities that only widened the gulf between the political class and the ordinary people.

After the election was over and the new parliament duly sworn in, President Sharmarke was assassinated by one of his bodyguards, apparently for a grudge tied to the elections in his own district. This incident added a new unsettling element to the country's already volatile political situation. Suddenly, the highest political office in the country was vacant, and a mad backstage marathon started to fill the new position. There could have been no better political situation for the army brass and its Soviet advisers to hatch a coup d'état.

The history of the plotting that led to the fall of the civilian government has never been written down. One fact that is well known is that Premier Egal had antagonized the commander of the army General Siad Barre by allusions to his inadequate education in military science and wanted him to retire. According to one version of the plot, a junior northern officer Captain Khaawe, with the support of General Barre, side-stepped the higher-ranked but militarily less-educated southern officers and went about organizing the coup in a methodical manner. He did this by recruiting some of his former classmates and fellow officers, such as Ismail Ali Abokar, Mohamed Ali Shire, and Ahmed Suleiman Abdalle.[56] Then Siad Barre and the young officers co-opted a few of the senior officers. The plotters had not given any information as to whom was going to be in their junta council a whole week after the coup.[57] Apparently ardent discussions were going on between the young junior officers and the old guard who had the benefit of better-known names. Thus, on the first press conference, Siad Barre and General Ainanshe, both of the old Italian police force, were present.[58] The young officers saw in Siad Barre a transitional compromise figure, an old rustic of no particular keenness of mind, to be conveniently replaced later on. Unluckily, what the promoters of the coup did not know was that behind the rustic figure of Siad Barre was a mind endowed with enough talent to sow suspicion among strong friends and hatred between brothers.

After the soldiers had staged their coup without any bloodshed, they arrested members of the government and parliament and suspended the parliament and the constitution. Then, taking a leaf from a trend that was common in the Third World, they constituted the SRC (Supreme Revolutionary Council) and started governing by simple decree without consulting anyone except themselves. Barre, the chair of the SRC, was named the president of the Republic, renamed appropriately in the same military-leftist style of the era, the Somali Democratic Republic. Unfortunately, the population tired of the inefficiency and corruption of the civilian regime, and, seduced by the propaganda of the military leaders who promised a new era of justice, discipline, efficiency, and development, poured out into the streets tacitly endorsing the coup.

THE YEARS OF THE DICTATORSHIP AND CIVIL WARS

In the first two years, the military regime had genuine popular support. Basing their speeches on populist socialism and nationalist ideals, the junta leaders exhorted the population to reach self-reliance. Popular slogans such as *Hadal yar iyo hawl badan baa horumar lagu gaadhaa* (Less speech and more work is the way to progress) festooned all public places. The Somali urban elites, schoolteachers, civil servants, and students were caught in the populist movement as the military leaders promised justice and advancement through merit and hard work. On the first day of the anniversary, Somalia was officially declared to be a socialist country; nationalizations of the banks, insurance companies, fuel distribution companies, newspapers, the sugar refinery, and any enterprise of importance were carried out. State companies were set up to import and export items. Unemployed youth were rounded up and organized into agricultural teams known as crash programs to increase food production and decrease urban unemployment. Multiplying egalitarian steps

Typical propaganda poster of the Barre regime.

in a country where egalitarianism was a reality by the near absence of a significant bourgeois or a landed gentry class, the regime, in the fashion of the Paris Commune, declared that from that time on everyone should be addressed as *jaalle* (comrade) without distinction to rank, age, or sex.

The propaganda machinery through the state-owned media (private media being forbidden) was relentless in inculcating upon the people the arrival of a new era and the banishment of corruption, *afmiisharnimo* (rumor-mongering, literally having a serrated mouth), and tribalism. Public ceremonies were held in which effigies of tribalism were burned and then publicly buried. All the while, however, Barre was consolidating power into a clique of his own making; his first scheme was to divide the SRC by winning to his side those who shared clan roots with him. Soon, a joke was circulated that when the effigy of tribalism was buried, Barre sneaked out in the middle of the night, dug out its skeleton, and placed it in his cupboard.

At the same time, repressive measures were put into place: the right of habeas corpus, the freedoms of political association, public expression, and the right to form labor unions and to strike were suspended and made an offense punishable by death in some cases. Advised by the security services from the Soviet bloc countries such as the Soviet Union itself, East Germany, and Romania, a new security service, the National Security Service (NSS) was created. Its followers would show, in the coming years, that they were

the equals of Hitler's Gestapo in sheer brutality and cold-blooded murder—
the very mention of the NSS became enough to make someone break into
a cold sweat. Next, a popular militia, the *Guulwadayaal* (Pioneers of the
Revolution), was created with chapters in almost every village of the country.
The Guulwadayaal, recruited from among the members of the illiterate urban
youth and from common criminals, were trained in rudimentary military
techniques and uniformed in green fatigues, a dress which earned them the
derogatory name of Green Dog, whose utterance was punishable by a harsh
sentence. Their task was to spy on the members of every household and on
ordinary people, freeing the NSS to pursue the more educated enemies of
the regime. One of the common pretexts that the NSS or the Guulwadayaal
used to arrest someone was to state they heard that person utter the word
Af-weyne (big mouth), Barre's sobriquet. This was the childhood nickname
given to him by his fellow camel boys in Shilaabo in eastern Ethiopia where
Barre was born.[59] Farah Galooley, the wit of Mogadishu, a man whose pungent political satire was couched in fables and aphorisms, summed up the
repressive atmosphere in these words: *Ama Af-weyne amaan, ama Afgooye
aad, ama afkaaga hayso* (Either sing Big Mouth's praises, or go to the Afgoye
prison [literally the mouth cutter] or shut your own mouth).

By 1974, barely five years after the coup, Barre had firmly established the
basis of his system, Siadism if it could be called a system.[60] The keystone of
the system was put in place in 1976 by the creation of the SRSP (Somali
Revolutionary Socialist Party). The central members of the SRSP were chosen
in a by-invitation-only meeting attended by members handpicked from the
Guulwadayaal and government-controlled organizations such as the Workers'
Union and various groups previously established by the propaganda office of
the junta for women and youth. The criteria for inclusion into the party
membership was an obedient temperament or blood links to Barre.

The army, on whose strength Barre's power ultimately rested, was given
a special consideration. Officers judged to have a mind of their own and
those not related to the inner circle of Barre's power base were dismissed,
retired, or assassinated. The cadets who applied for admission to the military
academy were henceforth to be from loyal clans, which meant the Marehan,
the president's paternal clan, the Ogaden, his maternal clan, or the Dhulbahante, his son-in-law's clan; the alliance of those clans became known as
MOD. The National Army was restructured in essence as an instrument for
internal oppression; gone was the professionalism of the army whom the
people of Somalia used to be immensely proud of and rely on in moments
of disaster; in its place was a ragtag army headed by hastily trained semi-
illiterate cadets who did not hesitate to destroy whole towns and villages.

Over the years, Barre would create a class of semiliterate apparatchiks who owed their food, homes, and luxury to Barre. His circle of family members and hangers-on had one aim in mind—to stay in power and endure. Nothing was too sacred to profane, no massacre too heinous to ponder to ensure the interests of the "family." The circle that ran the country had become a mafia, a *cosa nostra*. Gone were the ideals and the legacy of *somalinimo* "somalism," bequeathed by the Somali patriots from the colonial era. One by one, Barre and his inner circle cut all the bonds that held Somalis together as a nation: solidarity, compassion, decency, humanity, and sacredness of life and property. In short, the values of the Somali society were turned upside down. The Somali nation-state was in shambles, burnt by the idiosyncracies of a crazed old man and his greedy relatives, who let go only when flames from the burning *aqal* (house) fell on them.

But many who knew Barre from his boyhood and during his stint in the colonial police under the Italians were not that surprised. Barre was not a normal person; he was a psychopath whose mercurial spirit vacillated between raving hatred in one moment and words of praise and reconciliation the next moment. He was said to have witnessed the murder of his own father when he was only ten years old during the turbulent year of 1921, when the clan conflicts instigated by Mohamed Abdulle Hassan were raging across the land (Hassan was also an orphan of clan wars). Barre was reportedly forever after deeply marked by the murder of his father. He became sadistic, and as a member of the fascist colonial police, he had the ear of his Italian commanders. He was subsequently trained in interrogation and intelligence methods as a "special branch" police in the colonial era.[61] As a commander of a police station, he was said to practice torture, especially on nationalist Somalis. He had a particular liking for deriding and intimidating his colleagues, even his most ardent followers. He rewarded the corrupt and the embezzlers; it was publicly said that if a particular minister was not corrupt, he would soon dismiss him for fear that the honest minister would witness against him one day.

It seems that, early in his life, Barre took to heart the lesson that craftiness and guile were more rewarding than honesty and hard work. He was fond of retelling how he "craftily earned" his first promotion in the colonial police and how a "clever man," possibly an allusion to himself, stole another recruit's hat and ended with two hats while the guileless recruit went without one.[62] To the end of his life, he ostensibly thought he could remain the "clever man" and would outsmart everyone else. The personality cult he developed around him was much to his liking; he was called among other eloquent names "the father of the nation," and "the father of knowledge." His portrait

was mandatory in all public and private establishments; every public institution had an illuminated concrete and glass structure in its front yard where
an immense portrait of the *macallinka* (the teacher) was displayed, and this
in a country where most people were poor and without electricity. Instead
of being the redeemer the people were dreaming of in 1969, he became the
monster child born to the woman of the African legend who had incessantly
bothered God for the gift of a son.

In 1977, with Barre's popularity waning, he sent the army into Ethiopia
to lend a hand to the guerrillas of the Somali region in Ethiopia. The Ethiopian army was quickly pushed back. Uniting Somali-speaking territories
had always been popular with Somali masses, and with a victory to show,
Barre improved his popularity overnight. But the victory would be a short-
lived one. The Soviets, who had been the country's ally and major arms-
supplier since the 1960s, switched their friendship to Ethiopia, now ruled
by the Marxist regime of Colonel Mengistu. The Soviets saw Barre's socialism
as a facade for his clan dictatorship; in contrast, they saw in Colonel Mengistu
a younger and more knowledgeable leader, more committed to communism,
than the colonial policeman that Barre was. Additionally, Ethiopia was the
bigger country and, therefore, the bigger catch, and the more so since it was
being stolen from the Western camp. What happened next was a replay of
a scenario right out of the sixteenth century—a foreign ally was coming to
the help of the defeated of the Amhara-Tigreans, now of course ruling a
larger country, Ethiopia, with many nationalities including Somalis. The
Soviets mounted their largest military campaign since World War II and
airlifted a huge arsenal of weapons and thousands of troops, mostly from
Cuba and South Yemen, into Ethiopia. With veteran Soviet generals in the
war room, the operation "was almost over before it started."[63]

In 1988, the Somali army and irregulars returned to Somalia after having
incurred many losses. The Somali state was bankrupt. Additionally, as an
aftershock of the war, thousands of refugees of Somali or Oromo origin,
afraid of ethnic reprisals in Ethiopia, flooded Somalia. Barre's newfound
popularity vanished overnight, and Somalis wanted him to leave. But he
would find a new cold war patron in the name of the United States. For the
United States, this was a time perceived as an expansionist period for the
Soviet influence. With the Shah of Iran overthrown and Soviet troops in
Afghanistan, Washington felt the Soviets were getting too close to the oil
fields of the Middle East. An agreement was therefore reached with Barre
providing his regime with arms and other aid in 1980 in exchange for use
of Somali ports and airports, especially Berbera, the former Soviet naval and

air base in the north. For Barre, this was a godsend; once again, he had pulled an ace out of his sleeve. He felt more confident than ever and saw no compulsion to listen to his internal critics. He brazenly jailed seven members of his regime in 1982, including the popular former foreign minister Omar Arteh. The group included the most senior member of his regime from the north, Vice President Ismail Ali Abokar. The surprise move was designed also as a way of crushing Isaaq critics, whom he felt were becoming more daring in their opposition to him. Among those arrested were two members from his Marehan subclan, which was a Machiavellian maneuver intended to camouflage his objective of crushing the northern Isaaqs who had just set up a guerrilla movement across the border in Ethiopia.[64] Barre was a keen bluffer as a gambler—he had learned European card game techniques in his days as a colonial policeman.[65]

Barre's tactics and methods of rule deeply divided the Somalis. To those who opposed him, no punishment was harsh enough; to those who obeyed and served him, no reward was too high. By 1980, the Somalis were deeply divided; the clan, a minimalist association for pasture and conflict management in the countryside, had under Barre become transformed into social and political identities no different from the classical ethnic identities where language, religion, or physical appearance are the differentiating factors.

The year of 1981 is important in Somali history. It corresponds to the foundation of the Somali National Movement (SNM) by members of the Isaaq clan. For sure, the SNM was not the first front to oppose Barre. The SSDF (Somali Salvation Democratic Front), a front set up by members of the Majeerteen subclan of the Darod, was in operation since 1978. But Barre, by playing his clan cards well, which meant calling for Darod solidarity against the other clan families, lured its fighters back into Somalia and sent them up north to fight the northern Isaaq insurgents who were becoming more and more troublesome. The northern Isaaqs are ethnically no different from the Darods, Barre's clan family, or the Hawiye, the major southern clan family, or any other clan for that matter. However, as the majority population of the north, they had joined the south in 1960. In the early 1960s they were fearful of southern domination; but those fears subsided in the late 1960s as the northerners became more integrated economically with the south. Now a combination of factors, all emanating from Barre's administration, alienated the Isaaq population. First the most important causal factor was political alienation. Northerners, who came from a different political culture than that of the south, where fascist Italian rule had rendered ordinary people to be less questioning of those in power, were less willing to accept Barre's clan rule.

Second, the northerners have historically been more of a trading society than the more hinterland Somalis as participants in the historical trade between sea ports and the Ethiopian highland. Barre's state-run enterprises and bureaucracy crippled their commerce. Third, the northerners were not blind to the fact that they produced the mass of Somalia's wealth in the form of livestock exports and workers' remittances from the Gulf countries but received in return an insignificant amount of government investment—invariably, major socioeconomic projects in the form of factories, hospitals, and institutions of higher learning would go to the south.[66] Schools and roads built by the departing British were deteriorating in the north. The worsening socioeconomic infrastructures led in 1981 to the formation of a self-help group in Hargeisa, the main northern city, by a group of doctors and teachers with the aim of improving conditions in the main hospital. They were tried for insurgency and sentenced to stiff prison sentences. But instead of silencing opposition in the north, schoolchildren held demonstrations and were met with bullets, leading to the death of several schoolchildren.

Fourth, the number of refugees from Ethiopia settled in the north was disproportionate in comparison to those resettled in the south. Nevertheless, the northern population had welcomed the refugees, many of whom were ethnic Somalis, and collected pots and pans for them. What happened next was mind-boggling and objectionable to the northerners: the refugees were recruited into the Somali army and stationed to interrogate and harass the local populations.

Finally Barre's viceroys in the north, first General Ganni and then General Mohamed Said Hersi (alias General Morgan), who were iron-fisted individuals with no compassion for their fellow citizens, used outright killings and exposition of the corpses of presumed guerrillas, who were nothing more than unlucky Isaaq nomads collected from the countryside, as the preferred methods of silencing the population. The two tyrants would both earn the names of "butcher of Hargeisa."

The irony was that ethnic cleansing was a reality in a country that had prided itself, to a xenophobic level, on the homogeneity of its people, and the enemy was now officially the country's northern citizens. But with no changes emanating from the regime, a largely unreported war was fought from 1981 to 1990. The regime's answer to popular challenge in the north would be scorched-earth tactics, and by all means the regime was by now a fascist one. As one British scholar wrote in a most revealing way, "the North began to look and feel like a colony under a foreign military tyranny."[67]

But events took a tragic turn in 1988. In that year, with the army increasingly bogged down with fighting the SNM, Barre made a volte-face and signed a peace agreement with Colonel Mengistu of Ethiopia; the deal suited both dictators, as each saw in it a chance to eliminate insurgency movements: the Northern rebellion for Barre and the Somali, Oromo Eritrean insurgency for Mengistu. Both agreed to cut off assistance to their respective client insurgents. This basically meant stopping assistance in arms and munitions, shutting propaganda broadcasts by rebel radios, and evicting the guerrillas from the safe bases in each other's territory. The Ethiopian groups had few safe bases in Somalia to speak of, so the latter point was aimed at evicting the SNM from their sanctuaries in the Somali region of Ethiopia. Before the unknown, the leaders of the SNM decided to take the initiative and risk all in their home territory instead of being reduced to a toothless tiger in Colonel Mengistu's lap. On May 27, 1988, the SNM seized Burao, the third-largest city in the country, and freed political prisoners including schoolchildren from the main jail. On June 1, they attacked Hargeisa, the northern capital, and captured it except for the airport in its outskirts. The regime was caught completely off guard.

The regime's response was swift and brutal; the plan followed was nothing less than a genocide. Earlier in 1986, Barre's viceroy in the north, General Said Hersi, who was the dictator's bodyguard before he married a presidential daughter, told some nomads at a waterhole, who were not even capable of distinguishing between government soldiers in camouflage from rebels also in camouflage, "if you Isaaqs resist, we will destroy your towns, and you will inherit only ashes." This same man in a policy letter written to his father-in-law, which came to be known as "the letter of death," proposed the foundations for a scorched-earth policy to get rid of "anti-Somali germs."[68] Those morbid words became a reality in the north, as the army directed its fire power against the civilian populations. Jet fighters would take off from Hargeisa airport and drop their deadly cargo a few miles away in downtown Hargeisa. Artillery units positioned on the ridges that surround the city would train their sights on the residential quarters of the city and fire round after round of shells. Then soldiers would go door to door to physically eliminate any remaining residents and to loot homes. In one month, Hargeisa and Burao were reduced to rubble and became ghost towns.

By then any surviving urban Isaaqs had fled across the border into Ethiopia, pursued along the way by fighter-bombers piloted by mercenary South African and ex-Rhodesian pilots paid $2,000 per sortie. About 50,000 to 100,000 were killed in the first two months of the conflict. But this was a war fought in obscurity, the regime not allowing any reporters into the region. Even the Red Cross was denied access to bring food and medicines to the civilian population. The survivors of that attempted genocide claim today that only the bravery of the SNM fighters saved them from an outright annihilation; but in reality, it was more than that. Every man and woman became a fighter with nothing to lose but everything to gain.

These events happened long before the word "ethnic cleansing" gained currency, long before "humanitarian intervention" was thought to override the prerogatives of sovereign states. This tragedy happened at a time when the cold war was still in effect, when a patron superpower would look the other way to keep the privilege of having a regime in its camp, even one that was massacring its own citizens. That is why at the height of the fighting, the United States delivered weapons "of obvious and urgent value to the Barre government, and no one in the United States doubted that they would be used to kill people."[69] The weapons were distributed to Barre's forces in the north.

Toward the end of 1988, the regime's forces, at the cost of total depopulation, recaptured the main towns from the SNM guerrillas; however, the SNM fighters, now no longer fighting a dictator for the sake of a better government in Somalia but a veritable liberation war to retake their homes, farms, towns, and land from a brutal occupying force, retreated to the mountains and to the countryside. This was the beginning of the end for the Barre regime; and the end would have happened sooner were it not for the external aid principally from the United States, Italy, and Saudi Arabia that kept flowing to the regime. Barre thought he had played his cards well and found a solution to the Isaaq problem, but he underestimated the resolve of a people pushed to the wall.

The war in the north was becoming an insatiable juggernaut in human and financial terms for the regime. Batches of fresh young conscripts would be sent up north while their wounded comrades would be brought to the capital. Soon the hospitals of Mogadishu ran out of beds and blood supplies. Inevitably open resistance spread to the south. The southern Somalis, in particular the Hawiye, on whose land Mogadishu lies, joined openly the rebellion in large numbers especially after the setting of the USC (United Somali Congress). Another important blow to the regime came from Colonel Omar Jess's defection to the SNM; later, he would set up his own front, the SPM (Somali Patriotic Movement). Suddenly, Barre's clan alliance centered largely on the Darod clan family, whose inner circle had been dubbed MOD (after the acronym for the subclans of the Darod: the Marehan, the Ogaden, and the Dhulbahante), which was falling apart as Colonel Jess, an Ogaden by his father's side but Isaaq by his mother's side, parted ways with Barre. By the end of 1990, the rebellion was reaching Mogadishu as USC forces approached the red sand dunes that mark Mogadishu's northern periphery. The legend of Barre's decreasing magic map was becoming more and more a reality. According to legend, in the early years of his rule, Barre paused in front of a map of Somalia in one of the rooms of his palace. While he was gazing at the map, the devil spoke to him and said: "Behold, President. This is a magic map; it will grant you any wish you may ask; but after every answer, it will shrink accordingly."[70] Barre's map of authority, after so much ill-use, had by now shrunk so much that he was dubbed the "mayor of Mogadishu."

As the guerrillas of the USC closed on him, Barre adopted the same methods of destruction. Artillery pieces from his hilltop palace-barracks shelled downtown Mogadishu. Civilians were tied together in batches and shot summarily by the members of his feared Red Berets presidential brigade, who were drawn to the man from a small Marehan subclan. To a group of Hawiye elders who asked him to step down, Barre stormed: "When I came to Mogadishu . . . [t]here was one road built by the Italians. If you try to force me to stand down, I will leave the city as I found it. I came to power with a gun; only the gun can make me go."[71]

On January 27, 1991, on a Friday to a Saturday night, the people of Mogadishu, who had been exposed to two months of artillery bombardment from loyalist barracks in the city, gave the final assault to the presidential palace in a popular revolt that eerily looked like the taking of the Bastille by the people of Paris. Before dawn, instead of facing the showdown, Barre fled in a tank. In the end, as his own prophecy would have it, Barre, who came with the gun in front of him, left with the gun in his back.

Unluckily the dawn that came to Mogadishu on January 28, 1991, did not lead to peace. The following day, without consulting either the northern SNM or the southern SPM or even with the central committee of the largely Hawiye USC, Ali Mahdi, a politically hitherto obscure man but reputedly a rich hotelier and a member of the Abgal subclan of the Hawiye, in a pre-emptive move that left the Hawiye insurgency movement utterly divided, self-proclaimed himself president of Somalia. To the northerners, who saw things rather in regional terms, this felt like an insult added to their grievous injury from Barre's depredations. In the USC itself, the main rift happened when General Aidid, who had coordinated the fight against the regime for the USC, felt himself cheated by a man who had been drinking *spremuta* (orange juice in Italian, as it is called in Mogadishu) while he had been fighting in the bushes and in the desert. With each man now drawing support from his own subclan militia and independent marauders lavishly armed with the spoils of the army—the Somali army's main arms depots have always been in and around Mogadishu—the two equally obstinate men crossed swords in 1991 in a bloody urban war that would destroy the remaining infrastructure of Mogadishu.

Meanwhile, the leaders of the northern SNM, taking note of the southern audacity, convened an assembly of the populations of the north, including those that openly fought on the side of the regime. The northern convention was attended by members of all the northern clans including the Gadaboursi, the Issa, the Dhulbahante, and the Warsangali. The assembly, composed of traditional and eminent leaders of northern communities, after having deliberated first in Berbera and then later in Burao, judged that the region was stepping back from the unconstitutional union it had in 1960 with Somalia. Accordingly, the region was declared on May 18, 1991, as an independent state to be known as Somaliland within the confines of the ex-British Protectorate of Somaliland and the State of Somaliland of 1960. Although no country has yet to recognize Somaliland, the existence of its administration has spared it the civil wars that continue to plague the south to this day. Reconstruction, fueled by livestock exports and workers' remittances, has started in the north, creating a boom economy that has attracted migrant workers not only from the south but from Ethiopia, Kenya, and Djibouti as well.

In the south, while the enemy Hawiye brothers, Ali Mahdi and General Aidid, were dueling in Mogadishu, Barre and his loyalist troops were attempting a comeback. When Barre fled Mogadishu, he set up shop, with the remains of his army, at Baidoa, the granary of the south and capital of the Maay. There, "General Morgan," in a manner reminiscent of his genocidal program in the north, hatched a plan for eliminating the Maay and other agricultural peoples from the fertile interriverine area.[72] A top-secret document carrying his signature said implicitly "to pursue a military campaign between the two rivers (Shebelle and Juba) in the south so that it will be safe for our people."[73] However, months before the planned ethnic cleansing was put down on paper, Barre's remnant army was already massacring and raping across the region with the wrath of a defeated army and the rapacity of unpaid soldiers. The Maay and other riverine leaders asked for Aidid's help; the Hawiye general credited with having thrown Barre out of Mogadishu, who, out of his own self-interest and fearing that Siad Barre would fight his way back to Mogadishu as long as he was in Baidoa, joined the fight. The *Economist* noted: "Mr. Aidid's forces were drawn from the Hawiye; Mr. Barre's from the Darod clan. Each side, in the course of advances and retreats across the farmland that feeds Somalia, looted without restraint. This was partly because the armies received no rations. The land they fought across belonged to farming clans that traditionally occupy the lower rungs of Somali society.

They were stripped of their crops and livestock. Today's awful famine is the result."[74]

Most of the actual looting was done by Barre's forces, but Aidid's militia, allies to the weak Rahanwein militia, SDM, contributed to the depletion of resources. In the end, after several pitched battles, Aidid and a coalition of the peasant communities, including the Maay and other riverine groups, chased Barre and his remnant army under Morgan out of the riverine region and into Kenya in April 1992. In October 1992, four months later, Morgan, rearmed by Kenya's Daniel arap Moi, a good friend of Barre's (since the day he was saved from a certain coup by a Kenyan general who happens to belong to the same Somali clan as Barre), was back in the region with a vengeance.[75] Soon he recaptured Bardera, massacred its population, and was on his way to Baidoa when the marines landed at Mogadishu in December 1992, bringing a temporary halt to his advance on Maay lands.

Throughout the fighting, four planting seasons, two per year, were missed in the Baidoa area as the farmers abandoned the villages, which were the first places where Barre's soldiers would forage for food. With underground grain silos, *bakaar*, empty, the young and the old journeyed on foot to Baidoa, which was secure from the attacks of Morgan. The problem was that there was no food in Baidoa; death was waiting for them at the end of the trek. As the dying peasants flooded in, the town became the epicenter of the famine and was dubbed the City of Death by the Western media.

As for Barre himself, after a brief stay in Kenya, he went into exile in Nigeria where he would die in January 1995. There ended the life of a man who had begun it, like most Somalis, as a nomad. His first break from a typical nomad's life came when he enlisted in the Italian colonial police by craftily hiding his birthplace in the Somali region of Ethiopia lest he be disqualified for not being a subject of the Italian colonial regime; he would then rise through the ranks of the colonial police by stoically obeying his superiors even if he had to harass and torture Somalis agitating for freedom. He would be promoted to chief of staff of the Somali army after independence, only to emerge as the strongman of the junta that seized power in 1969. He claimed to be a socialist but was known for his limited understanding of social theories, never having had the benefit of any formal schooling. In Somali history, only one man, who was a model to him, ranks close to him in brutality. That man is Mohamed Abdulle Hassan, known as the Mad Mullah. Both were orphans at an early age and were thus exposed to a harsh reality in their formative years—it is known Barre had witnessed his father's assassination by a fellow clansman. Both had a gift for rhetoric, Barre in prose and Mohamed Abdulle Hassan in both prose and poetry. Both were short in stature, obese, and had raspy voices. Both were short-tempered but otherwise, both had pleasing personas that could be taken for sincerity. Both cultivated personality cults: Barre dubbed himself *macalinka* (the teacher) and *aabaha aqoonta* (the father of knowledge); Hassan had his followers and anyone else address him only as *sayidka* (the master) in a land of "fierce republicans" where no one was a subject or a master. Incidentally, both stuck around in power, although Hassan's was only above his followers and cowered subclans in the far hinterland, for twenty-one years after which both were defeated and chose to turn tail instead of fighting to the bitter end. Both died in exile far from Somali inhabited areas.

Barre spent a lot of money glorifying Mohamed Abdulle Hassan, the Mad Mullah; he commissioned an expensive towering equestrian statue set on a marble pedestal as a tribute to him, while a campaign of revisionist history was launched to wash away the Mad Mullah's massacres. School manuals were written to teach that Hassan was a "hero of Somali nationalism" while Barre was the "father of the revolution." Perhaps one day, some deranged dictator would also restore Barre's image as another "hero of Somali nationalism." One thing is sure: Barre will always figure prominently in Somali history. "History is no more than the portrayal of crimes and misfortunes,"[76] at least in large measure. Within living memory, Barre compares only to Pol Pot of Cambodia or to Hitler in sheer madness and desolation visited upon a people. Somalis have already called him "Black Hitler" and no more fitting epitaph can be found.

By 1992, as a result of the fighting between Barre loyalist forces and those led by Aidid, the famine in the southwestern region between the rivers populated by Maay-speaking groups and other minority groups reached a climax and was viewed around the world. The emaciated faces of the interriverine peasants shown on Western television screens prompted humanitarian nongovernmental organizations and media crews to pour into southern Somalia. A change occurred at the UN, which under Perez de Cuellar, a man with little interest in Africa, had been largely indifferent to the plight of Somalis. The Egyptian Boutros Boutros-Ghali became the first African to head the world body; with his characteristic but undiplomatic candor, he accused the West of preoccupying itself solely with "the rich man's war" in the Balkans to the detriment of other troubled spots in the world. Suddenly, Somalia, was on the agenda in every Western capital and numerous parliamentarians and celebrities went to visit.

By the end of 1992 the famine in the southwest region had been largely contained by efforts of nongovernmental organizations both Somali and foreign; however, U.S. President Bush, then a departing president, offered to send the marines to Somalia under the auspices of the UN, initially with the objective of securing ports, airports, and highways to allow smooth deliveries of food to the famine victims. Earlier, on April 24, 1992, the Bush administration had opposed the idea of sending 500 armed UN troops to Somalia at a cost of $20 million, "arguing that Congress would not support another costly peacekeeping mission in an election [year]."[77] President Bush's sudden change of mind came, therefore, as a surprise to Somalia watchers and many motives had been advanced for his sudden decision; but on the whole it seems that American foreign policy, which has always fluctuated between isolationism and interventionism, was particularly conducive to interventionism at that moment, as a result of the Gulf War victory against Iraq.

On December 3, 1992, the UN Security Council unanimously adopted resolution 794(1992), welcoming the United States's offer to lead humanitarian intervention in Somalia and authorized, under Chapter VII of the Charter, the use of "all necessary means." Some Somalis had misgivings about the idea of sending foreign troops to Somalia, especially given the haste in which the operation was launched.[78] However, in general Somalis were about evenly divided on the issue.

The U.S.-led operation was code-named "Restore Hope." The marines landed on the beaches of Mogadishu on the cool night of December 9. They were welcomed by hordes of journalists and television crews in what was the first televised marine landing of all time, the warring factions of Mogadishu having decided in advance not to oppose them.

The international forces were militarily well equipped, but the politicians who sent them had not given much thought to the possible problems ahead. Were the factions going to be disarmed? Was an international tribunal going to be set up, as in the case of the former Yugoslavia? How were the revolt leaders and Barre's men, like Morgan, the butcher of Hargeisa, or Barre himself going to be dealt with by the UN forces? If the aim of the operation was the delivery of food to the famine-stricken southwestern region, why not create a "secure zone" in that area as suggested by Frederic Cuny, a consultant to the U.S. Agency for International Development?[79] How were the international forces going to react to the deaths of their soldiers? Answers to these questions probably were not explored beforehand. In short, the simplicity with which the operation started was worthy of the adventures of Tintin, the French cartoon character.

Unfortunately, this was not a cartoon expedition to Africa and mistakes borne out of expediency soon piled up. In the belief that Somalis obey only a superior force, the international troops were told to "shoot first, and talk later." "Somalis admire military strength and power. Ill-timed diplomatic gestures can be interpreted as a sign of weakness," the marine booklet instructed.[80] The guide book, on the other hand, glossed over in a half sentence how Washington and Moscow, armed to the tune of hundreds of millions of dollars, propped up the abominable Barre regime in the pursuit of their cold war objectives, frustrated Somalia's democratic forces, and helped create the conditions that led to the armed insurgency.[81]

The supporters of Aidid of the USC and his ally, Jess, became suspicious of the actions of Unitaf (Unified Task Force), as the operation was renamed later, soon after the forces of Morgan took Kismayu with the tacit approval of Unitaf, shortly after Jess's own forces had been ordered out of the town by a Unitaf commander. Demonstrations were held with banners stating "This is not [Operation] Restore Hope, this is Restore Morgan."[82] That the operation could be referred to as "Operation Restore Morgan" even in jest should have been a serious cause for concern to the international community—Gen. Morgan, as Barre's right-hand man and as his viceroy in the north, is second only to Barre for having led Somalia into the very violence from which the world was trying to rescue it. Suspicions of unfair conduct were also aroused by the uncoordinated disarmament efforts that happened to target the forces of the Aidid-Jess alliance in Mogadishu and in Kismayu.

On the other hand, some progress was made in the first few months to reconcile the factions of Aidid and Ali Mahdi in Mogadishu through the good offices of Ambassador Robert Oakley, the U.S. representative in Mogadishu, and the "green line" dividing the city was erased. The situation, however, deteriorated after the command of the operation, now officially a UN operation under the name of UNOSOM (United Nations Somalia Mission), was passed, in May 1993, to Admiral Jonathan Howe, a U.S. retired navy general, who had practically no experience in Somali politics or any civilian diplomacy at all.

With the supporters of Aidid already suspicious of the true objectives of the mission and feeling targeted, the shots that would set the whole mission on the slippery path of war with Aidid's faction were fired on June 5, 1993. On that day Howe sent a group of Pakistani soldiers to Radio Mogadishu, which the mission had accused of spewing anti-UN propaganda. Word soon spread that the Pakistanis had come to shut down the radio. Officially, the UN would claim that it had dispatched its troops to inspect a nearby arms cache. A crowd of Somalis gathered informally from all around to watch the operation. Tensions were running high. No one knows who fired the first shot but shooting started. One version of the events says that the Pakistanis fired the first shots and killed some Somalis, which only infuriated the Somalis and encouraged them to take on the Pakistanis before and after the inspection.[83] In the ensuing battle between Somali irregulars and the Pakistani troops, the Pakistanis sustained twenty-four deaths; but the Somalis being just armed civilians sustained a far greater amount of fatal casualties. The whole event was just an accident; it had not been planned in advance, as some claimed in the rush to condemn Aidid. If it were General Aidid would have sent his veteran fighters and the deaths among the lightly armed UN troops would have been much higher. However, on June 6, less than twenty-four hours later, the Security Council hurriedly passed resolution 837 putting the blame squarely on the Aidid camp, without even so much as starting an investigation.[84] A military solution was to be privileged in Somalia and the Somali gnat was to be stricken with a sledgehammer.[85]

On June 11, the UN forces launched a coordinated attack on what was perceived to be Aidid targets. Shells and missiles fired from Cobra helicopter gunships hit densely populated areas. Radio Mogadishu, housing a hallowed site of Somali culture, the audio-visual tape library, was destroyed. Many Somalis died. The war was now officially on between the UN and the Aidid camp—the UN had just become another faction in the Somali civil war, albeit a better armed one. The hunt for Aidid was officially launched and Howe, whom the nickname-loving Somalis soon dubbed "Animal Howe," added a Wild West dimension to the manhunt when he threw in a bounty worth $25,000 and had "wanted" posters plastered all over Mogadishu.

The Pakistani soldiers would get their chance to have another encounter with the Somalis; on June 13, 1993, they simply fired volley after volley into an unarmed crowd of protesters consisting mostly of women and children. The Pakistani commander, Brigadier General Ikram ul-Hassan, would claim that his troops were provoked by shots fired at their bunkered positions, but Paul Watson, a reporter from the *Toronto Sun*, who certainly was not a Somali, and who happened to be in the unarmed crowd of demonstrators, gave an eyewitness report of a Pakistani contingent simply avenging their fallen comrades from June 5.[86] It was clear that the UN forces were not acting in coordination at all but rather that each contingent was acting independently in many ways and sometimes engaging in vengeful shootings with Somalis.

Unluckily, more bloody operations would follow; one of the worst, called a massacre by the Vatican paper, the *Catholic Register*, happened on July 12 when U.S.-UN forces, acting on mistaken information, showered missile and cannon rounds from Cobra helicopters on a meeting of elders, religious men, and intellectuals in a "conference center."[87] The death toll among conferees, who ironically were trying to come up with ways to reduce tensions with the UN, was high with 100 dead.[88] Aidid was not even at the conference center.

By that time, Howe had alienated all of the people he needed to help him work with the Somalis; earlier, the Italians had to recall their ambassador, the only Western ambassador who had stayed in Mogadishu since the downfall of Barre, to "avoid a head-on confrontation with Admiral Howe."[89] Howe next hounded the Italian commander, General Bruno Loi, out of Somalia, accusing him of complicity and leniency toward the Somalis.[90] Loi's mistake seems to have been walking among Somali crowds, microphone in hand, while Howe was staying longer and longer in his bunker, which was said to remind him of his submarine headquarters.

It seemed the Italian call for moderation was forcefully put down by Howe and U.S. officials, who were pursuing "Rambo" policies and had no patience for the Italian "Machiavellian" diplomatic approach.[91] Howe also won support for his "hardline approach" from the UN Secretary General Boutros-Ghali,[92] who had an "animus against Aidid" and was equally obsessed with his capture.[93] The secretary general had suffered humiliation at the hands of Aidid supporters on January 3, 1993, the day when his historic visit, capping his activities in favor of Somalia, was rudely disrupted by Aidid supporters, who threw stones at his car.[94]

The French defense minister Alain Juppé reminded Howe that several French soldiers had been killed in the Balkans, but that they were willing to implement a peace agreement.[95] Howe seemed to have no ears for calls for moderation; he was said to be obsessed with Aidid and to have adopted him as his "great white whale."[96] Howe was a key man in the capture of Noriega in Panama and might have thought that he was in familiar terrain again.[97]

However, Somalia was more akin to Afghanistan or to Vietnam in terms of locals with fighting experience or tenacious guerrillas than the Panama enclave, historically under close U.S. guard. Nothing, in the end, succeeded in swaying Howe's hardline approach in Mogadishu. Yet warnings of an impending crisis were abundant. As early as July 1993, *Newsweek* had written, "The mess in Mogadishu is the result of a team effort at mismanagement that would be comical if lives weren't at stake."[98] Two journalists called for a change of approach and head of mission at about the same time, in an article aptly titled "Talk, Don't Shoot in Somalia," writing: "The only way to restore UN credibility is to drop Howe's militaristic approach. A trusted outsider must be appointed to restart political and disarmament talks."[99]

Neither the manhunt for Aidid nor the punitive measures that brought death to so many civilians and more damage to a battered city eased until the final fatal encounter of October 3, 1993, when a terrible firefight erupted between a group of American soldiers dispatched to grab the elusive Aidid and Somali militiamen. Among the resulting casualties on the American side were 18 dead and 70 wounded. The Somali casualties, mostly civilians as the battle happened in an urban setting, were in the hundreds—the estimates vary from 500 to 3,000 dead. The sad events have been explored by a Philadelphia *Inquirer* reporter in "Blackhawk Down: An American War Story."[100] It tells a story of young soldiers, unsure of what to do, who, being shot at, blasted away in turn every living target in sight including men, women, children, and animals.

Four days later, President Clinton announced that he was ordering U.S. troops out of Somalia by March 31, 1994. With the pullout of American forces, who were the linchpin of the international intervention, the UN operation collapsed. The U.S. forces pulled out in March 1994 after their worst losses in battle since Vietnam. The rest of the UN peacekeepers left in 1995. The final death toll on the UN side was 135 dead, with several hundred wounded.[101] The Somali casualties were much higher at around 6,000 killed.[102]

After the departure of UN forces, it was thought that fighting would erupt all over again; but that did not happen, although sporadic fighting had been reported, major flare-ups of violence have not happened. But still no central government has been formed. For the moment, the old Somali state does not exist anymore; in its place are two lands corresponding to the old colonial borders. One, the north, calls itself Somaliland and is a de facto state with a government, a parliament, a constitution, a fledgling economy, and two newly opened universities. Its people, who created their own peace without international help and started reconstruction on their own, resent being routinely lumped together with Somalia by the UN and other international organizations. The Southern Somalia still has no peace nor governance and is fragmented into several faction-held territories.

The UN has held several conferences with the aim of helping the Somalis to set up a government; at the same time, several countries such as Ethiopia, Kenya, Djibouti, and Egypt have also held conferences with that objective. So far nothing has come of all those endeavors. The main reason is that the conferences were trying to set up a government without having closure on the past; in short, Somalis were being asked to make peace among themselves without justice for war crimes. Heinous atrocities had taken place in Somalia and Somalis needed some kind of a healing act to bury the past. In particular, Somalis needed a war crimes tribunal like the one set up for Yugoslavia or Rwanda and even a "Nuremberg." It did not happen. In the absence of peace with justice, another centuries-honored alternative of the Horn, time, a greater healer but a slow one, has been left to take care of wounds. With enough time, the rancor of war has always disappeared among Somalis, and this time, it seems the process might even be faster due to a new breed of Somalis—businesspeople.

Unfettered by bureaucracy and guided only by the bottom line, Somali businesspeople are cutting across all communal divides; they have set tele-communications, fishing, trading, and transport companies including the largest private airline companies in the Horn of Africa. They have introduced wireless telephone and the Internet to Somalis. Lured by the new prospects, the Somalis in the diaspora have in return started drifting back, often to invest and prosper. Therein lies the Somali hope and perhaps the only thing Somalis need from others the most is to be left to themselves. Over millennia, Somalis have endured and adapted; they will surely overcome their present disorganization.

NOTES

1. However, it appears northern Somali ports were only half-way depots for much of the cinnamon that found its way to the Roman world and to Europe; no cinnamon has been known to grow off Somali coasts, unlike frankincense and myrrh, which are indigenous to the region. See Lionel Casson (1989). *The Periplus Maris Erythraie.* Princeton: Princeton University Press.

2. Richard Burton (1987, 1856). *First Footsteps in East Africa.* New York: Dover Publications, 17.

3. Thomas J. Abercrombie, "Arabia's Frankincense Trail," *National Geographic,* 168, no. 4 (October 1985): 474–513.

4. Per Claeson, "Pharmacognostic Studies on Scented Myrrh with Emphasis on the Biological Activities of the Isolated Sesquiterpene T-cadinol." Fildr Degree Dissertation: Uppsala Universitet (Sweden), 1990.

5. Aubrey De Sélincourt (1972). *Herodotus: The Histories.* London: Penguin Books, 114.

6. Samatar and Laitin compare, for example, the "homogeneity" of Somalis with the "plethora of tribes" in other African countries. Said S. Samatar and David Laitin (1987). *Somalia: A Nation in Search of a State.* Boulder, Colo.: Westview Press, 21.

7. I.M. Lewis (1961). *Pastoral Democracy.* London: Oxford University Press, 12.

8. I.M. Lewis (1955). *The Peoples of the Horn of Africa: Somali, Afar and Saho.* London: International African Institute.

9. Some writers spell Sab as Saab, to avoid, it is said, confusion with Sab, a word which refers to low-caste groups among Somalis.

10. The Cushitic languages are a group of languages spoken in the Horn of Africa; as part of the Afroasiatic superfamily of languages, they are related to ancient

Egyptian, Semitic languages (Arabic, Amharic, etc.), Chadic languages (Hausa, etc.), and Berber group of languages.

11. Cerruli, cited by Lewis. See I.M. Lewis (1955), 32.

12. George Peter Murdock (1959). *Africa: Its Peoples and Their Culture History.* New York: McGraw-Hill, 302.

13. I.M. Lewis (1955), 42.

14. Herbert S. Lewis (1966). "The Origins of the Galla and Somali." *Journal of African History* 7, no. 1: 27–46. E.R. Turton (1975). "Bantu, Galla and Somali Migrations in the Horn of Africa: A Reassessment of the Jubba/Tana Area." *Journal of African History* 16: 519–37.

15. Isidore Dyen (1956). "Language Distribution and Migration Theories." *Language* 32, no. 4: 611–26.

16. B.W. Andrzejewski (1971). "The Role of Broadcasting in the Adaptation of the Somali Language to Modern Needs," in Whiteley, W.H., ed., *Language Use and Social Change: Problems of Multilingualism with Special Reference to Eastern Africa.* London: Oxford University Press for International African Institute, 263–73.

17. Herbert S. Lewis (1966), 41.

18. I.M. Lewis (1960). "The Somali Conquest of the Horn of Africa." *Journal of African History* 1, no. 2: 213–29.

19. Margaret Castagno (1975). *Historical Dictionary of Somalia.* Metuchen, N.J.: Scarecrow Press.

20. Casson (1989), 7.

21. Burton (1987), 122.

22. De Sélincourt (1972), 212.

23. A. Hersi (1977). *The Arab Factor in Somali History.* Unpublished dissertation, University of Los Angeles.

24. Ibid., 52.

25. Castagno (1975), 103–4.

26. M.R. Basset, trans. (1897). *Histoire de la conquête de l'Abyssinie (XVI siècle) par Chihab Eddin Ahmad Ben 'Abd El Qader.* Paris: Ernest Leroux.

27. R.W. Whiteway, trans. and ed. (1902). *The Portuguese Expedition to Abyssinia in 1541–1543 as Narrated by Castanhaso with Some Contemporary Letters; the Short Account of Bermudes, and Certain Extracts from Correa.* London: The Hakluyt Society.

28. Hersi (1977), 229.

29. I.M. Lewis (1955), 46.

30. Cited by Hersi (1977), 196.

31. G.S.P. Freeman-Grenville (1962). *The East African Coast: Select Documents from the First to the Earlier Nineteenth Century.* Oxford: Clarendon Press.

32. Samatar and Laitin (1987), 12.

33. Lord Curzon (1907). *Frontiers.* Oxford: Oxford University Press, 41.

34. Dileef Patwardhan (1981). "Imperialism by Proxy: Aden and Somaliland." *Indica* 18, no. 2: 105–120.

35. Samatar and Laitin (1987), 52.

36. H.G.C. Swayne (1895). *Seventeen Trips through Somaliland.* London, Rowland Ward, Ltd.

37. Ibid., 121.

38. Ibid., 226–27.

39. Conversation with a former Somali diplomat, Ismail Mohamed Diriye. Montreal, 1999.

40. Lee V. Cassanelli (1982). *The Shaping of Somali Society: Reconstructing the History of a Pastoral People, 1600–1900.* Philadelphia: Pennsylvania University Press, 202.

41. Touval (1963), 45.

42. Cassanelli (1982), 204.

43. Ibid., 227.

44. Ibid., 202.

45. Conversation with a former Somali diplomat, Ismail Mohamed Diriye, Montreal, 1999.

46. Castagno (1975), 71.

47. Ibid., 147.

48. Victor Anant (1960). "The Colony that Rejected Freedom," *The Herald,* (London) June 29.

49. Touval (1963), 110.

50. Farah Hersi, October 25, 1999. Somaliland Forum (somaliland@yoyo.cc. monash.edu.au). No records of course exist, as written documents in several areas of Somali history do not exist; but according to Farah Hersi that is what Colonel Musse Rabile Goud, a northerner who was present at that midnight meeting, said was exchanged between the two parties. In particular, the colonel was the one who asked the head of the northern delegation, Egal, what the word *hal* meant.

51. Anthony J. Carroll and B. Rajagopal (1993). "The Case for the Independent Statehood of Somaliland." *Journal of International Law and Politics* 8, no. 653.

52. Ibid.

53. Touval (1963), 121.

54. M. Hussein Adam (1994). "Formation and Recognition of New States: Somaliland in Contrast to Eritrea." *Review of African Political Economy* 59, 21–38.

55. Carroll and Rajagopal (1993), 14.

56. Ali K. Galaydh (1990). "Notes on the State of the Somali State." *Horn of Africa Journal* 11, no. 1 and 2: 1–28.

57. *Jeune Afrique* no. 462, (November 5, 1969).

58. Ibid.

59. Richard Greenfield (1991). "Siad's Sad Legacy," *Africa Report* (March–April).

60. See I.M. Lewis (1994).

61. Galaydh (1990), 24.

62. Jama M. Ghalib (1994). *The Cost of Dictatorship: The Somali Experience.* New York: Lilian Barber Press.

63. "The Ogaden Debacle" (1978). *Newsweek* (March 20).

64. Samatar and Laitin (1987), 157.

65. He was reported to be playing cards even after his ouster to while away his boredom in the Gedo region.

66. See Hannah Lawrence (1989). "Somalia's Troubled North," *African Business* (January), 9–10.

67. I.M. Lewis (1990), 58.

68. R. Greenfield (1987). "Somalia's Letter of Death," *New African* (July), 14.

69. Colin Campbell (1988). "Libya, Mercenaries Aiding U.S.-Supported Somalia," *The Atlanta Journal-Constitution* (October 6).

70. Serge Michel (1990). "La somalie en peu de chagrin," *Le journal de Genève* (May 15), 2.

71. Richard Greenfield (1991). "Siad's Sad Legacy," *Africa Report* (March–April), 13–18.

72. Richard Greenfield (1992). "Siyad's Plan to Seize Power Frustrated," *New African* (June), 18.

73. "Secret Document Reveals Siad Barre Aides' Tactical Plan to Retake Somalia" (1992). *The Estimate* 9, no. 7 (March 27–April 9).

74. "Somalia: A New Shadow" (1992). *The Economist* (October 17), 52.

75. Jane Perlez (1992). "A Somali Place that Even the Alms Givers Fear," *New York Times* (November 9) 3.

76. Voltaire, *L'Ingénu.*

77. "If Sarajevo, Why Not Somalia?" (1992). *The Globe and Mail* (July 22), A18.

78. Hassan Hirave (1992). "No One Invited U.N. Troops to Somalia," *Toronto Star* (November 27), 31.

79. Leslie H. Gelb (1992). "Shoot to Feed Somalia," *New York Times* (November 19), 27.

80. "Somalia: Hopeful Handbook" (1993). *Africa Confidential* 34, no. 8 (April 16), 8.

81. Ibid.

82. Geoffrey York (1993). "Coalition Hits Somali Faction," *Globe and Mail* (January 26) A9.

83. Robert M. Press (1993). "UN Calls Off Manhunt for Aideed in Somalia," *Christian Science Monitor* (November 18), 6.

84. Richard Greenfield (1994). "Somalis on Their Own Terms," *Africa Report* (May–June), 23.

85. For example, General Mackenzie, the former UN commander in Bosnia, stated: "Unlike Bosnia, Somalia is a relatively easy military problem to deal with. They (UN) have to make the point . . . and this is the place to make it." Andrew Bilski and Hilary Mackenzie (1993). "On The Attack," *Maclean's* (Toronto) (June 28), 19.

86. Paul Watson (1993). "Reporter Watches Troops Even Score Against Unarmed Civilians," *Ottawa Citizen* (June 14), A7.

87. "Somalia: Hope Denied" (1993). *Africa Confidential* 34, no. 14 (July 16).

88. Ibid.

89. Francis Kennedy (1993). "Rambo versus Machiavelli in Africa," *Globe and Mail,* (July 23), A15.

90. Donatella Lorch (1993). "Disunity Hampering U.N. Somalia Effort," *New York Times* (July 12), A8.

91. Kennedy, "Rambo versus Machiavelli," A15.

92. "Somalia: If You Are Not Part of the Solution . . . " (1993). *Africa Confidential* 34, no. 19. (September 24), 1.

93. Elaine Sciolino (1993). "UN Chief Warns U.S. Against Troop Pullout From Somalia," *New York Times* (October 1), A8.

94. Allison Mitchel (1993). "Angry Crowds of Somalis Disrupt Visit to Mogadishu by U.N. Chief," *New York Times* (January 4), A1.

95. Elaine Sciolino (1993). "Pentagon After Goals in Somalia Failure," *New York Times* (September 28), A17.

96. Michael R. Gordon and John H. Cushman Jr. (1993). "U.S. Supported Hunt for Aidid; Now Calls U.N. Policy Skewed," *New York Times* (October 18), A1.

97. Patrick Cockburn (1993). "Somalia: U.S. Lashes Out at UN's Envoy," *Ottawa Citizen* (October 8), A6.

98. "The Pitfalls of Peacekeeping" (1993). *Newsweek* (July 26), 32.

99. Karl Maier and Richard Dowden (1993). "Talk, Don't Shoot in Somalia," *Ottawa Citizen* (July 13), A8.

100. Mark Bowden (1997). "Blackhawk Down: An American War Story," *Philadelphia Inquirer* (Nov.–Dec.).

101. Robert M. Press (1995). "Retreat from Somalia," *Christian Science Monitor* (February 27), 9.

102. Ankomah Baffour (1994). "A Great Wrong," *New African* (May): 8–9.

SUGGESTED READING

Africa Watch. 1990. *Somalia: A Government at War with Its Own People.* New York: Africa Watch.

Carroll, Anthony J. and B. Rajagopal. 1993. "The Case for the Independent Statehood of Somaliland." *Journal of International Law & Politics* 8, no. 653.

Cassanelli, Lee V. 1982. *The Shaping of Somali Society: Reconstructing the History of a Pastoral People, 1600–1900.* Philadelphia: University of Pennsylvania Press.

Castagno, Margaret. 1975. *Historical Dictionary of Somalia.* Metuchen, N.J.: Scarecrow Press.

Hersi, A. 1977. "The Arab Factor in Somali History." Doctoral dissertation, University of Los Angeles.

Jimale Ali, Ahmed, ed. 1995. *The Invention of Somalia.* Lawrenceville, N.J.: Red Sea Press.

Lewis, I.M. 1955. *The Peoples of the Horn of Africa: Somali, Afar and Saho.* London: International African Institute.

———. 1960. "The Somali Conquest of the Horn of Africa." *Journal of African History* 1, no. 2:213–229.

———. 1961. *Pastoral Democracy: A Study of Pastoralism Among the Northern Somali of the Horn of Africa.* London: Oxford University Press.

———. 1994. *Blood and Bone: The Call of Kinship in Somali Society.* Lawrenceville, N.J.: Red Sea Press.

Samatar, Said S., and David Laitin. 1987. *Somalia: A Nation in Search of a State.* Boulder, Colo.: Westview Press.

Touval, S. 1963. *Somali Nationalism.* Cambridge, Mass: Harvard University Press.

2

Religion and Thought

TODAY'S SOMALIS are 100 percent Muslims. The word Islam means "submission to God" and the word Muslim means "one who submitted to the Supremacy of Allah." For Somalis, as for Muslims the world over, Mohamed is the Messenger of Allah (*rasuul*) and the Prophet of Islam (*Nabi*). Early in their history, Muslims split into two camps over a question of leadership succession: Sunni and Shia. The Sunni believed Muslims should elect their rulers, while the Shia believed that successions should follow along the lines of descent from the prophet's family. Sunni means "the beaten path" and refers to following the examples and sayings of the prophet, while Shia came from *Shiat Ali* (the party of Ali, i.e., the supporters of Ali, the prophet's cousin). Somalis belong to the Sunni branch of Islam, to which the vast majority of the world's Muslims belong. The Shia branch of Islam has few adherents among Somalis. Additionally, Somalis adhere to the Shafi'i school of Islamic jurisprudence. Therefore, Somalis can be said to adhere to the Sunni Shafi'ite denomination of Islam, although among Muslims denominations are not as closely segregated as in Christianity, for lack of theological differences. Followers of other religions among Somalis are numerically insignificant, much less than 1 percent. These usually consist of the members of a few families whose grandparents were brought up by Catholic missions as orphans.

No exact date can be set for the arrival of Islam among Somalis. But given the nearness of Arabia and the constant travel between Arabia and the Horn, Islam came early among the Somalis—that is probably soon after the start of the Muslim calender, the Hejira, in the first century of Islam, which corresponds to the year 622 of the Christian calendar now in common use around the world.[1] Islam was by no means the first religion to have reached the Somali shores from the Middle East. Judaism and Christianity earlier had penetrated the Horn and were being practiced. However, by the tenth century, Islam had sufficiently diffused to many coastal communities and many more in the interior as to warrant the attention of the practitioners of other faiths, mainly Christianity.

Likewise, no single proselytizer is credited with being the first to bring Islam to the Somalis. However, among the early Somali holy men of Islam the name of Sheikh Yusuf al-Kownin stands out for having made a significant contribution to the spread of Islam. The *sheikh* (priest) was given the name of al-Kownin (he of the two worlds). He is popularly known as Aw-Barkhadle (the Blessed Father). According to a well-known legend, al-Kownin rid the country of Mohamed Hanif, a chief priest of a pre-Islamic cult. Mohamed Hanif is said to have challenged the Muslim priest to equal his own magical powers and to add action to his words he entered the flank of a mountain and came out from another flank twice. Al-Kownin asked him to repeat his feat a third time, and this time, while Mohamed Hanif was still inside the mountain, he prayed to Allah that his opponent may never emerge from the mountain; thereupon the mountain closed upon Mohamed Hanif, and thus the old cult was forsaken in favor of Islam. Mohamed Hanif's clan, the Yibir clan, then demanded blood money from Yusuf al-Kownin and the good priest asked them what kind of compensation they would like to receive. Thereupon the Yibir asked that they be given a gift (*samayo*) at the birth of every male infant. Al-Kownin granted them their wish, and even today, even though the practice is dying, at the birth of a son, a member of the Yibir clan is supposed to come to the door and collect the gift due to his clan.

From that legend, we learn that al-Kownin was a very active proselytizer who probably irked the priests of the older cult. However, today he is remembered for another of his feats, which is the invention of a unique method of teaching the complex Arabic alphabet to Somalis. His method, virtually unaltered even after several centuries, is still in use today. It can be described as a kind of vulgarizer system that uses Somali words in a mnemonic way to help young Somalis master the Arabic alphabet and its diacritics. After having learned al-Kownin's method of vulgarization, a Somali is able to easily read the Koran or any Arabic text with diacritics.

The Somali practice of Islam is in substance the same as that of other Muslims around the world. The main tenets of Islam, *arkan* (pillars in Arabic) are five: Belief in the oneness (monotheism) of Allah, and belief in Mohamed, as the *rasuul* (messenger); Saying a prayer five times a day; Fasting in the month of *Ramadan*; The offering of *zakat* (alms); The *Haj* or the pilgrimage to Mecca when possible.

These tenets and the rituals related to them are taught to young children as soon as possible and are part of the socialization process that imparts values and customs to young minds. Only a small number of Somalis learn about Islam in a formal catechistic method. To be sure, there are religious schools known as *mal'aamad* or *dugsi* (Koranic schools), but these usually have a vocation of training young would-be *wadaads* (priests), although today they also function for urban populations as a kind of preschool or kindergarten, helping children memorize the Koran, but more importantly the discipline of handwriting and learning in a formal setting. In a *mal'aamad*, children learn to write the characters of the Arabic alphabet on wooden slates that are usually taller and wider than the children themselves; after mastering the alphabet, the youngsters go on to learn how to read and recite the Koran in Arabic. Arabic is the only liturgical language among Muslims (all rituals are said in Arabic and the Koran is in Arabic); while translations of the Koran exist, they do not supplant the original in Arabic. Learning to read and write in Arabic is therefore essential for Somalis, as it is for other Muslims.

The beliefs and practices of Somalis as Muslims have their basis, as elsewhere, in the Koran (the Muslim scripture), as revealed to Prophet Mohamed, the *Hadith* (Prophet Mohamed's sayings and actions), and the *Sharia*, a body of jurisprudence commonly referred to as "Islamic law." However, spirituality and holiness among Somalis is not just following the five tenets, the Koran, the Hadith, and the Sharia. The spiritual life of Somalis is rather a complex amalgamation that includes many elements that are carryovers from indigenous practices that predate Islam; it also includes elements from Islamic mysticism and philosophy, commonly known as *sufism*.

These tiers of spiritual practices coexist in such a way that the whole is harmonious and yet complex. For example, a Somali will go to the mosque and pray as is formally required. Then in the evening he or she might belong to a *sufi* brotherhood where group meditation and the recital of litanies of saints such as that of Sheikh Abdulqadir Al-Jilani are performed, usually with the accompaniment of a drum. Yet in another evening, we will find the devout Muslim offering *du'o* (sacrifice and incantations) to his or her ancestors in a ceremony of psalms and incantations presided over by the local *wadaad* (priest). Islamic mysticism and the veneration of saints and ancestors are therefore as much a part of Somali spirituality as the strict orthodoxy of Islam enshrined in the Koran, the Hadith, and the Sharia.

This system of spiritual tiers is not, of course, peculiar to Somalis as localized versions of it exist in almost every Muslim society. However, worship is offered strictly to Allah; what Somalis ask from saints and ancestors are *barako* (blessings). For someone who is not familiar with this system of spirituality, it might be difficult to understand the difference between ritual worship and submission to Allah during a prayer and supplication of saints and ancestors. There are two major differences. The first is that in a ritual prayer a Muslim submits to Allah and states that there is but one Allah; he or she therefore recognizes the supremacy of Allah. The second major difference is the assumption that when one asks for the blessings of a saint or ancestor one is still addressing one's requests to Allah, the saint or ancestor being considered as merely a conduit. Were it not so, one would be liable to a charge of *shirka* (idolatry). This does not mean that there are no purists who abhor these parallel practices, for they have always existed. In consequence, there has always been an ideological opposition between traditionalists (i.e., those *ulema* [clergy] who tolerate the complex system of spirituality), and purists, who at times call the traditionalists heretics and soothsayers.

THE WADAAD: RITUAL EXPERT, STELLAR CONSULTANT, AND PHYSICIAN

In Islam there is no organized clergy with a hierarchy—there is neither pope nor bishop and no intermediaries are supposed to mediate between the Creator and the created. All Muslims are therefore supposed to be participants in all practices and if necessary to be capable of leading the prayers. However, in practice, among Somalis as among other Muslims, certain people are more knowledgeable in religious matters and rituals than the rest of the population; among Somalis these people are usually referred to as wadaad or sheikh.

The wadaad is an expert, not clergy, as is understood in Western church organizations. The wadaad, always a male, starts first as an *arday* (student or wadaad in training) and through a process of training under well-known experts accumulates considerable knowledge in the Koran and Islamic jurisprudence. Later, if he is very widely acknowledged for his learning and wisdom, people may refer to him as *ʿaalin* (scholar). Still, he is not part of an organization that pays him a salary nor does he need a diploma to obtain this position; rather he is an individual professional in much the same way the local shoemaker is a professional in the community. However, while the shoemaker makes and sells shoes, the wadaad meets all the services required of him for free and people decide themselves what they may offer him in kind or cash. Many wadaads exercise regular self-employment in other areas and in some villages the wadaad doubles as the shoemaker of the village.

Nevertheless, wadaad is a profession and an institution among Somalis in a class of its own.

The profession, despite the lack of a hierarchy, has developed certain norms and strategies for declaring its presence in the society. In the countryside, the wadaad is recognizable usually by the items he carries, including most notably a copy of the Koran, carried in a cloth bag and slung over the shoulder, a *masale* (prayer rug), traditionally of fine leather, an ablution jar, *weyso*, a rosary, *tusbah*, and some paper for writing. Itinerant wadaads often carry additional books with them and a number of personal items; they usually travel from community to community preaching and teaching. Sometimes a wadaad and his students travel together as a kind of traveling college, preaching and teaching along the way. At other times, a group of senior students, called *her*, travel around communities practicing and perfecting their knowledge. The itinerant wadaad or the her carry no food supplies of their own, they depend entirely on the charity of the rural communities and families they encounter. Because of the sanctity that surrounds them, people receive them well and they were traditionally not subject to hostilities between clans and communities on account of their holiness; in fact, a family usually butchers the fattest ram in the herd for a visiting wadaad or the her. Exempt from vengeful animosities and vendettas, they could thus travel unmolested across the vast stretches of the Somali territories helping reinforce cultural and linguistic ties among Somalis.

In towns where large mosques are to be found, a wadaad is usually appointed as the caretaker of the mosque and is usually given a stipend either by the benefactors of the mosque or the government. People refer to such caretakers as *imam*, although anyone leading a prayer anywhere can be called an imam; the same word also refers to a charismatic religious political leader among Muslims. Also in the cities, some wadaads are appointed by local governments to enforce family law, such as marriages, divorces, and inheritances. These are called *qadis* (judges); they receive a salary from the justice department, a practice that started when they were formally incorporated into the justice system by the colonial administrations. Traditionally in the city-states and sultanates, a qadi was the chief justice officer and adviser on religious matters to the ruler.

In the countryside, the local wadaad is a very important person; he not only performs the rites of passage (births, marriages, and funerals), but also mediates in disputes if asked by the parties concerned. However, unlike a qadi, who is a justice officer, he cannot enforce his decisions to be binding upon the contestants. Elders might also seek his advice when they are deliberating on questions of communal importance.

It is important to note that a wadaad's expertise is not confined to the religious domain. The wadaad was historically the keeper of science and knowledge, imparted only to those who went through a long apprenticeship. The wadaad therefore performs important functions, which the profession probably inherited from a pre-Islamic cult.

In the past, stellar consultation was much more in use and probably regulated all forms of rituals such as marriages; today, however, it is a declining practice and few wadaads practice it. As a stellar expert, the wadaad consults the Somali stellar and solar calendar as well as the Muslim lunar calendar and accordingly gives advice on propitious moments to break camp and migrate or to start the livestock breeding season. By no means is the wadaad the sole stellar expert; there are others who are by profession stellar and weather experts known as *hiddigo-eege* (star gazer or astronomer).

Although, divination (*faal*), is strictly not in the field of practice of wadaads, some wadaads, true perhaps to the roots of the profession in pre-Islamic cults, do some divination through a body of written works in Arabic or through the reading of geometric designs. Other parareligious services provided in the countryside include the *arba'uun*, a kind of protective spell recited for a lost camel. The spell is supposed to protect the camel from wild animals and from thieves until its master finds it. The owner of the camel usually promises a gift to the wadaad in the event that the camel is found alive.

As a traditional medicine expert, the wadaad is a herbalist and a bonesetter; by no means is he the exclusive expert in this field as there are expert bonesetters and traditional medicine experts who have established their reputation without being a wadaad. Additionally, obstetrics and treatments of infant diseases were and still are in the countryside the domain of female practitioners known as the *umuliso* (midwives). On the other hand, traditionally many wadaads were physicians and surgeons, especially before the arrival of modern Westernized medicine. Traditional medicine drew upon a body of knowledge dating back thousands of years; some elements of that knowledge were local in origin and handed down by word of mouth, while some of it was gained from Islamic written sources.

The wadaad used, and still does in rural areas, rational medicine when examining for symptoms and prescribing cures; he also used and still uses a large measure of pyschotherapy by means of blessings and amulets, the latter as a kind of palliative in cases where his physical medicine is of no avail. Amulets contain some Koranic verses and are worn around the neck or waist. The blessings of renowned wadaads are especially sought after, and people suffering from infertility and chronic illnesses often constitute the main beneficiaries of psychotherapy from the wadaad.

While the blessings of a wadaad are sought, his displeasure and curse are to be avoided. The curse of a holy person is thought to be capable of causing damnation and all kinds of afflictions on the offender; especially feared is the *asmo*, a severe curse. The holiness that surrounds a person of religion starts as early as the *arday* (student) stage. Somalis, for example, say that if the thorn of an acacia tree grabs the cloth of the arday, the impious tree will in due time wither and die. It might be said that the wadaads, deprived of any temporal power, which is the domain of the *waranle* (the warrior), exercise spiritual power by virtue of their holiness.

TARIQA AND SUFISM

Islamic mystic philosophy, *sufism*, rose in the ninth and tenth centuries as a way of elevating the soul by following the correct path (*tariqa* in Arabic). Elevation of the soul is sought through forms of asceticism and ritual prayers in addition to the prescribed five a day. The root meaning of sufism comes from the Arabic word *sufi*, meaning wearer of wool—wearing wool was in the old days a sign of poverty as wearing silk was a sign of riches.

From its original sites in Arabia and surrounding areas, sufism then diffused to the Somali populations. Since then religious orders have always been part of Somali religious life. The *tariqa* orders, sometimes called *jama'a*, are headed by a spiritual head, called also a sheikh. There are many such orders in the country, although most orders belong to one of three movements (*Qadiriya, Ahmediya,* and *Salihiyah*), but there are no central organizations or headquarters that oversee the tariqa communities in any of the movements. Rather, the tariqa orders in each movement share a common founding father and viewpoints but are independent of each other. However, the orders in each movement exchange information on points of interest to them. Of the three main movements, Qadiriya is the most important one not only among Somalis but also in the Muslim world. Its founder, Abdulkadir Al-Jilani (1077–1166) has his tomb in Baghdad, Iraq.

Life in a tariqa community is centered around religious rituals, the incantation (*dikri*) of panegyrics to saints or to the prophet (*nabi-amaan* in the case of the prophet), the saying of litanies or repetitive incantations (*wardi*), and spiritual reflection and study. Life in the order also means one must partake of physical work in the communal fields of the order. Religious orders generally try to be self-sufficient and independent from the communities and clans around them and to whom usually the land where the tariqa is located belongs. Having no allegiance to any clan, they were thus neutral communities and were spared the feuds and vendettas endemic in the countryside.

The members in the order, who ethnically belong to the surrounding larger communities, are encouraged to renounce their communal and clans ties and to consider their fellow members as their new brothers and sisters. Each tariqa therefore cultivates a different kind of genealogy, a spiritual one compared to the blood ties of the Somali clans. This spiritual genealogy is called *silsilatu albaraka* (the blessed chain) and the members are supposed to learn its components just as ordinary clan folk are supposed to memorize the names of their ancestors in their genealogical tree. The spiritual genealogy consists of the names of saints who had played an important role in the development of the tariqa and in the particular sufi movement of the order; ultimately, the prophet himself is supposed to be the last link in this blessed chain.

Admission to a tariqa requires a ritual and the administration of an initiation rite conducted by the sheikh of the order. The new member or initiate then starts at the bottom of the spiritual rung or at the first station of the spiritual journey. From this first stage, the murid (the initiate), has to progress through hard work and perseverance into advanced philosophical and mystical stages. However, there is no last station, as spiritual advancement is theoretically possible until the last breath of life. In practice, the one who succeeds the sheikh of the order might have reached the highest post in the order. Those who believe that they may have reached a high level of knowledge leave the order to find their own independent order while still maintaining spiritual ties with the sheikh of the order. Few might also claim to have found mystical knowledge (*asraar*) through exegesis and asceticism; some might also be ascribed to have spiritual power (*karaama*) and be capable of performing miracles through prayers, in which case the sick and those with a request to make (*muraad*) might flock to their door.

VENERATION OF ANCESTORS AND SAINTS

In orthodox Islam the veneration of saints and ancestors is objectionable as a practice; moreover, the prophet is said to have warned his followers against glorifying his tomb. Thus, Muslims do not have a beatification process as is known, for example, to Catholicism. In spite of that, veneration of saints and ancestors, no doubt inherited from a pre-Islamic stage, is still practiced among Somalis, as among other Muslims.

Saints are venerated yearly on the date of their deaths, if known, otherwise on a date fixed by convention. The most well-known saints have shrines that are maintained by a resident sheikh and his entourage. The shrine usually consists of the tomb of the saint (*qudbi*), which might be a mosque (*masjid*), and quarters where the residents live.

There are generally two types of venerated personages among Somalis: ancestors (*waalid*) and saints (*wali*). In practice, however, this division is not very strong, and some ancestors are venerated as saints by their descendants; obviously the more numerous the descendants, the more likely that an ancestor will be venerated. Therefore, many clans and subclans venerate their legendary founder. However, few venerated ancestors have shrines and sanctuaries, for proper saints far outnumber those for clan ancestors.

Saints proper are those who have been "beatified" popularly because they were held in high esteem in their lives and were associated with a high *karaama*. To this category belong the saints from the first period of Islamization and saints from sufi movements or tariqa communities. The tombs or the shrines of saints are the object of annual pilgrimages, *siyaaro* (visit). At these events, which are a kind of festival, thousands of people congregate for several days at the shrine and marathon recitals of panegyrics to the prophet (*nabi-amaan*) or to the saint (*manaqib*) are held. People bring food and animals to be sacrificed for the occasion. The sick and those with requests, ordinary people just partaking of the spiritual communion, as well as the very poor who just come for the free food all gather on the location chanting and swaying in unison. Strips or bands of cloth worn on the arms sometimes identify those who have done the pilgrimage. Tombs of highly venerated saints are said to glow at night and such a saint is referred to as *wali siraata*.

An example of an early saint and proselytizer who is much venerated is Sheikh Yusuf al-Kownin, *Aw-Barkhadle* (the blessed father), the inventor of the method for facilitating the learning of the Arabic alphabet. Al-Kownin's shrine is near the main northern city of Hargeisa, and his annual pilgrimage is a huge festival attended by thousands. A curious custom associated with his pilgrimage is the marking of crosses on the foreheads of the pilgrims. One might wonder if this custom got transferred from a cult older than Islam, such as Christianity, that had reached the Horn before Islam and is still practiced by the Highland Amharas and Tigreans of Ethiopia and Eritrea. In the south, the saints who attract the largest number of visitors are Sheikh Uways and Sheikh Ali Mayow. The shrine of Sheikh Uways Mohamed of Barawe is a recent addition to the Somali saintly pantheon (he was assassinated in 1909 by followers of Mohamed Abdulle Hassan, presumably for differences of opinion on theological and political points).[2] Sheikh Uways was the founder of a tariqa, and his followers now belong to the Uwaysiya order. His yearly tomb visit at Biyoley draws large crowds. The crowds chant, dance in a rhythmic way, and work themselves into a delirium that makes some individuals experience spontaneous spasms. Some people call him *Sheikh Uways Buubaye* (Sheikh Uways, the flying Saint), which is an indication of the strength of the passion and veneration he arouses among his followers in the south.

Some of the early proselytizers were grafted both into the saintly pantheon and into the genealogical trees of Somali clans; these might be called genealogical saints; one of them is Sheikh Ishaaq, the mythical father of the Isaaq confederation, who probably was an early proselytizer who over the years became transmogrified into a genealogical father. Sheikh Ishaaq has a shrine in Mait along the northern coast where an annual pilgrimage takes place. Another example of syncretism between a clan genealogy and a holy person or an early proselytizer is that of Ismail Jabarti and Darod. Here it seems Ismail Jabarti, who is venerated as a saint even by non-Somalis, was fused with the clan figure of Darod, whose pre-Islamic name suggests a Cushitic personage ennobled as a Muslim saint, a process adopted also by the other clans and confederations in a fashion similar to the procurement of letters of nobility in medieval Europe. Ismail Jabarti (or Sheikh Darod) has his sanctuary in the same region as Sheikh Ishaaq, in the nearby Hadaftimo Mountains, and is also the object of a yearly pilgrimage.

Traditionally, religious orders were centered in the countryside and in villages, however, since the late 1980s, urban orders, disparagingly referred to as incense burners (*foohlay*) from their practice of engulfing themselves in thick fumes from the burning of frankincense while meditating and chanting, have mushroomed. These urban tariqas are different from the traditional tariqas in that they do not produce their means of livelihood themselves through work; they depend entirely on donations from members or charitable persons. Additionally, unlike the traditional orders that were founded by persons steeped in religion and sufism, most are run by people who quickly got into the mystic calling by accident—some claim to have dreamt of a saint or to have found inspiration suddenly; some have been founded by illiterate persons who can hardly read classical Arabic let alone understand the writings of sufi scholars. In many ways, the urban orders are like the cult associations of the West and the fact that they mushroomed in the 1980s points to a spiritual crisis that Somalis were undergoing then as a nation— perhaps this was symptomatic of an aversion to the increasing brutality and unholiness of the Barre regime. Such cult groups also have membership soliciting and marketing policies that target the rich and the powerful, a practice quite unknown to self-sufficient traditional orders.

INDIGENOUS BELIEFS AND PARARELIGION

No early indigenous cult has survived among Somalis of today; there is therefore no pantheon of ancient deities or spirits that is directly known to Somalis. What we know of early beliefs, after 1,000 years or so of Islam, comes from two sources: words and customs still existing among today's Somalis or practices found among other Cushitic peoples such as the Oromo, among whom indigenous beliefs have somewhat survived.

Among the words that reveal the existence of a pre-Islamic indigenous religion are *waaq, ayaan, nidar,* and *huur.* Waaq (sky-god) is an archaic Somali word for god and contrasts with the word allah (god), which came with the arrival of Islam. The waaq or waaqo, among the Oromo, is the only god of the Cushitic religion. Thus it can be safely assumed that the quick absorption of Islam among Somalis was facilitated by the monotheism of their ancient cult. The abode of the waaq is the sky and a season of good rains and prosperity is still known today to as barwaaqo, literally god's rain-drops. Early on in childhood, Somali children are taught, especially in the countryside, not to point a finger at rain clouds as it is said to bring bad luck and drive away the precious rain clouds. This tradition is also found among the Oromo,[3] however, the origin of this practice probably has to do with avoidance of offending the waaq that dwells in the sky.

Ayaan means good luck and destiny; someone who is in good luck and prosperous might be referred to as *ayaanle.* Ayaan is also a popular name for girls. In the ancient Cushitic religion, the ayaan, or ayana among the Oromo, are good spirits or angels that mediate between god and humans and whose blessings one seeks. As is known from practices among non-Muslim non-Christian Oromo, the chief priest of the Cushitic cult is the *qallu.*

The qallu presides over important ceremonies, grants blessings, and settles disputes. His function compares to the role that the Muslim wadaad fulfills among Somalis. Today there is no Somali word that directly refers to the qallu personage, but it might be said that the word *gaalo* (infidel), which is used pejoratively for any non-Muslim, has its source in the qallu personage; evidently Somalis, after having become Muslims, termed the followers of the qallu infidels. Obviously, there are also bad spirits in the ancient Cushitic religion. The word nidar refers to a kind of spirit or fairy who is a righter of wrongs, nowadays especially of the sentimental kind. *Nabsi* is also another word for nidar. The huur, the marabou, is the messenger of death.

Various rites and spirit possession practices also give us some information about the ancient beliefs of Somalis. One of these is undoubtedly the *zaar,* a ritual dance of spirit possession that comes under various names such as Borane in the south among the Rahanwein, a reference to the ancestral spirit of the founder of the Borane clan of the Oromo.

The zaar spirit usually visits only women, although some men are also said to be possessed by it. After its presence is acknowledged in the body of the person, a costly ceremony of spirit exorcism is then held in which feasting and ritual dancing are the main features. The ceremony is led by a ritual expert, *'alanqad*, who is usually a person who had suffered earlier from zaar possession.

Many people scoff at the idea of spirit possession and religious authorities openly discourage such practices. But for centuries Islamic orthodoxy and the parareligion have coexisted unofficially and continue to do so. One of the reasons why zaar has endured lies in its use as a form of psychotherapy for stressed individuals. A zaar ceremony is not an exorcist rite per se whose aim is to drive away an evil spirit from the body; rather, zaar is considered as a kind of companion of the body which must be placated and pleased so that it can coexist amiably with the body of the sufferer. Additionally, the zaar spirit is thought to be transferred along hereditary lines and one might inherit one's grandmother's zaar; there is therefore no emphasis on a permanent cure for the ailment.

Communion by dancing together and eating together are the main ingredients that create the relaxing ambience of a zaar ceremony. In an otherwise rigid society, where the roles and behaviors of women are strictly placed under an unrelenting code, a day or two of a zaar ceremony in which a woman may engage in "abnormal" behavior such as rhythmic dancing and smoking releases pent-up stresses and refreshes the soul. In this regard, the zaar is a healing experience at the personal level.

In many ways zaar can be characterized as a religious relic from the old deities. The old northeastern African deities were headed by two figures; Aw-Zaar (father Zaar), the male deity known in the West as Osiris, and Ay-Situ, mother Situ, known in the West as Isis. Ay-Situ is still celebrated in a fertility rite and given offerings by pregnant women so that she will facilitate childbirth. Of course, the fertility rite is now wrapped up in Muslim parlance as it is not only offered to Ay-Situ but also to Fatima, the daughter of the Prophet of Islam.[4] The rite itself is called either *kur* or *sitaat*. Additionally, the fact that zaar is celebrated and led only by older women closely corresponds to the ancient practice of older women as the priestesses. Among Somalis, younger women, and especially unmarried ones, are not thought to be deserving of a visit from the zaar. The zaar ritual is by no means confined to Somalia; its cultural domain historically covers all the northeastern African countries, including Ethiopia, the Sudan, and Egypt, although by now it has spread to surrounding regions. It is a lasting witness to a common culture of the region.

In southern Somalia, among the Bantu villagers and also among the Benidiris of the Benadir, a different kind of spirit possession known as *lumbi*, from the Swahili *umbia*, is practiced. Lumbi differs from zaar in several ways. First, unlike zaar, which is held inside homes, lumbi is held outside in the open or in the public square of villages. Second, in lumbi the objective is to drive away the evil spirit from the body of the possessed, and toward that end, the lumbi leader strikes repeatedly the body of the possessed with a whip. Third, the possessed dances alone in the middle of the ring until he or she falls into a trance and then falls down.

Spirits that existed in the old Cushitic menagerie of evil fairies are no longer in use among today's Somalis. The name for such evil spirits was *busho*, which today, as an archaic word, means only disease; among the Rahanwein the word *bushi* also means just disease and no longer evil spirit. However among the Oromo, the word bushi still refers to evil spirits. One well-known evil spirit is Hanfaley. If something disappears mysteriously, people say that Hanfaley must have taken it. Prayers and incantations existed to dispel evil spirits and the following cultural relic is an old prayer meant to ward against evil spirits.

> Evils lurking behind us, be ye halted there,
> Evils waiting before us, be ye forced to flee,
> Evils hovering above us, be ye suspended still,
> Evils rising beneath us, be ye blunted of spear,
> Evils treading beside us, be ye thrust afar.[5]

Today among Somalis, evil spirits are generally referred to as *jinn*, a word used among all Muslims. The jinn, the Semitic counterpart of the Cushitic ayaana, are mentioned in the Koran. They are said to be descendants of Iblis, an angel who fell from God's grace. Iblis was the only one of God's angels who refused to bow to Adam as God ordered. Iblis stated, as a creation from light, that he would not bow to a creation from mud, Adam. God punished him for his pride and banished him from heaven; ever since, Iblis had made it his endeavor to lead as many astray as he could until the day of judgment. Iblis is also popularly known as Shaitan (Satan). The pious Somali utters the Arabic formula *a'adu bilahi mini sheydani rajiim* (Oh Allah I seek protection from Satan) to banish the ever present evil spirit from his or her surroundings. This is the equivalent of the making of the sign of the cross by Catholic Christians.

Divination, Magic, and Myth

Traditional diviners, *faaliye* (*faaliso* for a female), practice the art of *faal*, divination, and use different mediums to interpret the esoteric and the future. Among these mediums are cowrie shells, geometric designs on fine sand, and smoke from burning incense. Crystal balls and palm reading are unknown among Somalis. Certain women diviners known as *taawilo* make noises and belches while in the process of divination. Officially, religious leaders frown upon faal; but nevertheless, it continues uninterrupted as it did centuries ago, mainly because it is seen as harmless and not a threat to Islam.

Especially, in southern Somalia, among the riverine populations or people from a Bantu cultural heritage, one finds persons who openly claim to be sorcerers and sorceresses. For a fee, they would perform magic (*sihir*) or cast a spell (*qataar*) on a third person. The magicians (*sihirlow*) keep a low profile and would not confess to engaging in magical practices in public for fear they would run afoul of religious authorities or local administrations. Some riverine villages are well known or feared for their magicians.

A small group of riverine dwellers, also Bantu of origin, are feared for their crocodile cult. They are believed to communicate with the crocodiles of the Shebelle and Juba Rivers. A typical myth related to them is that a crocodile man (*bihar*) may send his favorite crocodile to fetch the lady of his desire. First, the crocodile man casts a spell on the unfortunate lady who develops an irresistible urge to go bathe in the river where the crocodile is patiently waiting to whisk her promptly to its master.

Among pastoralist Somalis, a dying practice of magic is attributed to those who claim to understand the language of the hyena (*waraabe-la-hadal*); by listening to the howls of the hyena prowling around settlements, they are said to be able to understand the speech of the hyena and in turn they learn about misfortunes that might lie ahead for the area. Another mythical tradition among Somalis concerning hyenas is that of the hyena-man, *qori-ismaris* (literally he who rubs a stick on himself). As the name indicates, the hyena-man, who is the Somali equivalent of the Western werewolf, transmogrifies himself into a hyena by rubbing a magical stick on his hindquarters at nightfall, and before dawn he does the same action and is reversed into his human shape.

A living tradition that certainly comes out of the pre-Islamic age is the giving of the *samayo* (birth gift) to a member of the Yibir clan, as had been mentioned earlier. The person who collects the samayo is appropriately known as ʿ*aadoqaate*, the collector of tradition. In exchange, after being paid in kind or cash, the ʿaadoqaate gives the parent an amulet to be worn on the baby's neck. The amulet is at once a receipt of service and a talisman (*hirsi*) against evil spirits. If the ʿaadoqaate is not paid, it is believed harm might come to the baby.

According to the legend of Sheikh Yusuf al-Kownin and Mohamed Hanif, this tradition was instituted as a compensation for the death of the latter, as has been mentioned above, entombed inside a mountain by virtue of the former's prayers. However, this tradition is much older than Islam itself. Already, the ancient Egyptians knew such talismans as *sema*. What this tells us is that at it widest limits, traditions among the Somalis link up with those in the whole region and are due to common cultural origins that go back thousands of years, something that is not surprising as the languages of the region belong for the most part to one super-family of languages known today mostly as the Afroasiatic family of languages.

NOTES

1. The first year of the Hejira, the Muslim calendar, corresponds to the migration of the Prophet Mohamed and his followers from Mecca to Medina in the year of 622 A.D.

2. The two men were theologically at odds: Sheikh Uways was a sufi (mystic) while Mohamed Abdulle Hassan was a follower of a puritanical sect that abhors mysticism and veneration of saints. Additionally, Sheikh Uways refused to give support to Hassan's political and clan wars, seeing him as nothing but a power-hungry man. In turn, Hassan called him "a weak man" (*candho dogob leh*) (literally an udder with a log). See Said S. Samatar, "Sheikh Uways Maxamad of Baraawe (1847–1909): Mystic and Reformer in East Africa," in Hussein M. Adam and Charles L. Geshekter (1992). *Proceedings of the First International Congress of Samal Studies.* Atlanta: Scholars Press, 224.

3. G.W.B Huntingford (1955). *The Galla of Ethiopia.* London: International African Institute.

4. This rite has its parallel in Atete, the fertility deity of the Oromo.

5. Margaret Laurence (1954). *A Tree for Poverty: Somali Poetry.* Hamilton, Ont.: McMaster University Library and ECW Press, 52.

SUGGESTED READING

Cassanelli, Lee V. 1975. "Migrations, Islam, and Politics in the Somali Benaadir, 1500–1843." In Harold Marcus, ed., *Proceedings of the First United States Conference on Ethiopian Studies, 1973.* East Lansing: Michigan State University African Studies Center, pp. 101–15.

Huntingford, G.W.B. 1955. *The Galla of Ethiopia.* London: International African Institute.

Lewis I.M. 1955–56. "Sufism in Somaliland: A Study in Tribal Islam." *Bulletin of the School of Oriental and African Studies* 17: 581–602; 18:146–60.

———. 1966. "Conformity and Contrast in Somali Islam." In I.M. Lewis, ed., *Islam in Tropical Africa.* London: Oxford University Press, pp. 253–67.

———. 1969. "Spirit Possession in Northern Somaliland." In J. Beatrie and J. Middleton, eds. *Spirit Mediumship and Society in Africa.* London: Routledge, pp. 188–220.

Samatar, Said S. 1992. "Sheikh Uways Maxamad of Baraawe (1847–1909): Mystic and Reformer in East Africa." In Hussein M. Adam and Charles L. Geshekter, *Proceedings of the First International Congress of Somali Studies.* Atlanta: Scholars Press.

3

Literature, Drama, and Media

LITERATURE of the Somalis can be approached from two divisions: oral literature and written literature. Oral literature refers to the fables, folktales, and poetry before the adoption of an official writing of the Somali language. Written literature might be termed as the works written and published in the official script since 1972, although this does not imply that no written literature was produced by Somalis before 1972. Just as medieval Europeans used to write in Latin, for centuries Somalis have been writing in Arabic. However, most of what was written in the past in Arabic was about religious matters, and the surviving texts in Arabic are mostly in the form of religious poems (*qasiido*) and panegyric ballads (*manaqib*) for saints. Nevertheless, the division between written and oral literature is not clear-cut and, as a nomenclature, this has more to do with Western traditions than with Somali tradition. Among Somalis, many works including long plays and poems are still written only after they have been entirely orally composed; others have been collected and written down after listening to memorizers (*hafadiyaal*) long after the death of the composer. Many poets, even if they are literate, prefer to record their poems with a cassette recorder and thus can disseminate their work without ever writing it down because, even today, the voice of a poet reading his or her poem is vastly preferred to reading a poem from a book.

THE WRITING OF THE SOMALI LANGUAGE

It might be asked why Somalis who were acquainted with writing systems for a long period did not adopt a common script for Somali. This has much to do with Arabic and its use for both religious and official purposes—until the nineteenth century, the learning of Arabic and the religious books were the core of education just as learning Latin, Greek, and the scriptures were for a long time the core of European education. The average Somali, a pastoralist, had little incentive to write; if a Somali wanted to have a letter composed, he or she would turn to one of the learned men of religion who knew how to read and write. These men of religion were the custodians of the cult but also of the occult, and writing was both part of the cult and the occult. Reading and writing in Arabic was the key to their profession and to their status in the society; therefore, they saw no urgent need to vulgarize their science in the language of the common people just as the church in Europe for centuries saw no need to vulgarize its religious works in the local tongues.

The lack of a strong centralized state, and it might be said that writing and accounting systems, being the backbone of a taxation system, are essential to a centralized state, contributed to the lack of a common writing code for Somali. For comparison, we may note that the largely agriculturist Amhara, neighbors of the Somalis, developed a writing system and a feudal system of governance as well as land ownership; but Somalis did not develop any powerful systems where hierarchy and class were of importance. They were, despite the existence of numerous sultanates and city-states, "a race of fierce and turbulent republicans," until the arrival of the colonial European state.[1]

The story of the codifiers of Somali (i.e., those who attempted to invent a script for Somali) is long and includes both Somalis and non-Somalis. Among the Somalis were Sheikh Mohamed Abdi Makahil, Muse H.I. Galal, Sheikh Abdirahman Sheikh Nur, Yusuf Keenadiid Osman, Shire Jama Ahmed, and Sheikh Ahmed Kadare. Among the non-Somalis were notably such persons as J. K. King (1887) and B. W. Andrzejewski. These various scripts fell into three types according to the characters they used: Arabic, Latin, and unique. Sheikh Abdirahman Sheikh Nur and Yusuf Keenadiid Osman's systems were unique endeavors of their own making. However, the unique scripts did not make much headway, and by the 1950s, the promoters of a script for Somali were in two camps: Arabic and Latin.

These two script camps began ideological battles in which linguistic and nonlinguistic arguments were exchanged.[2] For example, those who were favoring the Arabic script took pleasure in pointing out that their characters had the advantage of being largely known to the public through the teaching of Arabic as a liturgical language as well as of being of Muslim origin—in fact, they predate Islam. The confrontation between the two groups, in the end, got so heated that the Arabists adopted the slogan *laatiin waa la' diin* (Latin is heathen), a play on the words *laatiin* (Latin) and *la' diin* (without a religion), implying the Latin characters are used by non-Muslims. The Latinists argued that the simplicity of the Latin script and the availability of Latin-based printing machines and typewriters already in the country should be considered.

Thus the apparent lack of a consensus among Somali educators on a script translated into the fact that there were no plans for a common system of writing Somali on the birth of the Somali Republic in July 1960. Shortly after independence, the Somali Language Committee was instituted with the purpose of finding a solution to the lack of a common orthography. It was headed by Muse H.I. Galal, the first Somali professionally trained in modern phonetics. In 1962, the committee recommended a Latin script alphabet, after viewing the various competing scripts. However, no action was taken to adopt an official script, as the civilian politicians were not willing to risk alienating one or the other script camp.

The quest for an official orthography for Somali had to wait until 1969, when the military junta came into power. In 1971, the junta, having silenced all potential opposition with the barrel of a gun, could afford to reach whatever decision it wanted on an issue that nine years of civilian regimes could not solve. The Somali Language Committee was revived and in 1972, on the third anniversary of the coup, a Latin script was announced as the official orthography of the Somali language. This measure was accompanied by another edict making Somali the sole official language. The historical development of the script has been largely attributed to one British linguist, B. W. Andrzejewski, and two Somali scholars, Muse H.I. Galal and Shire Jama Ahmed.[3] These three men might therefore be rightly called the fathers of the Somali Latin script.

In further attempts to spread quickly the use of the new orthography, government workers were asked to become literate in it in six months. Subsequent alphabetization campaigns in the towns and in the countryside raised the level of literacy to double digits for the first time. By 1980, Somali was not only the official language but also the language of instruction up to grade twelve, the terminal school grade.

While the Somali language became the language of public, business, and government transactions, as well as the language of education in schools, the use of other languages—notably Arabic and English, and to some extent Italian—continued and in some cases even increased. First to have increased its share of public usage was Arabic, as a result of several reasons. It must be stated that Arabic, unlike European languages that came with colonialism, had a long history of existence and use among Somalis. Arabic had always been the language of religion among Somalis; before the arrival of European languages, it was the only written language in use among Somalis.

However, what increased the use of Arabic during the 1970s and 1980s lies in the increased emigration of Somalis to the petrodollar-rich countries of Arabia. It is also due in part to the admission of Somalia into the Arab League, in spite of Somalis being not Arabs. As a result of that membership, the government of Siad Barre had to show some zeal in encouraging the use of Arabic in public life by organizing Arabic literacy classes on the radio and in classrooms in urban centers.

A NATION OF POETS

One Italian scholar, seeing the lack of written Somali in magazines and books, noted in the 1950s, "This is a language without a literary tradition, a scholastic discipline and without official functions."[4] True, written media in Somali was rare until recently; but writing on paper is only a recording of artistic speech creations, and Somalis certainly did not lack "literature."

Somalis have a tradition of oral poetry, poetic combats, and poetic series in which several poets hundreds of miles away from each other participate. The series of poetic contests known as *Guba* (1920–40s), *Silsilada haydha* "The Chain of Fat" (1940s), *Halla'-Dheere* (c. 1910s), and the more recent *Siinley* (1973) and *Deelley* (1979–81) show that poets and rhetoricians were highly admired, commented upon, and were well known to people who never saw them. This aspect is not much different from learning and admiring a poet's work in a magazine. One writer observed rightly in 1854:

> It is strange that a dialect which has no written character should so abound in poetry and eloquence. . . . The country teems with "poets, poetasters, poeticos, poetaccios": every man has his recognized position in literature as accurately defined as though he had been reviewed in a century of magazines—the fine ear of this people causing them to take the greatest pleasure in harmonious sounds and poetical expressions, whereas a false quantity or a prosaic phrase excite their violent indignation.[5]

Poetry is just one part of the Somali literature; however, it is poetry that has caught much attention of foreign students and admirers of Somali literature. Margaret Laurence, a Canadian novelist and scholar, called Somalis a "nation of poets" while Andrzejewski and Lewis could, with some modesty, proclaim: "It is perhaps not too much to claim that the Somali are a nation of bards."[6]

Why is poetry so important and central to the Somalis? Several non-Somalis have tried to answer this question; for example, Margaret Laurence, one of the first to introduce Somali poetry to the outside world, suggested the "barren" nature of the Somali landscape, affording little "materials for painting, sculpture, weaving or pottery-making" explains the preponderance of the verbal arts among Somalis.[7] She also suggests that the Islamic abhorrence of image depictions is a further contributing factor. However, as Laurence concedes in the next sentence nonverbal art forms do exist among Somalis. Indeed, Somalis have always woven, carved, sculpted, and produced pottery, among other things; however, they did not carve or paint human figures like many other Muslim peoples. The popularity of poetry among Somalis is a social phenomena, and the environment of the land does not afford an ample explanation. In other words, the different usages of poetry among Somalis are the cause of its importance. A poem could be used to encourage warriors, to avenge an insult, to teach a moral lesson, to record a historical event, and to express sentiments. This was made possible by the fact that poetry was easily memorized and propagated quickly across the land by groups of memorizers and reciters (*hafidayaal*). Today, the cheap cassette recorder has replaced the memorizers and reciters but poetry is still important among Somalis, and renowned poets command respect that their Western counterparts would envy.

Genres

There many ways to categorize Somali poetry. But let us first state that the generic name for poetry is *maanso*. Poetry is then subdivided into several categories or genres depending on form (meter, style, and length). The most important forms of poetry are *gabay, jiifto, geeraar, wiglo, buraanbur, beercade, afarey,* and *guuraw*.

The gabay (epic or grand) is the most complex form in both meter and length—a gabay might be longer than 100 lines. It is considered the form that marks the highest perfection in the art, and young poets are supposed to have reached poetic maturity when they can compose a gabay. Traditionally, gabay was mostly composed by men, while buraanbur, which is of a lighter measure (*miisaan*), was mostly composed by women. In theory, there were no explicit rules that forbade women from making a gabay. But the unwritten rules were such that women should not compose gabay, and even today the masters of the buraanbur are still mostly women and men the masters of the gabay.

The geeraar and the jiifto come next in complexity and length. The rest of the genres might be called light genres. Geeraar has subpart divisions or strophes while the others have no subpart divisions. Some of the best known geeraar poems are in praise of horses.

The ordinary people usually divide all verse into gabay (serious poetry) and *hees* (song). The only distinction between gabay in the popular sense and hees is that the latter is expressly set to music; in other words, hees or *balwo*, as popular song was known in the 1950s, is poetry accompanied by music. In turn, there are several kinds of genres proper to the hees as a category depending on the style of music, among them the balwo genre of the 1950s.

Poems can also be classified by theme (i.e., the main subject of the poem). There are as many themes as can be imagined; however, some of the main categories of themes in Somali poetry are: *baroorodiiq* (elegy), *amaan* (praise), *digasho* (gloating), *jacayl* (romance), *guhaadin* (invective, diatribe, assault), *guubaabo* (guidance). At the death of a well-known personality or a poet, a moved poet usually composes baroorodiiq, encapsulating the good deeds of the deceased and expressing pain at the loss of such an illustrious person. Digasho is composed after the fall of an enemy and guhaadin refers to poems of which the aim is to incite a feud, insult an enemy, or verbally assault someone or a clan. Guubaabo refers to any poem of which the aim is to uplift, reconcile, and teach; it is the opposite of guhaadin. A late addition to the Somali poetic genre is *jacbur* (the motley). Jacbur is a light, humorous, nonsensical poem, the equivalent of the English limerick, which is intended to make people laugh even if presenting some truism; the best known masters of this genre are Abdi Shube and Abdi Moallin Ibrahim (Dhoodaan).

The poet generally suits the form to the theme. For example, all elegiac poems are gabay, since the occasion and the subject are serious, and a light form of poetry would not be appropriate; on the other hand, romance poems are generally light in form. Most poets cannot be attached to any particular theme. However, some poets are well known for a dominant theme in their works. For example, Elmi Boodhari was a romantic poetic; he is often called *boqorkii jacaylka* "king of romance." Mohamed Abdulle Hassan and Abdi Gahayr were the masters of the invective and the diatribe against individuals as well as entire clans. On the other hand, Abdillahi Suldaan (Timacade) was well known for guidance and patriotism.

Today, the trend in poetry is toward lighter verse, although free verse (i.e., versification) without alliteration does not yet exist in Somali. Even so, we can discuss poets as contemporary poets and bards of old. The bards of old preferred the gabay as a genre, which is why sometimes the gabay is called today classical poetry; but many contemporary poets have a preference for the lighter meters in their compositions.

Reciting poetry is done either by the poet himself or a reciter. A good reciter has a large repertoire of poems and is a kind of walking library whose presence is appreciated. When poetry is recited there is no music or clapping that accompanies it; the audience may, however, repeat or hum chorus lines, when present. On the other hand, if someone is reciting a song, people join and sing along.

A line of verse has meter (*miisaan*) (i.e., a particular arrangement of words and syllables) as well as alliteration (*qaafiyad*). In the study of Somali poetry, scholars have emphasized the role of the relationship between syllables and long vowels in a line of verse. On the surface, this is true and poets maintain an equilibrium between syllables and long vowels; but an easy way to have an understanding of Somali scansion is through beat groups or breath groups that give rhythm or a beat to the poem or song. Simple forms have two beats and more complex forms as many as six beat groups. An example would be the following lines from a folk poem chanted when on the move from one settlement to another.

Maqaley (1)	*Warlaay* (2)	Ye, unwary young of sheep and goats
Ma laguu (1)	*Waramay* (2)	Have ye received the tidings
In Cali (1)	*la dilay* (2)	That Ali has been slain
Oo Cumar (1)	*la dilay* (2)	And Omar has been slain too
Oo waran (1)	*Dhul galay* (2)	And that spears have struck earth.

In a complex form, the beat groups are increased. An example would be the following four lines from Ahmed Mohamed Qaadi's gabay, "Geel" (Camels), in praise of camels, extolling their resistance to the ardors of jiilaal, the dreaded season.

> Jillaal muddada dhigay, dhulkoo mudhux abaaroobay,
> Markuu adhigu mayti u batee, lo 'ina naafawdo,
> Madiix[8] waxay ku fooftaa, Gobliyo, meerisyada Hawde,
> Maraagiyo waxay goosataa, midho cambuuleede

> When the time of Jiilaal has come, and the land is barren from
> the drought (*abaar*)

When sheep and goats are mostly dying, and cattle is weak
Madiix (a she-camel) sails forth to the land of the high trees,
    and the farthest Haud[9]
She chews on the acacia tree and its thorny produce (Author's
    translation)

The beats of the first line can be analyzed as follows:

Jiilaal (1) *muddada dhigay* (2), *dhulkoo* (1) *mudhux abaaroobay*
    (2).

Young poets learn how to compose by listening to recitals either by reciters or by older poets, or, as is more common now, by listening to the radio or a recorded tape or even by reading poems at school or at home. Most young poets, before they fall into a style of their own, consciously or unconsciously mimic the style of a particular poet. When the source model of their style is evident to everyone, it is said that they have composed a *gabay-dheeg* (derivative poetry). Gabay-dheeg is not an appreciated genre; but some imitations have achieved acclaim either because of the new metaphors they introduce or because of the humor that results from the difference between the seriousness of the theme in the source model and the frivolousness of the one in the imitation composition. The effect is a parody or a burlesque.

The role of the poet in Somali society is very important, and, therefore, a particular poet could choose to advance either the forces of good or those of evil. This polarity between the functions and roles of the poet have been best expressed by the lines of one contemporary poet, Ahmed Ismail Diriye, known as Qaasim, in a poem titled "I Am," which starts with the following lines:

The bitter-tasting aloe sometimes shoots forth flowers
And you can drink its sweet nectar
I am both sweet and bitter-tasting
My right and left hands are twins
One gives succor to travelers and to the weak
and the other one is sharp knives (Author's translation)

Qaasim is also best remembered for his apt lines that decried the behavior of the new Somali elites soon after independence. In now famous lines, he stated:

Is there a difference here
Between the colonialist I sent home
And the new occupant of his mansion
In manner and skin, you'd think he is a Somali
But he is not one to warm our hearts
And he is verily of the colonialist Karale's ilk [a colonial
    administrator in British Somaliland] (Author's translation)

Qaasim's critical verses are very pertinent and insightful in that the new
Somali state, like many others in the third world, had retained administra-
tively the same methods of governance and administration as the colonial
state.

Among the poets of the past century, a poet who has gained the hearts of
all Somalis in every district is Elmi Boodhari. Many major poets, such as
Mohamed Abdulle Hasan and Gahayr, aroused resentment among some Somalis, as they addressed diatribes against the members of a certain clan or
urged bloodletting among the clans; such poets are known as viper tongues,
and the poems of such poets have been known to cause feuds and clan wars.
But not so with Elmi Boodhari—his subject was romance, and only that.
While the poets of his day were addressing more serious subjects such as war
and feuds, Boodhari composed all his poems for the lady of his affection,
Hodan, who was given in marriage to a man wealthier than him (Boodhari
was a poor baker in the town of Berbera). Instead of getting literary kudos
for his beautiful verse, Boodhari was made the object of public ridicule.
Somali society had not been, of course, devoid of romance either in song or
in prose in any age, but to publicly proclaim the object of one's love was
frowned upon in the social mores of Somalis. That fact of culture did not
escape Boodhari, as these two lines amply tell:

If a man has a wound he is taken to the doctor
But the braves of Daud are ridiculing me (Author's translation)

It was enough that Hodan's relatives were infuriated and felt that their daughter's name had been soiled by a man who was proclaiming in public his love
for her. But Boodhari also had to face the fury of his kinsmen, the Daud,
who altogether disowned him for spending his days pining for one woman
when they could get him a girl as beautiful or more beautiful than she.
Boodhari tried in lament, as in the above lines, to remind his kinsmen that
the wounds of the heart merit the same attention as the wounds of the

flesh. He died in 1941—no one knows his birth date since traditionally Somalis do not record birth dates.

In his life Boodhari might have been a poor forlorn poet who reaped ridicule and banishment for his poetry; but after his death, he became very popular. His romantic poetry inspired a new generation of song composers and poets in the 1950s who wove his name again and again into their verses— in fact, the song composers and poets who flowered in the 1950s and popularized the balwo romantic song genre owe much to him. Since his death, he has become the lover's patron saint, and romantic souls visit his grave near the city of Berbera to pay him homage and seal their love. Finally, Boodhari might be thought to have gotten his poetic justice when the son of Hodan, the lady whose love made him suffer, collected his poems and published them in an aptly named book, *Ma Dhabaa Jacayl Waa Loo Dhintaa?* (Is It True that One May Die of Love?)

Obviously, there are many great Somali poets; therefore, only a few will be mentioned here. In the following poem, Ugaas Nuur (c. early nineteenth century), speaks of how through patience and wit one may entrap one's enemies.

> Oh God! How often have I let a man who is inimical to me
>   sleep in my best room
> How often have I let speak to me a man from whom my flesh
>   would cringe
> I am not hasty in affairs
> How often have I put up with nasty personalities
> How often have I fed honey copiously to a man plotting to
>   hurt me.
> When I hem him in and play out my noose.
> When he bumps his haughty chest against the trap that I had
>   set for him.
> How often have I struck him suddenly. (Author's translation)

Geeraar Poems

Many geeraar poems praise the horse. In the past the horse was central to the pastoral way of life as a means of transport and as a means of waging war. Equestrian poems were therefore much in vogue before the early part of the twentieth century. One of the most well known of such poems came from the tongue of Ali Bu'ul (c. 1900–1920) of Borame.

In Praise of My Horse

From the seaside Bulahar
to the corners of the Almis mountain
and Harawe of the pools
Hargeisa of the Gob trees
My horse reaches all that in one afternoon
Is it not like a scudding cloud?
From its pen
A huge roar is heard
Is it not like a lion leading a pride?
In the open plains
It makes the camels kneel down
Is it not like an expert camel-rustler?
Its mane and tail has white tufts on the top
Is it not as beautiful as as a *galool* tree abloom? (Author's
     translation)

Mohamed Abdulle Hassan is perhaps the most controversial poet of the past
century, as a poet with a "viper tongue." In the following poem, recited after
the killing of a British officer, Richard Corfield, in an engagement with his
roving bands, he uses vivid imagery that does justice at once to his poetic
skills and to his violent and sanguinary nature. It has been said that he
composed it while contemplating the severed head of Corfield brought to
him from the battlefield.

Corfield (Mohamed Abdulle Hassan)

You Corfield, you're out of this world
You will take the road of no return
When you reach your hellish destination
Our slain who went to paradise will get news, God willing
If perchance, on your way, you see the crowds and the valued
     ones
Tell them how God's displeasure fell upon you
Say "the dervishes have not ceased harrying us yet"
Say "by powder and bullet the English had been routed"
Say "they attacked us to avenge you"
Say "in an early morning they laid siege upon us"
Say "in the thick of jihad, they hit me"

Say "their bullets struck in the thighs"
Say "the sticks they whipped me with became flayed of bark"
Tell them the grind of the blades that they slashed you with
Show them where the gashes of the knife are
Say "out of self-preservation I cried 'friend spare me' ' "
Say "when I looked around a piece of my heart broke away"
Say "my eyes were popping out so much they were upturned"
Say "I did not get remission for my soulful pleas"
Say "whenever I uttered a word they hit me in the mouth"
Say "I moaned much but they never heeded my cries"
Say "when I started shaking I lost hope of life"
Say "like the previous generals my plans were narrow"
Say "I have been rewarded for the advice the devil gave me"
Say "when the nerves of pain where twisted"
Say "the groans I made kept the people from sleeping"
Say "when the soul quit me, they let loose joyous shouts"
Say "wild beasts feasted on my body and dragged away the
    carcass"
Say "the hyena bolted down morsels of flesh and fat"
Say "the sinews and the tough tissues were left for the crows"
Say "Without denial, my kinsmen have been beaten"
Say "They are always routed in pitched battle"
Say "The dervishes are like the trees and the grass that grow
    again" (Author's translation)

Unlike Hassan, Abdillahi Suldaan (Timo-ʿadde) is best known for the gu-ubaabo (guidance) theme. In his "Dugsi Ma Laha Qabyaaladi" (Clannism Has No Warmth) of 1967, he warns Somalis of the dangers of clannish factionalism. Among its famous lines recited orally now almost everywhere:

If we don't stop abuse and slaughter
If we don't stop favoritism
The reward of such deeds is hellfire
And burning timbers
Clannism has no warmth only destruction (Author's
    translation)

Baroordiiq (Elegy) Poems

Ali Jama Haabiil was one of the great poets of the early nineteenth century; he is well known for engaging Hassan in poetic combat. According to folk history, Hassan was said to be so concerned about this poet's ability that he asked his entourage to say prayers requesting that Ali Jama Haabiil be stricken dead. Most of this poet's poems have been lost for lack of collection, unlike those of Hassan, whose poems have been collected and written down, under the obvious encouragement of Siad Barre's government. The verses in the following poem by Ali Jama Haabiil illustrate the baroorodiiq (elegy) genre. They belong to a long poem, gabay, in which he laments the death of an esteemed friend.

Oh Farah (c. 1905)

O Farah, I tossed from side to side sleepless
Evil vipers infested my bedding
And of the food placed in front of me, my teeth would not bite
They had brought me news of Hirsi's death,
May the messengers be bereft of kin
May they lose all their children
Those who brought me tidings of disaster and tragedy
Darkness has settled on the families resident on the grounds of
    Boo
Men have always died, but this one is a calamity
Let me mention six of his particular trait
First if skirmishes occurred and camels were looted
When rapid force to rescue is a must
When finally we catch up with the fleeing looters
When the coward steers away from contact with the enemy
He knew how to counter-attack and improvise
Am I brooding too much? Maybe
In difficult cases of arbitration when the elders don't agree
When the council is gathered beneath the tree
When each of the disputants insisted on his rightness
When discussions get heated but no decision was reached
On occasion he would whisper advice
And if need be raise his voice like a hero
People used to abide by his just sentence (Author's translation)

Among today's poets, Mohamed Ibrahim, popularly known as Hadrawi, is the poet's poet. He is not only a prolific poet but he is also probably the most eloquent living poet. His style is more light and more vivid than that of the classical poets, and this quality has endeared him to the younger generations. He is also different from the old bards in that, as a literate person, he writes his poems. Hadrawi first gained public fame through his lyric poetry, which was set to music and was sung by popular artists. For this reason he has been dubbed the "king of romance"; but in the following lines, composed at the grave of Elmi Boodhari, he rightly passed that honorific title to Boodhari, the man who gave Somali romantic poetry its letters of credence.

(At the Grave of Elmi Boodhari, 1971)

O King of poets!
....
O Elmi, you who died from passion's anguish,
You are the very masterpiece of love!
....
Accept my greetings, praise and homage. (Author's translation)

A keen observer of Somali society, Hadrawi is also known as an astute social critic and the master of the *sarbeed* genre (coded poetry). His use of coded poems was culturally a continuation of the Somali poetic tradition of coded poetry (cryptic verses that could be understood only by a person highly adept in the Somali culture and language); but the reason why Hadrawi employed cryptic poetry in much of the 1970s had to do with the fact that any overt criticism of the Barre regime could lead straight to a pole in front of the firing squad. During those years, Hadrawi's verses became so cryptic that they became a challenge to comprehension, and everywhere people were engaged in competitions to decipher them with the effect that, far from being banished from Somali society, as the Barre regime wanted, the poet's words were in every household. In 1972, he initiated the poetic series known as *Siinley*. One of the most enigmatic poems of that era is "Hal la Qalay" (The Slaughtered Camel, 1973). Among its lines:

A serpent is in the room
But there is a thorn below it
The Quulle berries have refused to be despised
The Brave have been vanquished
And the horse has bartered its value for comfort
Pride has crossed pride
And laughter has become cause for suspicion
But the unfinished is still out there (Author's translation)

In long debates, Somalis would try to explain what the poet possibly meant by these lines. Generally, it was accepted that the snake was Siad Barre and the thorn opposition; the quulle wild berries, which indigent nomads collect, symbolized the changed state of Siad Barre and his inner family members bent on monopolizing power. The horse was said by many to symbolize a civilian popular politician who swapped his integrity for the comforts offered by a top post in the military regime. As to the question whether that was what he meant in those verses, the poet answered cannily that the "the people had the right of interpreting his verses." Even if some verses were obscure to the public, everyone agreed that the image of laughter becoming grounds for suspicion and state persecution graphically depicted the fact that people were being persecuted without recourse, the right of habeas corpus having been suspended. Finally, everyone agreed that the unfinished business of modernization and civic construction were altogether forgotten by Barre and his cronies in the pursuit of perpetuating their rule.

As could be expected, the eyes and ears of the regime in the name of the state security agencies were fully aware of the debates aroused by Hadrawi's verses and soon accused him of making poems and songs with hidden political messages. He was expressly asked to make songs in praise of the "revolution" (i.e., the military junta), as some of the lesser poets and artists were doing. But he would not accept that and in 1973 he was exiled to what became known as Barre's "gulag" for defiant artists, which was a lonely village in the upper Juba region by the name of Qansax-Dheere, where he continued to make public more critical verse bemoaning how the regime was straying from its statements of justice and equality. In prison and conscious of the physical danger he was exposing himself to but yet true to his conscience, he stated his convictions in a poem called "Deyn Maayo Heesaha" (1973) [I Will Not Cease Verse-making].

My mouth is bubbling
It is telling me to speak
And I am blocking it
But as long as God's gift
And the lines of verse
Are on my sides
As long as my spirit is alit
As long as my desire is alive
And there is a subject to vocalize
I will not cease verse-making

Subservience to others
Is not what my mother bequeathed to me (Author's translation)

Hadrawi was released in 1978 and made a director in the Academy of Arts
and Sciences. The junta thought they had broken him into submission, but
Hadrawi was not cowed, and he continued writing his cryptic verses. Within
the same year of his release, he produced a poem called "Dhahar" (1980) in
which he resumed his codified criticism of the regime and the new social
class of exploiters it was fostering.

O Mohamed Hashi, the perfect [Mohamed Hashi Dhama' is
    another well-known poet]
Behold this *dhilowyahan* [a parasitic plant]
Growing on the blood
And the sap of the umbrella acacias
Entwined on their tops
Should I enumerate the genealogies of trees
And how they behave? (Author's translation)

MODERN PROSE WRITING—NOVEL AND STORYWRITING

It can be that Somali prose came, before the official adoption of an orthography, in the form of oral stories and legends. Folk stories about Queen
Araweelo and Igal Shideed, a comical figure, were the staples of storytelling
to children for ages and still are. As literacy in Somali increased, two types
of writers emerged: the preservers and the creators.[10] The preservers set about
recording oral literature to preserve it for future generations; whereas the
creators wrote new fiction and produced stories, novelettes, and novels. The
preservers collected not only prose but poetry as well, and their work did not
start with the official writing of the Somali language. Indeed, men such as
Muse H.I. Galal and Shire Jama Ahmed were engaged in collecting Somali
literature in the 1950s and in the 1960s; whereas Omar Aw Nuuh might be
said to be one of the new preservers.

Among the new literary creations in written prose after 1972 are numerous
short stories, novelettes, and novels. The first full-scale novel of the period
has been written by Farah M.J. 'Awl. With the lofty name of *Aqoondaro waa
u nacab jacayl* (Ignorance is the enemy of love), his novel is a baroque work
that contains both prose and verse forms and in which the themes of love,
hardship, and tragedy are played out amid propagandistic idealization of a

violent period (1900–1921)—the era of Hassan's wars; both the prose and verse forms in this half-fiction half-propaganda work display the fine forms of Somali oral literature.

The most influential novel so far and without doubt better understood by the younger generation is Mohamed D. Afrah's *Maanafay*. Published first in serialized form in the government-owned daily *Xiddigta Octoobar*, it became an instant hit among the general public of Mogadishu. It was subsequently published in book form. The reason why this novel proved more popular than 'Awl's novel lies in its themes, characters, and language. First, instead of a baroque language in which prose and poetry alternate, Afrah uses language that ordinary people can understand. Additionally, the themes of his novel are everyday themes that modern young city-dwellers can understand: conflict between tradition and modernity, conservatism and liberalism, the corruption and the riches of the new rulers versus the poverty and innocence of ordinary persons. The main character Maanafaay is a young schoolgirl who, against her wishes, is to be married off to the man chosen for her by her father; but her heart belongs to a young modern Somali, Ahmed, whose father happens to be one of the corrupt old men who had capitalized on their connections to reach positions of power and who visit brothels stocked with young women from poor families. When Maanafaay runs away to escape the forced marriage, madame Beydan, who makes her living from the procurement of young girls to the immoral men of power, lures her to the "green villa" where Ahmed's father is waiting for his prey; she is rescued by Ahmed and her sister, acting on a tip from the disgusted sister of madame Beydan.

DRAMA

Somali performance theater is a very important aspect of the cultural life of Somalis. In small provincial towns with no permanent theater or performance groups, the arrival of a touring theater troupe is an event that brings immense excitement to the locals. Suddenly, the seemingly tranquil town wakes up from its provincial stupor as the arrival of the troupe spreads by word of mouth, and soon the *riwaayad* (play) and its stars become the talk of the town. Such itinerant troupes are large enterprises, since they also include musicians and their equipment.

An evening at the theater is a special occasion. People dress in their best and the theater, usually a community center or a schoolyard in small communities, becomes a place to admire the finery and elegance of others. The play usually starts at 8:00 P.M. and runs for two to three hours. Going to the theater is a family affair, and young children are brought to the play so they can learn the subtleties of the language as well as the moral lessons displayed.

The modern Somali theater is said to have evolved from modest beginnings in the 1940s in the north and has since continued to occupy a prominent place in Somali arts. One of the reasons why the theater still ranks as the first venue for entertainment is the lack of an indigenous film industry. But that cannot be said to be the main reason. The success of the Somali theater lies in its nature and packaging as a cultural commodity. The Somali play is not only some text and some characters; it is also part pure drama in the form of alliterative text, part singing show, and part comedy show. All these different components are integrated in a way that provides a complete entertainment and cultural package. The Somali riwaayad is therefore a synthesis of old, in the form of versified text and songs, and new, in the form of comedy and music.

The cast consists usually of one main actor and actress, one supporting actor and actress, as well as two sets of parents, usually the parents of the actors and actresses. Miscellaneous roles are played either by different actors or the same actor. A typical play has a cast of no less than ten persons and each actor might play more than one role. The stars are also called to be the main singers and consequently the best-known singers are also the best-known theater stars. In the early days of modern Somali drama, female artists were unheard of, and some of the male artists had to play female roles. That period, however, did not last long after Shamis Abokor "Guduudo Carwo" become the first female performance artist and vocalist in the north. Khadija Abdullahi Daalays played the same role in the south.

Somali plays are not just art for the sake of art or presentations about surrealistic explorations; they deal with societal problems, the lofty ideals of nationhood, patriotism, morality, and human sentiments while still providing entertainment. Thieves get caught; false lovers are punished by *nabsi* (the righter of wrongs), and corruption gets exposed.

The composers are persons who have mastered the art of versification and poetry, since plain prose alone is not the stuff of a Somali play. The composers are therefore also prominent poets and song composers. A few like the prolific Abdillahi Diriye (Sooraan) have been alternatively composer, actor, singer, and comedian. As such, they are persons who have an immense knowledge of Somali culture and language. Their learning schools are in the company of the other artists and composers and not the classroom of a university. However, lack of higher education, rather being a handicap, gives them the ability to be one with the people and their feelings; they are able, as a result, to compose works that are a barometer of popular sentiments. This inevitably turns the composers into social critics and political commentators of the day, which in turn puts them at loggerheads with rulers. The 1960s, during the time of the civilian governments, might be said to have been the golden era of the Somali play. During the twenty years of Siad Barre's reign, political persecution kept good composers from critical works, although by making use of *sarbeeb* (hidden messages), a number of works were staged; some of which were pulled off the stage when the censors finally caught with up with the meanings of the metaphors.

The current repertoire is a large one but few have been transcribed and written in a book form; this is because the Somali play, much like Somali poetry, has tended to be entirely composed orally and then either memorized or recorded onto tape. Even less have been translated into foreign languages. One play that has been translated into English is a play titled "Shabeel-naagood" (Tiger Among Women) and composed by Hassan Sheikh Mumim, a prominent composer. Some other prominent composers are Ahmed Saleebeen Bidde ("Alla Aamin ma Iisho" [The Innocent Never Regret, 1964]), Abdi Adan Qays ("Sarreeye Hoose" [Up and Down, 1967]), Mohamud Abdillahi Sangub ("Qabrigii Jacaylka" [Love's Grave, 1973]), Abdillahi Diiriye (Sooraan) ("Lama Huraan Waa Cawska Jiilaal" [Necessity Is Like the Hay of the Dry Season, 1967]), Abdillahi Qarshe, Huseen Aw-Farah, Mohamed Omar (Huryo), Ismail Ahmed (Hadhuudh), Mohamed Ismail (Balo'as), and Abdi Amiin, whose play "Muufo" (Bread, 1979) promptly earned the displeasure of Siad Barre, who was in the audience, and prison for its author.

BROADCASTING—RADIO AND TELEVISION

The first Somali language radio broadcasts date from the period of World War II, when the Italians and the British were vying for the attention of Somalis, by broadcasting respectively from Addis Ababa and Aden.[11] However, the first regular Somali-language radio station came into being in 1943 in Hargeisa and was "accepted by the public as a welcome innovation."[12] Initially called Radio Goodir (Kudu), it became known later simply as Radio Hargeisa. Ever since, the radio has become a major source of news and entertainment for Somalis. With the introduction of cheap portable transistor sets in the 1950s, radio broadcasting reached even the most isolated pastoralists, so much so that it is a common sight to see a group of nomads huddled around a radio listening to the news or a poem.

The first broadcasters at Radio Hargeisa had a difficult task of translating news items from English into a language with no modern technological and political terms; but making use of the linguistic methods of innovation and word formation inherent in the Somali language, they initiated a movement of modernizing the vocabulary of the Somali language long before the adoption of an official orthography in 1972. Additionally, by integrating the cultural instructors of the people such as poets and wadaads into their programs, they transformed the new technology into a new channel for the diffusion of the Somali culture. That trend still continues today and the cultural content of Somali radio broadcasts might be said to be all Somali. Somali radios exclude, for example, all types of foreign music and songs and, as a result, the Somali public is blissfully unaware of major musical or pop trends from the outside.

Later, a second Somali-speaking radio station was opened in 1951 in Mogadishu. These two stations then became the main centers of Somali language broadcasts. Today, Somali language broadcasts are carried by radio stations in several countries: UK (BBC World Service), Egypt, Italy, Saudi Arabia, Kenya, Ethiopia, Djibouti. Somali-speakers therefore have a variety of stations both local and international to choose from; but of all the outside stations, the Somali BBC World Service is the most popular.

Although Somalis own their fair share of television sets and VCRs, as is evident from video leasing outlets in the main towns, television broadcasting came late to the Somalis. The first television station was set up in Mogadishu in 1985. It was a government-owned station whose broadcast zone was limited to the capital. After the fall of the Barre regime, there was no television station in Mogadishu for some time until 1999 when a private station came into being. In the north, some enterprising businesspeople founded the first television station in Hargeisa in 1996. Both television stations have, however, limited diffusion and television as a mass medium does not yet exist, thus the radio remains the only mass medium for entertainment as well as for the propagation of educational and political programs.

THE PRESS

If the radio largely replaced the Somali news troubadours, the people who used to transmit news from one locality to another in the old days, the introduction of Somali-language newspapers made them even more redundant. Before 1972, there were no Somali-language newspapers. There were, however, newspapers in Arabic, English, and Italian; but their circulation was handicapped by the limited number of Somalis able to read well in these languages. For some reason, be it the oft-cited pride of Somalis in their culture or some socioeconomic cause, among Somalis, foreign languages never reached the same levels of currency as, say, English had in Ghana or in Malaysia or even in neighboring Kenya.

However, written Somali did not flower much when the official orthography was adopted. This was largely due to the military junta's debilitating hold on all media in the country—even private printing machines had been confiscated and nationalized. Consequently, the choice of newspapers was a hobson's choice: you bought and read the government-owned *Xiddigta Oktoobar* (October Star), named after the day of the coup that curtailed parliamentary democracy in the country, or none at all.

However, even without competition, the circulation of *Xiddigta Oktoobar* was always dismally low and never exceeded 50,000. The reason for such a low publication figure was not that Somalis did not like reading, but that the newspaper was a government mouthpiece full of dreary propaganda articles and speeches by the president or other government functionaries. It soon came to be known as *'ar-I-Dhamee* (I Dare You to Finish Me) newspaper.[13] No matter how low its price (at invariably 50 cents a copy), it was said to be the lowest-priced commodity in Mogadishu, but still at the end of the day, unsold copies had to be given away to party functionaries and the paramilitary forces.

After the fall of the Barre regime, despite the chaos and the destruction in the major towns, enterprising Somalis started new publications in every major city, and the Somali consumer had at last, despite all the problems facing him or her in the absence of a central government, particularly in the south, a choice as far as newspapers were concerned. After a trial period which saw the startup and the closing of many newspapers, several newspapers have now a solid foundation and a significant readership in their area of circulation. An influential newspaper in Hargeisa is *Jamhuuriya*, which has a far larger circulation than the government-owned *Maandeeq*—"government" here means government of the Republic of Somaliland in the northern regions, the rest of the old Somalia still lacking central governance, although by no means completely devoid of local administrations. Two of the main papers in the south are *Qaran* and *Xog-Ogaal.*

NOTES

1. Richard Burton (1856, 1987). *First Footsteps in East Africa.* New York: Dover Publications, 47.

2. Denis Herbstein (1991). "The Alphabet War," *Africa Report* 36, no. 3 (May–June), 67–69.

3. Mohamed Farah Hared (1993). *Modernization and Standardization in Somali Press Writing*, dissertation, University of Southern California, Los Angeles, p. 29.

4. M.M. Moreno (1955). *II somalo della Somalia, grammatica e testi del Benadir, Darod e Dighil* (Roma: Istituto Poligrafico dello Stato), iv. (Author's translation.)

5. Burton (1987, 1856), 81–82.

6. Margaret Laurence (1954). *A Tree for Poverty: Somali Poetry and Prose.* Hamilton, Ont.: McMaster University Press and ECW Press, p. 23; also see B.W. Andrzejewski and I.M. Lewis (1964). *Somali Poetry: An Introduction.* Oxford: Clarendon Press, p. 2.

7. Laurence (1954), 24–25.

8. *Madiix* is a proper name for a she-camel. Somalis gives names to their favorite camel, cow, sheep, or goat.

9. The poet alludes here to the fact that camels can be taken to grazing areas far from the main nomadic encampments, while goats, sheep, and cattle, easily perishable animals, have to remain near wells.

10. B.W. Andrzejewski (1975). "The Rise of Written Somali Literature," *African Research and Documentation* 8, 7–14.

11. B.W. Andrzejewski (1971). "The Role of Broadcasting in the Adaptation of the Somali Language to Modern Needs," in Whiteley, W.H., ed., *Language Use and Social Change: Problems of Multilingualism with Special Reference to Eastern Africa.* London: Oxford University Press for International African Institute, p. 263.

12. Ibid., 265.

13. Mahamuud Siyad Togane (1990). "High on Marxist Humbug," *Horn of Africa* 21, no. 1–2: 104.

SUGGESTED READING

Andrzejewski, B.W., and Sheila Andrzejewski. 1993. *An Anthology of Somali Poetry.* Bloomington: Indiana University Press.

Andrzejewski, B.W., and Musa H.I. Galaal. 1963. "A Somali Poetic Combat." *Journal of African Languages and Linguistics* 2, pt. 1, pp. 15–28; pt. 2, pp. 93–100; pt. 3, pp. 190–205. East Lansing: Michigan State University, African Studies Center.

Andrzejewski, B.W., and I.M. Lewis. 1964. *Somali Poetry: An Introduction.* Oxford: Clarendon Press.

Galaal, Muuse Haaji Ismaa'iil. 1956. *Hikmad Soomaali.* London: Oxford University Press.

Johnson, John William. 1974. *Heellooy. Heelleellooy: The Development of the Genre Heello in Modern Somali Poetry.* Bloomington: Indiana University Press.

Laitin, David D. 1977. *Politics, Language and Thought: The Somali Experience.* Chicago: University of Chicago Press.

Laurence, Margaret. 1954. *A Tree for Poverty: Somali Poetry and Prose.* Hamilton, Ont.: McMaster University Library Press and ECW Press.

Loughran, John, Katheryne Loughran, John Johnson, and Said S. Samatar, eds. 1986. *Somalia in Word and Image.* Washington, D.C.: Foundation for Cross-Cultural Understanding.

Mumin, Hassan Sheikh. 1974. *Leopard Among the Women: Shabeel Naagood, Somali Play.* Translated by B.W. Andrzejewski. London: School of Oriental and African Studies, Oxford University Press.

Samatar, Said S. 1982. *Oral Poetry and Somali Nationalism.* Cambridge: Cambridge University Press.

4

Art, Architecture, and Housing

SOMALI VERBAL ARTS such as literature, especially poetry, have found mention in the outside world for more than a century now; less so other forms of art, especially material art, the assumption being the majority of Somalis, always on the move as nomads, possessed little material art. A catalog of material art and artifacts in 1986 represented the first serious survey of material art among Somalis and may have already corrected some of the false impressions.[1]

Somali material art is just as important, if not more so, that Somalis might better be called "art-loving people" instead of a "nation of poets."[2] In fact, far from being rich in only verbal art and poor in material art, the materials of everyday use among Somalis represent high forms of indigenous craft. The carved and woven implements and materials of a traditional Somali *aqal* (the portable nomadic home) are themselves a rich illustration of the fine tradition of carving (*qoris*), weaving (*soohid*), leather-making (*madgin*), and dyeing (*aslid*). Somali material art also manifests itself in the urban centers, whether they date from ancient times or whether they are relatively new.

Most artifacts and material art forms are traditionally utilitarian in origin; however, demand for art objects and artifacts from tourists and from a new generation of Somali collectors has led to the production of for-sale pieces from artists and artisans. One field in which professionals today make a living out of their production is painting. All other fields are artisans' work.

What is common to objects of material art, whether the piece is a carved comb, a woven mat, a worked leather, a gold ornament, or the walls of a building, is an embellishment pattern consisting of lines and geometric pat-

Geometric designs on a wall and door.

terns. Figures of animals or humans are not used; this has been attributed to Islamic influence but it is not known whether that assumption is actually true and it might well be that the lines and geometric designs of Somali art work have existed prior to the arrival of Islam (the Old Cushitic religion itself was monotheistic and used no iconic depictions for god).

Regional variations of material art do exist, although some patterns are to be found almost everywhere. Two different zones—although there is much blending—from the main dominant Somali culture exist: the riverine zone and the Benadir zone. In the riverine zone, conical huts (*mundul*) and dancing masks, pottery-making, and musical instruments such as the lyre (*shareero*) are a carryover from the previously dominant agricultural Bantu populations of this zone. The blending of material cultures in the riverine zone is signified by the fact that the Rahanwein majority, even where village inhabitation and agriculture has occurred, keep the elements of their pastoral culture at the same time; for example, they may reside in a permanent *mundul* (conical hut) but close by they still erect a portable nomadic hut. Other various objects unknown to the majority of Somalis such as hoops for river fishing are found in the riverine zone.

Among the Benadiris of the Benadir, or coastal southern town-dwellers, traces of material culture that link up with the material culture of the Swahilis of East Africa are to be found. These include niches in the interior of walls,

Cabinetmaker works outside his workshop to advertise his product.

huge beds, and various other household objects. A noticeable craft, which is dying now in the Benadir and in the riverine zone, is weaving *allendi* cloth, which parallels in texture and artistry with the *kente* cloth of West Africa.

WOODWORK AND CARVING

Traditionally, all woodwork and carving is done by men, whereas weaving is done by women. The man of the household, among the pastoralists, is supposed to cut wood and carve it into implements. While every man can cut out a branch and turn it into a shepherd's crook (*hangool*), not every man is capable of producing a finely carved camel's bell. A good master carver is therefore recognized by his community. However, most master carvers work only for their own material needs or for that of their relatives and friends. The carved objects are such things as wooden spoons (*fandhaal*), water ladles (*kalah*), bowls (*heedho*), troughs for watering the animals (*qabaal*), water or milk vessels (*haan, dhiil*), camel-bells (*koor*), walking sticks (*bakoorad*), combs (*saqaf*), wooden slates (*looh*) for learning, and wooden lecterns for holding the Koran. In urban centers, any carving is more likely to be done by professional carvers and these are seen on such items as door and window panels, furniture pieces, or stools. However, nowadays, carving of furniture, doors, and windows has disappeared as furniture and fittings are produced in workshops using electric machinery.

Wooden milk vessels and spoons with geometric designs.

Dabqaad: meerschaum incense burners and incense.

Meerschaum (sepiolite), a white mineral of hydrous magnesium silicate, is carved into incense burners, kitchen stoves, and sometimes art relief. The the district of Eilbur is the center of meerschaum quarrying and crafts where a pipemaking industry started.

WEAVING

Among pastoralists, weaving is done by women, just as all carving is done by men. Many of the materials used in the portable home (*aqal*) are woven mats (*'aws*). The making of these mats is time-consuming and some weaving goes on at all times in a pastoral household. The mats are woven from certain types of grass and are adorned with lines and geometric designs threaded into them.

A particularly labor-intensive woven piece is the kabad, which is woven from long fiber filaments, string, and colored thread. The finished product is a rug with plush fibers on one side and a smooth upper surface. The kabad, which might be called a "camel rug" because of its rough surface, is used as an inner wall mat for the aqal; it is also used as a protective cover for the back of the pack-camel or as a seating mat. The making of this piece is usually a collective effort by the women of a settlement. The piece to be worked on is placed under a temporary shelter such as that afforded by a leafy tree where it is set up straight so a group of women can work on it. Much singing, as an encouragement, goes on while work continues. When the piece is finished, a ceremony is held by the women to fold up the rug (*furid kabad*).

Other woven items in a pastoral setting include the *alool* (bamboo grass mat), a piece whose main support is bamboo grass. The threads are different colored ribbons from clothing, usually from wornout clothes. The purpose of this hardy mat is to serve as an exterior wall for the portable home; it is also used as portable walls when a quick meeting place (*gole*) is being marked off in villages and towns. A large variety of ropes and strings are also woven from the bark fibers of acacia trees and in the old days from the fibers of a type of sisal (aloe) plant (*hig*). A particular plant (*qabo*) also provides, after a conditioning process, a much appreciated wicker used in the making of milk and water vessels (*dhiil, haan*). Sleeping mats (*darmo*) and praying mats are woven from palm leaves. A variety of baskets are also woven from the same material or from slivers of bamboo or sugarcane. A particularly beautiful handbag (*qandi*) is made from acacia fibers and string but is now a rare item.

Traditional cloth weaving with looms was widespread in the past, especially in the Benadir coast and in the riverine areas of the south. In fact before the introduction of the cheap American cotton cloth (*maraykaani*) in the nine-

Woman with a traditional pouch (*qandi*).

teenth century, Mogadishu was the textile manufacturing center and its cloths were sought not only in the Horn but were exported to Red Sea, Gulf, and Indian Ocean rim countries. Some loom-made cloth, known locally as *al-lendi*, is still being produced mainly to supply the local market for use as drapes and cultural clothes.

LEATHERWORK

Leatherwork is one of the traditional occupations and in some areas was exclusive to certain groups of people. Sandals, bags, ropes, and other items are made from leather. In the south, stools (*gambar*) and as well as some beds (*jiinbaar*) with a leather top and wooden frame are found. Some leather items, such as saddles for horses or leather praying mats, are seldom produced anymore.

Gambar: a leather and wood stool.

METALWORKS

Traditional artisans that work with metal include goldsmiths and black-smiths. The goldsmiths, who have shops in major towns, produce necklaces, rings, and decorative pieces from gold and silver and the craft is usually passed from father to son. Traditional blacksmiths work with blow-pipes and produce knives and other pieces of metalwork. A particularly well-known product, which is still produced by blacksmiths, is the Somali dagger (*tooray*). This is a short, curved dagger, although in some areas, such as among the Issa Somalis, it can be fairly large. The handle is made from a cattle horn, and in the old days from a rhino horn, which is inlaid with metal lines for embellishment. The dagger is carried in a leather sheath, which is worn around the waist, and is a common sight in the countryside.

Today, traditional blacksmiths are dwindling in numbers and most metalwork is done in metal shops which produce a variety of items such as iron gates, windows, and other goods.

PAINTING PICTURES

Painting pictures as a profession is relatively new to Somalis; however, the use of painted posters for propaganda purposes by the government of Siad

Barre as well as the demand for decorative paintings from the general public made it possible for painters to live as professionals and open artists' shops in the 1970s. The inhibition against making "images" is long gone and portraits and pastoral scenes are popular, with paintings of camels and herders being the most common—a revealing testimony to the profound pastoral origins of Somalis. Most of the painters are folk painters who have learned their trade by apprenticeship, and many of them paint from memory.

ARCHITECTURE/HOUSING

In the old coastal towns, soft limestone as well as sun-dried bricks were the common building materials. Building on the rubble of older buildings is also fairly common and the old coastal towns can be said to have been rebuilt again and again over their previous ruins. Some of the architectural styles as well as, oddly enough, origins of the coastal towns were in the past attributed to be the work of outsiders as part of a fairly common colonialist mentality that attributed anything of value to someone other than Somalis. However, the accounts of medieval Arab travelers who came to visit Somali towns always wrote of the towns as "Berber" towns, the word for Somali before the fifteenth century. Nevertheless, the architectural style in ancient Somali towns such as Zeilah or Mogadishu reflects some influences that spread from other Islamic countries. This is to be expected given the proximity of the land of Somalis to the Arabian coast. But to attribute Somali ancient towns to outsiders is just of the same kind of opinion as that which in the past denied Africans their cultural heritage and ancient civilizations including that of ancient Egypt.

In the modern cities, just as in the past, stones and bricks are the main building materials; however, concrete roofs and pillars are now fairly common and are used in storied buildings. In Mogadishu and the coastal areas, soft limestone is still quarried and used for walls. Italian architectural styles now have some influence in the south, a remnant of its past history as an Italian colony. That influence is most noticeable in Mogadishu and it manifests itself as colonnades and embellishments. In the north, because of the mountainous terrain and the availability of stones, stone is the main building material for homes and one-story buildings. The different patterns of the stone work, the colors of the stones themselves, which range from pinkish to white hues, as well as colorings applied to the layers of stones give northern towns a distinctive look and warmth. In the country, permanent constructions include wattle and daub homes (*'ariish*), round homes (*mundul*) (riv-

Villa construction combines traditional and modern methods.

Round wattle and daub homes of a southern village.

Adobe building of a northern village.

erine areas of the south) and adobe (sun-dried bricks) buildings (*dargad*) in the north.

Traditional Portable Nomadic House

The traditional portable home is a familiar sight in the countryside; it is the home of the pastoralist. It consists of the frame of semicircular supports and a middle pillar (*udub-dhehaad*). The semicircular supports (*dhigo*) are made from light-weight wood from the branches and roots of certain trees; the covering, as we have said, consists of woven mats; for additional impermeability a tarpaulin is draped on the top.

MAIN FEATURES OF URBAN AND RURAL HABITATS

The Somali home is an oasis from the outside world; Somalis do not like passersby to see them in their homes eating or going about their home routines. Homes are to provide shade, sanctuary, and security from prying eyes; thus open porches and see-through bay windows are not found in Somali homes. Whether the abode is a nomadic homestead (*guri*) or a townhome, fences and walls that keep the outside world at bay are part of the Somali habitat. Courtyards and high ceilings are also another feature of townhomes. Areas such as courtyards are neutral zones where male strangers might sit and have a cup of tea.

Aqal: traditional nomadic home.

In a nomadic homestead, the aqal constitutes the inner area accessible only to family members; strangers, especially men, are bound by protocol to the courtyard afforded by the fence surrounding the homestead and the men's fire corner (*ardaa*). Even if there is no fence surrounding the homestead, as now is the case in many places, male strangers have to stay outside the portable house at all times. The nomadic house is divided into two parts: an atrium (*dadab*), which forms part of the entryway, and an inner area where the family members sleep. Usually older male children and the father sleep,

Modern multistory building in downtown Hargeisa.

Downtown Mogadishu combines colonial Italian architecture with local design. (Note that the cathedral has been
destroyed since the war.)

except when it rains, in the men's fire corner. Older daughters and grand-
mothers sometimes have their own portable houses that are smaller in size
(*buul*).

The ardaa is an open space in the settlement (guri) protected from the
winds by some thorn bush fence; a mat or two for sitting and sleeping at

Building that survived the bombing of 1988 in Hargeisa shows the arches and
embellishments of an earlier period.

Hargeisa square: downtown squares are usually spacious.

night is always found in this place. The mats are folded during the day and unfolded in the evening for use. A large fire is lighted at night in this area of the settlement; the purpose of the fire is to keep away wild animals—today mainly hyenas and foxes—and to act as a beacon to travelers and family

Suuq (market): open markets and bazaars are lively places to shop.

members. In this regard, there is nothing more joyous to the weary traveler than to see the fire of a settlement at night because giving shelter and food to the traveling visitor (*marti*) is a cultural institution among Somalis, and traveling nomads and priests (*wadaad*) depend entirely on the charity of settlements for survival. Male visitors as well as men of the settlement (the father, older male children) sleep and eat in this area while the womenfolk and younger children eat their meals inside the aqal. Finally, the ardaa is where stories are told and men discuss affairs; thus today, the very word means a forum.

In towns, the thorn-fence of the countryside is replaced with high walls of stones, bricks, or wattle. An interior courtyard, which might be covered, is the equivalent of the pastoral or country courtyard. Children play in this courtyard; clothes are hung and strangers and peddlers might come into this area. Many townhomes have four rooms; one master bedroom for the couple, one combination dining-sitting room, and two other bedrooms, which are divided between the female and male offspring. Any relatives visiting the family sleep with the children in these two bedrooms, depending on the gender. The latrine, which is more widespread, and a kitchenette are to be found tucked somewhere in the courtyard.

In towns, large squares are a main feature. The squares permit a lot of activity; peddlers hawk their wares there; children play in them; and people who know each other might just stand there speaking to one another for a long time. A visible structure in any town is a mosque with its minaret.

NOTES

1. John Loughran, Katheryne Loughran, John Johnson, and Said S. Samatar (eds.) (1986). *Somalia in Word and Image.* Washington, D.C.: Foundation for Cross-Cultural Understanding.

2. Mohamed D. Afrah (1993/94). "A Nation of Poets or Art-loving People? The Role of Literature in the Present-day Somali." *Hal-Abuur* 2, nos. 2 and 3: 32–37.

SUGGESTED READING

Lewis, I.M. 1961. *Pastoral Democracy: A Study of Pastoralism Among the Northern Somali of the Horn of Africa.* London: Oxford University Press.

———. 1955. *The Peoples of the Horn of Africa: Somali, Afar and Saho.* London: International African Institute.

Loughran, John, Katheryne Loughran, John Johnson, and Said S. Samatar, eds. 1986. *Somalia in Word and Image.* Washington, D.C.: Foundation for Cross-Cultural Understanding.

5

Cuisine and Traditional Dress

CUISINE

THE SOMALI CUISINE is one that the world has yet to discover mainly because of the lack of books on the subject—Somali cuisine remains today largely a knowledge system that is acquired by practical learning and apprenticeship. Another reason why Somali cuisine has remained so hidden is because tourist hotels tended to serve European food to Europeans—colonial Europeans (the Italians, British, and French) tended to stick to their own eating habits and modern hotels have continued to serve European food to European tourists. Another reason why Somali cuisine remains a secret is because Somalis do not cook or eat on the street. It is against Somali culture to eat in public, not for fear of an evil eye seeing you eat but rather because of a cultural stipulation that eating alone when others are not doing likewise is selfish; therefore, no one cooks in street stalls and no smells of cooking food greet the international visitor on the streets.

Although unique in many ways, Somali cuisine is in many other ways typical of the Horn of Africa. Like all cuisines in the world, it has, however, incorporated different elements from near and even distant cultures over the centuries. The influences are mainly from the Swahili coastal peoples in East Africa, India, and Arabia. European influences are perhaps a minor element overall but include spaghetti dishes (Italian influence) and some desserts such as pudding (British influence). Somali cuisine might also be easily divided up into rural and urban fare, with rural fare being more simple in style and less copious in vegetables and fruit servings.

Dinner: meals are traditionally eaten sitting on floor mats.

Zonal variations in Somali cuisine follow the cultural zones such as Benadir, southern riverine, and northern. These zones are more a result of the use of some ingredients and dishes than about differences in styles. Broadly speaking, the northern cuisine, which corresponds to the ex-British Somaliland and today's Republic of Somaliland, differs from the southern cuisine by the predominant use of rice and rice dishes. Northern cuisine has now largely diffused to the south due to the northerners opening restaurants and residing in the south. Likewise, the use of spaghetti and spaghetti dishes, an Italian influence, is more prevalent in the south, although spaghetti use has now diffused to the north. In the same manner, in the Benadir coastal region of the south use of fish and fish dishes is more prevalent than in other areas. In the riverine zone, among the cultivating communities of Bantu and Rahanwein villagers polenta (*soor*), a thick mush made from corn or sorghum meal, is the staple food. To obtain the mush, corn or sorghum grains are coarsely ground and boiled and then served with various accompaniments (*kusaar*).

Given these few basic differences in regional fare, we will speak of Somali cuisine in general in the following pages, and merely point out where a particular style or dish is used.

First the ingredients of the cuisine are cereal-based products (rice, spaghetti, sorghum, corn, and beans), fresh vegetables and fruits, a wide variety of spices sold by weight in markets, and fresh meat products (mutton, beef, camel meat, fish, and chicken). Among meats, mutton is the favorite and dominates the use of all others; goat meat is the second most popular, with beef somewhere in the middle and camel meat being the least favorite. This order does not correlate to any perceived qualities of the meat but is mostly about availability. Very little fowl, mainly chicken, is consumed. Somalis do not eat any other bird meat. Fish is consumed only along the coasts, mainly because of the lack of cold storage in towns far away from the coast. Game meat from different types of deer is rarely consumed and usually exclusively in the countryside out of necessity, except of course, among the few remaining hunting communities in the riverine areas because hunting carries a stigma in traditional society. Pork or meat from carnivores or from horses and donkeys is forbidden (*haaraan*) by the religion; reptiles such as lizards and snakes are not eaten.

Meat is consumed only if the animal has been butchered according to Muslim practice (*halal*). This means that the animal was slaughtered swiftly with a stroke of knife across the throat while a short prayer was said. The anecdote of a nomad who would not eat fish because he thought the fish, which still had its head intact on the plate, had not been slaughtered in the Muslim way testifies to the strict adherence of the halal practice among Somalis (fish is not in the category to which the halal custom applies). The brain and viscera, with the exception of liver, kidneys, and tripes, are not consumed. Meat dishes are cooked well done, and rare or uncooked meat is not consumed. The only meat eaten raw by nomad connoisseurs is the bloodless fat in a camel's hump (*amaan*); however, this is now more of a cultural history than an existing practice. Today's urban Somalis may not even be aware of this ancient delicacy. Camel hump fat, however, when cooked, is still consumed with hot bowls of soup and heaps of flat *injera* bread.

Rice and spaghetti are served with a meat sauce (*suugo*). Somali meat sauce, which is by itself a dish when served with bread, might be very spicy or mildly spiced according to the taste required. Onions, garlic, cardamom, ginger, cinnamon, fresh local parsley, and several other vegetables and condiments give the Somali meat sauce a strong pungent smell that lingers in the kitchen long after the meal has been consumed. As soon as the sauce meat is ready, it is poured on top of the rice, spaghetti, or corn meal dish. Hot ground peppers are usually served in a small bowl so that individuals can spice their plate according to their tastes. A special paste of ground peppers, other condiments, and lemon juice is used in the north (*duqus*).

A variety of stews and soups are known through combinations of different types of meat and vegetables. A particularly common stew is known as *fahfah* in the north and *kalaankal* in the south. To obtain these stews, a variety of vegetables, large pieces of meat, and condiments are simmered for a long time until the meat is tender. The meat pieces are then separated and either served as they are or dipped in a red sauce or fried. The liquid is served as a broth (*maraq*). This is the common way of preparing meats in the country-side, although pastoralists and even traditional cultivators, who cultivate only cereals but no vegetables or fruits, usually do not have access to vegetables. Riverine cultivators add the broth to the corn or sorghum mush to soften it. Purely vegetable soups are not a Somali tradition, Somalis being great consumers of meat; however, in the south where Italian culinary influence exists, vegetable soups are known and are served mostly in restaurants. The name of one such vegetable soup, *manistroni*, is itself of Italian origin. A particularly common vegetable and meat stew dish is called *suqaar*; accompanied by bread, it is a part of the evening menu of all Somali restaurants. Meat is roasted in large wood-fired ovens and is served in many roadside eateries. Tallow (*haydh*) obtained from animal fats and bones is sometimes used by poorer families in cooking. A thick fat (*badhi*) is obtained from the rump of the Somali black-headed sheep and is used in foods and as a medicine for certain ailments in traditional medicine. Sometimes the rump fat is cut into small pieces and fried into small puffy balls (*shariiryo*) that are eaten as a side dish.

Rice and pasta dishes come in different styles. A particularly well known rice and meat dish is known as *isku-dheh-karis*, which translates as mixed cooking. Isku-dheh-karis is a dish of vegetables, meat pieces, and rice cooked together in a process that starts with the browning of the vegetables and meat. This dish when cooked in a clay pot is called *baris-dhari*; it is said that the clay pot imparts a certain flavor lacking in rice cooked in metallic pots. A rather colorful rice dish is the *surbiyaan*, which is obtained when white rice and colored rice, prepared separately, are mixed together to produce a colorful dish. Until recently when rice cultivation was introduced in the riverine areas, no rice was cultivated anywhere; however, rice had been a staple import from Asia for centuries and the *Periplus*, the Greek document from the first century A.D., mentions it as an import for northern coasts.[1] In contrast, pasta or spaghetti is a relatively new addition to Somali cuisine as it dates from the Italian colonization of the southern areas in the beginning of the twentieth century.

Vegetable oils as well as clarified butter or ghee (*subag*) are used in Somali cooking. It is the use of ghee that gives a distinct flavor to foods. All ghee is made by rural families who bring it to the markets in villages and towns to sell. Ghee is obtained by melting fresh butter. The best ghee is obtained when a small amount of sorghum meal is added to the hot liquid butter. The sorghum sinks to the bottom and helps refine the ghee by absorbing milky substances and sinking down, as a sediment, to the bottom. The leaves of an aromatic shrub, a kind of a myrtle, are also added to give perfume to the ghee. After the ghee is drained, the remaining sorghum mush (*heemaar*) is considered a delicacy and is usually given to children.

Somali cuisine has perhaps the largest variety of breads anywhere in the world. The four main categories, each with different subvarieties depending on the shape and the flour used, are *injera, sabaayad, muufo,* and *roodhi* (*rooti*).

Injera, known in the north as *lahooh,* is a thin pancake that is made from batter poured in a circular pattern starting in the center of a hot greased flat pan. It is never flipped over, although lifting it from the corners is usual. Sorghum is the preferred flour for making injera, which is common in the countries of the Horn. There is a sweet variety and another variety that has eggs added. Injera has the widest usage of all bread types, and it is easy to make and does not require an oven like muufo and roodhi (rooti) types. A regular breakfast in a Somali family consists of three pieces of injera with ghee and a cup of tea. At lunch, which is the main meal of the day for a Somali family, injera might also be eaten with stew or soup.

Sabaayad bread is also round and flat as injera but is much thicker; it resembles Indian flat bread. Unlike injera, however, this bread is made from a slab of dough that is flipped over on a well-oiled flat pan until done on both sides.

A certain type of doughy bread (muufo) is also made from sorghum or corn meal and is found in Benadir and riverine cuisine. The word itself is from the Swahili language. Muufo has a rough surface and looks like pita bread from the Middle East except that it cannot be opened into a pocket. To make muufo, a ball of dough is flattened into a circular shape and slapped to attach to the sides of an oven that opens from the top; the oven (*tinaar*), which looks like a large-sized earthen pot, has live embers in the bottom. Most popular restaurants in the Benadir serve this type of bread with stews, soups, and steak dishes.

Bread that looks familiar to Western consumers is the roodhi or rooti. Traditionally, this type of bread is made by bakers using wood-fired ovens and there are still many family bakeries in the major towns. However, bakery plants have made some inroads in the 1980s, which pushed some of the family bakeries out of business in the main cities. The variety of baked breads ranges from loaves to several kinds of elongated breads or baguettes.

A great variety of fruits and vegetables are produced by Somali farmers and fresh produce is available year round. Somali grapefruit, papayas, and bananas have been exported to the Middle East countries and to Italy. Guava, pomegranate, and mango are grown and are available in the main markets. In the north, because of the temperate climate, there is a wider choice of citrus fruits.

Restaurants

There are many restaurants in all towns; most can be called traditional restaurants in that the foods and the setting are traditional. There are usually no printed menus on hand and the waiter when asked what is available belts out the menu in a rapid voice. Such popular restaurants are usually crowded and waiters do not stay very long with one customer; tips are not expected but would be accepted. More expensive restaurants have more spaces and may have printed menus; waiters spend more time with the customer and tipping is expected. On the streets one sees frequent commercial signs saying *bar*; the name, borrowed from the Italians, is misleading and does not refer to a drinking bar or a bistro but just a popular eatery. Camel-meat restaurants specialize in broiled camel, broth, and large slivers of camel hump, eaten with steaming mounds of injera.

Beverages

Bottled soda beverages, whether locally bottled or imported, that look familiar to the Western traveler might be found in towns. However, it should be said that Somalis, being Muslims, have no traditions of making alcoholic drinks. Nevertheless, sale of alcoholic drinks and some production of rum from sugarcane started in the colonial era and continued up to the fall of the Barre regime in 1991. Since then, consumption and the sale of alcoholic beverages seem to be forbidden by the different regional authorities and subject to severe punishment. Even if someone eludes arrest by the authorities, a whiff of an alcoholic beverage emanating from someone makes one liable to an instant mob justice and stoning by impish youngsters. Soda and fruit drinks, particularly lemonades, are popular. Freshly squeezed grapefruit juice (*isbaramunto*) in the south (from Italian *spremuta*) is sold by restaurants and soft drink outlets.

Coffee, a product of the Horn before it spread to the rest of the world, is drunk in two ways: traditional or European style. When traditional it is called *bun* and is made from home-roasted coffee beans and husks (*qashar*). Among the Rahanwein of southwestern Somalia and other riverine inhabitants, coffee beans are boiled in ghee, an ancient custom shared with the Oromo of Ethiopia. The beans are then consumed while the scalding ghee is used to anoint the body, especially the scalp. Somali traditional coffee is a strong brew. European-style coffee is brewed from machine-ground coffee and is available either as a regular coffee brew or as espresso coffee, another Italian influence. However, coffee use is marginal among Somalis and does not come anywhere near tea, the national drink.

Somali Tea

Somali traditional tea is a sweet and fragrant beverage. Among the ingredients that give it fragrance are cardamom, cloves, fresh ginger, and lemon. Strong tea leaves from Kenya or southern India and Sri Lanka are preferred. The leaves are infused in a large metal kettle (*kildhi*) and the various ingredients are added one after the other with the tea leaves being introduced first. Sugar is also added into the boiling infusion and not after. The choice of sugar level depends therefore on the person who is preparing the tea. Somali tea is usually sweet and syrupy; however, the spicy ingredients usually mask the sugar and the tea does not taste very sweet. After the infusion of tea leaves and the herbs and sugar have been added, milk may be added. If no milk is needed, a few drops of lemon juice may be added. The most preferred milk for tea is goat's milk; cow's milk might be used if no other type of milk is available. The tea is not served in a mug but in small glass cups.

The essence of Somali tea is not just the tea leaves but the other ingredients as well. A fragrant hot cup of tea is the preferred drink no matter how hot it is. In the arid countryside, a hot cup of tea is what the thirsty traveler gets first. Sugary tea is said to quench thirst better than plain water, which can cause stomach ache and distension in an overly thirsty person. That is why in the countryside tea shops you will see a weary pastoralist who might have walked thirty miles without a drop of water cradling not a cup of cool water but a steaming cup of tea. Tea also has therapeutic uses and when strongly spiced with fresh ginger is a folk therapy for common colds.

Tea is sold in all restaurants; it is also sold by stalls on the street as well as by itinerant sellers who push wheelbarrows full of thermos bottles containing the brew. In the countryside, the tea shop might be housed in an adobe or a wattle and daub building or even in a shade of bushes and wattle (*waab*) in temporary settlements. There, nomadic men gather, exchange news and information, listen to poetic recitations or fresh compositions of poetry, and drink cup after cup of hot tea. Round houses are sometimes offered by someone who might have made a good sale of livestock or who is visiting from abroad or from a large town. Paying for a cup of tea for a friend or a group of friends is common and reciprocity by picking up the tab in turn is expected and is received. A sly customer, who does not want to reciprocate for previous offers from friends, is said, as a joke, to secretly signal an order to the waiter and to exclaim loudly: "I wonder who has offered me this cup of tea!" In short, a lot of socialization revolves around the drinking of tea among Somalis just as a lot of socialization in the West revolves around drinking alcoholic beverages in a pub or a bar. The one noticeable difference is, however, that women do not frequent tea shops. Somali society is in many ways largely gender-segregated and women socialize among themselves by visiting each other's homes.

Somali Pastries

Somali cuisine also includes a significant number of pastries and cakes. These also show outside influences just like the rest of the cuisine. An indication of borrowing is the fact that the word for cake is *dolshe* (from Italian *dolce* "sweet") in the south, and *keeg* (from English "cake") in the north. A good amount of Somali pastries are oil pastries or oil cakes made from dough and other ingredients dipped in sizzling oil. These include puffy yellow cakes of various tastes and shapes, doughnut-like pastries, again of various sizes and shapes, patties containing ingredients that have been minced or ground previously. A particularly widespread patty pastry is the samosa (*sambuuse*) containing seasoned vegetables or meat; of Indian origin, it is now a staple of Somali cuisine and it is sold almost everywhere including by wheelbarrow vendors. During the fasting month of Ramadan, samosas are a regular part of the snack meal that marks the breaking of the fast at sunset in Somali homes. Among the cakes that would look familiar to a Western traveler is the spongy cake, a loose and fluffy cake, and the muffin, which have been borrowed from Western cuisine by the Somalis. Pastry shops in large towns sell a variety of pastries (*ma'ma'aan*), including the sweet meat pastry known as *halwad* and snack foods. Street vendors sell milk-based caramels, sesame-balls, and spicy puffy cakes of yellow colors produced by adding saffron to the dough and halwad.

MANNERS AND CUSTOMS OF MEALS

A noticeable custom among Somalis is the practice of eating food with the hands. Somalis believe that the Prophet Mohamed blessed the habit of eating with one's hands. Therefore, eating solid and semisolid foods with the hand is common among Somalis and it is considered rude to eat with a fork and spoon when everyone else is eating with their hands. Distinction must be made between eating individually and eating in a group. Somalis eating individually at home or at restaurants may use forks and spoons and many do that all the time. However, on occasions when there is a traditional banquet and large communal platters of rice, meat, and vegetables are presented to a group, one must eat from the common platter by using one's right hand.

To eat from a large platter, you dig into a mound of rice, sauce, and meat, twist it slightly into a ball, and place it into your mouth, or you pick a piece of meat from the platter and place it into your mouth. If a piece of meat is too large or too tough to come apart by tugging at it with the fingers, you may cut pieces off by using one of the knives provided by the host.

Eating from a common platter has its own etiquette. First you wash both of your hands before you eat; to reinforce this custom, a proverb says "you don't get into a platter by saying I was at the wells yesterday." The host provides a washing bowl or bucket, water in a container with a spout, and soap, and the host or a delegate or another guest holds the water container for you. You might also be asked to go and wash your hands in a bathroom. You eat from the area directly facing and you continue eating from the same spot until you are done and you have created a zone that looks like it has been strip-mined; touching different zones is bad manners. If you require additional sauce, you pour it on your area. Belching or making noises is bad manners as well as returning to the platter anything you picked up into the folds of your hand. After you are done, you wash your hands again; you then wipe your hands and mouth on the towel that is provided. Finally, it is good manners to express gratitude to Allah by saying *Alhamdu Lilaahi* (Gratitude to Allah). This might be a surprise to Westerners but it is a sign of humility and a way of expressing gratitude to the creator on behalf of the host; if you want to thank the host personally, that is done when you are about to leave by saying thank you (*Mahadsanid*) and "the meal was excellent" (*contadu way macaanayd*).

TRADITIONAL DRESS

Although only worn today during cultural festivals and special occasions, Somali traditional dress has changed little over the centuries. Among traditional dresses for women is the gareys whose modern adaptation is known as *guntiino*. This dress consists of several yards of cloth, which, in a technique that needs much practice to be mastered, like the wearing of the Japanese kimono, is knotted on the right or left shoulder, wrapped around the chest and waist, leaving a fold in the back of the torso that may be used as a hood when sand blows or when it gets cold. The edges of the dress almost touch the ground. A belt of camel thread is then tied around the waist—a particular type of belt with a tassel and bright colors (*boqor*) is worn by young girls who have come of age. A blouse, a long skirt, and a shawl for the shoulder are also a traditional urban dress. Another women's outfit is a long dress (*toob*) that touches the feet and is worn with a long skirt and a shawl. The *diri*, a missionary-style loose dress, brought from Djibouti in the 1970s, has been popularized to such an extent that it is almost universal among Somali women. The *hijab* (veil), a dress that covers a woman's body from head to toe, which is wrongly associated with all Muslims but which has its origin in Arabian tribes, has never been part of regular Somali women's dress, although it had some use in towns as a status symbol and was worn previously by the daughters and wives of rich merchants. Lately, it is seen being worn in communities or by persons of Islamic revivalist persuasion.

Traditional dress for men consists of a white cotton sheet worn around the waist reaching in length to slightly above the ankles; another cotton sheet is used for the top part of the body and is sometimes carried over the shoulder or shaped into a hood or draped across the shoulder depending on the temperature; tassels on the corners of the sheet are sometimes found as an embellishment. A sleeveless cotton shirt completes the attire of a traditional men's outfit. In current fashion the lower piece has been replaced by the sarong (*ma'awis*), borrowed from Muslim Asian countries such as Malaysia or Indonesia. With a sarong, one wears a shirt as the upper piece. However, in urban centers, trousers and a shirt are the most common dress for men. Traditionally, most clothes were fashioned by a tailor, but now most men's apparel is imported because it is inexpensive and there are far fewer people making a living from tailoring.

NOTE

1. Lionel Casson (1989). *The Periplus Maris Erythraie.* Princeton: Princeton University Press, 18.

6

Gender Roles, Marriage, and Family

PASTORALIST VALUES are at the heart of Somali culture, for most Somalis have origins in the pastoralist clans that have been wandering the land with their flocks for millennia; most of what is discussed in this chapter and the following one will mostly likely be true, therefore, of the culture of most Somalis.

In the Somali language the word *guur* has two meanings: to marry and to move away. Marriage in Somali society is therefore viewed as both a rupture and a renewal. It is a rupture because one is leaving one's parents' household, and it is a renewal because one is going to begin a new family. This dimension of rupture and renewal is true for both young men and women.

The socialization of a young man prepares him for that moment of "moving away and marrying," and in a traditional rural society until that moment arrives a young man is a member of his parents' household and therefore under their authority. He, therefore, might be said not to have progressed beyond "boyhood"; he is certainly not yet admitted to the club of household fathers, an informal council of men in a village or a rural area that deliberates on the affairs of the commune. Marriage is the first step in getting accepted in the *shir* (meeting), and to have fathered children and be of a certain age qualifies one as an elder of the community. But until the time when he establishes his own family unit, a young man might be referred to by household fathers and mothers as just *yarkii ina* (the young boy of).

In a similar manner, the socialization of a young girl prepares her for the day of *guur* when she will become the mistress of her own household. Until then, people will refer to her as *inantii ina* (the daughter of) and she will not be able to participate in gatherings held by married women such as showers held for pregnant women or spirit rituals such as the zaar. Marriage is therefore an empowering stage for the woman as much as it is an empowering stage for the man, and many young women see it as a means to escape the overpowering authority of their parents and an opportunity to manage their own households.

Managing a household means having responsibility over its immediate finances and day-to-day affairs; in a rural setting, this means the wife has to keep house, apportion tasks to the children, and so forth. In other words, as soon as the wedding is over, the young woman assumes the governorship of a household and she has complete freedom in the management of her household without interference from her husband's family or from anyone else except perhaps her husband. However, her husband recognizes her authority over inner-household matters just as she recognizes his authority in matters relating to the outside world such as representing the family in a community meeting. A husband who occupies himself with running the inner affairs of the household is considered a bad husband and is known as *qorqode*.

The role of the mistress of the home increases as the couple have children and the household members increase with relatives staying for long periods of time or with orphaned children from close relatives taken in by the family. Over time, it can be said that the young woman of the house becomes a veritable matriarch who rules a household as large as ten persons. The more successful her family is financially, the larger her household will be as less fortunate members of the extended family from her side and his side join the family. To help her with household chores such as housekeeping and cooking, she will count on her daughters or any females staying with the family or if the family can afford a maid or two whom she hires herself.

Children in a Somali family learn their respective and complementary gender roles from a tender age. A young boy is encouraged to develop qualities capable of sustaining and securing a livelihood for his family or ensuring the safety of his wife and children. Like his father or similar men, he has to learn how to carry out his familial responsibility (*hil*). The word hil (written as *xil* in Somali) interestingly gives us also the word *hille* (wife) (in Somali, *xille*) and the word *hilkas* meaning a responsible person (in Somali, *xilkas*). The correlation between hil (responsibility) and hille (wife) should not be construed as meaning that the husband is a lord to his wife and the wife is a possession of the man; rather it means that upon taking a wife (i.e., upon founding a new family unit), a young man takes on a new responsibility (hille) heavier than any carried before (hille is derived from hil and leh,

Matriarchs: married women play an active role in family affairs.

abbreviated as le, a suffix which means having, or bringing forth). As we shall see, far from being a possession of the man, a Somali woman has both freedom and responsibilities in the household and in society.

The significance of the word hil and its derivations means that when a boy grows up he has to find work or take care of his flocks or his piece of land to ensure an income for his family unit so he can be successful and become *ninka reerka* (the man of the household); therefore, a boy has to develop the qualifies that make him hilkas (responsible) long before he marries. To be successful as a family man, he should have a compatible wife that helps him in playing his role. It is acknowledged that a man who is not assisted by his wife in all family affairs and who is not morally encouraged by her will not prosper; to inculcate that point a Somali adage teaches the following wisdom in an enigmatic form (such enigmatic adages are common in Somali): There is a man you may not catch up with in a day, one you may not catch up within a year, and one you may never catch up with. The answer is: the man you may catch up with in a day is a man whose pack-camel is better than yours while on the move; the man that you may catch up with in a year is a man whose livestock had a better pasture than yours in a particular season; and the man you will never catch up with is a man who has a better wife than you. Another well-known proverb is "women make one man surpass another man."

In a rural setting, the division of physical labor, between man and wife, especially among pastoralist Somalis, might be said to correspond roughly to the following simplified schema:

women	*men*
home and sheep	outside world and camels

While all categorizations have the weakness of overgeneralizations, the above binary division broadly describes the division of labor between men and women in a pastoralist family unit. By "home and sheep" it is meant that women in a pastoralist settlement are responsible for running the inner affairs of the household, which include milking the goats and ewes. It also means women are responsible for child care. By "outside world and camels" it is meant that men are responsible for milking the camels and taking care of them and other outside affairs such as watering the animals, going to the meeting of the community, waging war or defending the settlement, going into a town and buying provisions for the family, scouting for fresh pastures (*sahan*), and constructing new pens for the animals at a new settlement. Of course, in real life, work roles overlap but this categorization gives the big picture of the division of labor in a traditional pastoralist society. Additionally, the above simplified schema easily adapts itself to the traditional city household division of labor if we discard "sheep" and substitute "camels" for a "job."

Somali society is not an exception in cultivating certain gender-related traits. Boys are, for example, encouraged to be strong and not to cry or show their emotions; girls may do so. Boys are encouraged to explore more of the outside world, be adventurous, and be brave; girls are encouraged to be more cautious, more home-bound or in a pastoral setting more settlement-bound, more obedient, and occupy themselves more with their personal beauty. Girls, of course, can be brave too, but the theme or rather social depictions of a brave young man and a beautiful young woman is a common one among Somalis, as much as for Americans. The toys of children, as is the case, say in the United States, also reflect this gender role playing. Since commercial toys are rarely available, children must fashion their own toys with help from older children and sometimes from parents. Boys make truck toys and slings or camels from clay in a rural setting, while young girls play house with a doll made of acacia sticks.

Teaching the mores of a society or socialization is a long process that turns young children into the men and women of the society. Children learn what is expected or acceptable from the parents, and relatives, who are ready to dispense lessons to them if the occasion arises. In some ways, everybody expects good behavior from a child, and among Somalis, it is entirely normal for a total stranger who sees, for example, a child smoking not only to yell at the child for engaging in such a behavior out of conformity with what is expected of a child, but also to ask the child to take them to the child's parents so he or she could inform the parents of the deeds of their child. This aspect is more true now in small localities than in large towns where anonymity and the problems of city life render people more occupied with their own problems than with the care of others.

Passing from childhood into adulthood is not ritually celebrated among Somalis as Somalis do not have an age-set system that formally marks the passing from one stage to another. However, it can be said that the passage is more marked when it concerns girls. Traditionally, young girls had their hair shaven before puberty. The hair was all shaved or else a ring of hair was left on the top of the head much like that of Christian monks. Then at or about the time of puberty, the hair was let to grow long and was thereafter worn in plaits without any head cover until puberty. This practice still subsists somewhat in remote areas; but in other areas little girls may keep their hair and girls who have attained puberty wear bright scarves on their heads (married women wear less bright covers). But the transition from young child into a well-bred or proper lady is a whole art, as Isak Dinesen (Karen Blixen), a Danish baroness who employed Somalis on her Kenyan coffee farm, noted with much insight in the 1920s in a chapter devoted to Somali women in her famous book *Out of Africa*. She noted, referring at first to the case of one young girl, and then in general about Somali ladyhood:

> With time, and under the influence of the grown-up girls, she was transformed, and was herself fascinated and possessed by the process of her transformation. Exactly as if a heavy weight had been tied on to her legs, she took to walking slowly, slowly; she held her eyes cast down after the best pattern, and made it a point of honour to disappear at the arrival of a stranger. . . . The novice gave herself up gravely and proudly to all the hardships of the rite; it was felt that she would rather die than fall short in her duties towards it. . . . Here were three young women of the most exquisite dignity and demureness. I have never known ladies more lady-like. Their maiden modesty was accentuated by the style of their clothes. They wore skirts of imposing amplitude; it took . . . ten yards of material to make one of them. Inside these masses of stuff their slim knees moved in an insinuating and mysterious rhythm.[1]

This style of the socialization of girls still applies today to a remarkable degree; except for the attire, skirts being less voluminous today, not much else has changed. Girls who have come of age are always expected to walk slowly in a dignified manner and not scamper or walk fast.

At a certain age girls and boys are asked to do some chores and participate in the activities of the family. The kind of chores or activities done by children are marked according to age and gender but generally there is no child labor to be deplored among Somalis—although, in large towns, there may be street children or children of poor families who work in restaurants as dishwashers or shine shoes. At home, young girls always help with the cooking and the preparation of food or with housekeeping activities. Generally, in towns young boys do not do housekeeping or cooking activities, but they may be asked to run errands to the corner store or to do other assignments such as bringing a pail of water from a communal water-tap or taking the grain to the miller so that injera bread could be made from the dough. If the family has a store or restaurant, ordinarily it is the young boy who may stand behind the counter or help with the business in his spare time or if he has stopped attending school or never formally started school. He would be groomed to take over the business at some future point (this is not an absolute custom and girls may exercise these same activities).

In the countryside, the same difference in household chores is observed with the young girls closely helping their mothers in their activities of house-keeping, cooking, weaving, or milking the sheep. Likewise, the young boy is drawn increasingly into the activities typically done by his father. If the family has some camels, the young boy would be sent to become a camel-boy (*geel-jire*), herding the camels in the company of the other camel-boys, far away from the household (*reer*) and his mother. The camel herds which the camel-boys look after are usually not one family's property but consist of the herds of close relatives banded together in a large herd and then sent to grazing lands far away from the sheep pastures where the household settlements are. It is thought that the rigors of the camel camp will harden the character of a young boy and wean him from the pampering of his mother and sisters. If the family has many camels, the young boy will, except for occasional visits to his parent's household, be away with the camels until such a time when he comes of age and is ready to marry.

The life of camel-boys is one of constant hardship; they don't carry cook-ing utensils but only a few milk vessels (*gorof, gaawe, dhiil*) which have the dual function of milking and drinking vessels. Camel-boys may also have a skin pouch (*sibraar*) for camel milk on which they mostly survive. Their most important tools are guns and daggers for the defense of the camels from marauding thieves, camel rustlers, and wild beasts. These are carried by the older young men of the camel group, which consists of boys as young as eight years old to young men twenty-four years old. In such a group, the older young men are responsible for the defense of the group and the camels, for the milking, fencing and watering of camels, for watching out for marauders and rustlers, and as well as for scouting for good pastures. The youngest boys may watch the young camels that stay around the camel camp or may go out with the main herd according to their ages. To bring the camels to water points, the camel-boys drive their herds great distances. Sometimes, they will become involved in fighting and shooting either to defend the camels against rustlers or as a result of a dispute over watering rights at wells and pools. Skirmishes between groups of camel-boys might also develop out of more trivial affairs such as taunts, shooting competitions, or theft of a camel-bell. In short, the life of a camel-boy is harsh and it happens that sometimes young boys of tender age run away from the camel camps back into the parental household only to be brought back to the camel camp.

It might be said, in a superficial manner, that Somali traditional fathers favor begetting male offspring over female offspring. This is, however, a simplification of a complex issue; it is more correct to say that it is thought desirable to have at least a son or sons in a household because the son carries the patrilineal (descending from male) line further as the proverb says: *wiil dhalayaaba ab durug* (It is a boy and the genealogical tree will grow). However, in a traditional Somali society a good balance of children of both genders is still preferred over gender imbalance for three reasons: a gender-balanced household is suited to the traditional division of labor; in a gender-balanced household in which the number of boys and girls are equal, the bride price paid by the family would be offset by what the family receives; and having a married daughter means having relatives (in-laws) in another settlement or town (*hidid*) whom one can draw on for help in times of need.

When it comes to gender relations, Islam, which early in its history had banned female infanticide in Arabia and championed women's rights, and *heer* (Somali customary law) protect women's rights, which includes protection from frivolous divorce as well as protection from cruel abuse. For example, if a man beats his wife severely in a village or a settlement, she may take the matter to the elders or to the local wadaad and may win her case against the husband who might be asked, perhaps, to make amends to her (*haal*) by selling a few animals and giving the money to the wife to use however she wanted, or he may be reprimanded or, in the old days, he may, if especially recalcitrant, through an order of the elders, be tied to a tree infested with biting ants. In Somali society, women are always part of the paternal clan even if they marry into another clan; this is evident in the distinction between *dhihid* and *dhalasho*; the former means an overnight stay and signifies the transient nature of marriage, the latter means birth and signifies inalienable and inalterable rights of birth invested in her family of birth. Therefore, it is incumbent upon a woman's paternal relatives to periodically check on her by visiting her or allowing her to visit them. In the old ways, the custom of ensuring the safety and the well-being of a daughter was sometimes carried further by obliging the husband to reside with his wife's family for up to a year or more. This is known as *inan-la-yaal* (residence with the wife's people). This is less of an institution today; nevertheless, in case of need, a Somali woman can always turn to her brothers and paternal relatives for protection or for seeking reparations, and usually in the countryside the threat of violence or retaliation from her paternal relatives is sufficient to instill respect and fear into the heart of a violent man. This is especially true when the two families are from neighboring clans. If, however, a woman marries into a clan whose area of habitation is far removed, it is impossible for paternal relatives to keep an eye on her, and this is one of the reasons why parents prefer to know beforehand whom the suitor of their daughter might be. In short, in cases of severe abuse or murder, the husband and his clan would have to reckon with the relatives of the woman, and more recently with statutory law.

Women were always allowed to possess wealth and to trade in villages and towns or to possess land in cultivating communities. One of Islam's first women, Khadija, the prophet's first wife, was a trader herself (trading by women has always been seen as a normal activity). In towns and cities, there are no restrictions on the professional activities of women. However, there are categories of jobs or professions in which one gender might predominate. Many women are now more than ever employed in that sector of the economy known as the informal sector; these are usually women who are the sole household heads due to the death of the husband or other circumstances or may be women from poor households in which the men are unemployed or receive small incomes. These women work as vendors mostly of vegetables or household and food items; they work from small stalls or even on mats spread on the street.

FAMILY LIFE AND FILIAL DUTY

Somalis are brought up to respect their parents and to seek advice and blessings (*du'o*) from them. Lack of deference for parents brings forth *habaar* (curse). To secure blessings from parents, a sixty-year-old Somali may be seen asking an aged parent for blessings and even advice on how to deal with certain matters. Old parents whose own offspring have started their own households are viewed as the center of the extended family. They are asked to arbitrate in disputes between brothers and sisters. At other times, the old parents may ask for contributions from their grown offspring to help a member of the family who is not doing well. In other words, parents in their senior years never retire from family management.

Children of both sexes are supposed to take care of old parents when the need arises. However, in cases when an old parent is staying with his married children, the custom is for mothers to reside with the daughters while the father would normally reside with one of his sons. This type of arrangement was found to have some practical benefit. First, gender socialization makes it easy for a mother to confide in her daughter or a father to confide in his son; second, such an arrangement mitigates tensions in the house, as a man whose mother-in-law or father resides with him would be less likely to be violent.

Marriage Ritual

In the past and even today, whatever the circumstances, marriage, on a societal level, is perceived as a relationship between two families, that is between two clans, and only at the personal level is it considered a relationship between husband and wife. This does not mean that the family or clan picks out who should marry whom; in fact, young people are expected to select their own mate, and that was more often the case than not in the past. However, families usually are heavily involved in what happens when the young man, or sometimes the young woman, makes the chosen person known.

In the countryside, young people get ample time to get to know each other; however, opportunities for courting are not limitless and aspiring young men on the lookout for a wife, *guurdoon* (literally he who is looking for marriage), have to make ingenious use of all occasions to get to know young women of marriage age. Among one of the favorite occasions, and one which marks the coming of age of young women among pastoralist Somalis, is the leading of the water-camel to the wells. For this occasion, the young woman dresses in her best clothes and jewelry, takes the halter of the camel, and leads it to the wells where gallant young men hang out for the chance of filling her water jars. For the joy of conversing (*haasaawe*) with a young woman, a young man would not only fill the water jars, but do all the work necessary until the water-camel is fully laden and is ready to be led back. For a particularly beautiful girl, it is said the young men at the watering point will literally throw themselves into the well to get water to fill her containers.

Perhaps, the greatest occasion for young pastoralist men and women to assess each other is the marriage dance. Dances are held at the home of newlyweds for several nights and the young and unmarried are allowed to dance. Such dances allow the young poet and composer of both genders to sing his or her piece and to expose his or her intelligence and verbal artistry to his or her peers, with an eye, of course, to attracting a mate. A more in-depth conversation between a young woman and man might occur when the young woman is watching the sheep near the settlement (young marriageable girls are relieved of this duty and usually do not watch the sheep in the pasture). However, this type of innocent conversation, when the partners-to-be share each other's views in private without the presence of others, is officially unacceptable to the parents and the male relatives of the girl, but it is a common norm and a kind of game in which the young man tries to stay one step ahead of trouble by vanishing at the approach of any male or older relative of the young woman. It is during such one-to-one conversations when the young man pops the question and if the answer is yes, the young woman reminds him that he would have to make a formal request to her parents.

Sometimes a whole rural community might know when a young man is looking for a wife. He might suddenly be seen dressed in new clothing or spending fewer days taking care of his usual activities and prowling around settlements of families with marriageable young girls. Such young men, when wandering far away from their settlements, are usually accompanied by a trusted friend or two from his own kinsmen (usually similarly unmarried young men). The reason for such escorts is for companionship and as well for security—the enraged brothers or cousins of the girl might oppose the young suitor (*guurdoon*), even if they themselves engage in the same behavior of wooing and conversing with young women attending sheep. The friend or friends also counsel the aspiring husband-to-be in matters related to the selection of a wife. The group of men might as a whole converse with the young woman since she can sense their purpose at first sight. Verbal artistry and the solution of enigmatic questions are considered, more so in the past, as ways to assess the intelligence of one another in such courting games. Accordingly, a proverb says "a woman converses with a thousand men but picks out only one," which attests to the fact that the selection process is a mutual process in traditional Somali society.

Likewise, young people in towns benefit from all social occasions, such as going to the market, school, work, or ceremonial occasions, such as marriages, to meet others and converse. Certainly, in towns the atmosphere of personal relations is less rigid than in rural areas and there are more opportunities for conversing with a member of the opposite gender.

It is at the stage of formal request for marriage that the parents and relatives of the young people get involved in the process that would lead them to marriage. The young man first contacts his father or, if his father is not available, an uncle or just about any close older kinsman; if all else fails he may ask just a male friend to do him the honors of request. From that point, and up to the point of the wedding, the relatives direct everything. If the young man's family judges that his choice is fine, then preparations are made to formally contact the girl's kinsfolk. Sometimes a young man might be advised that the would-be in-laws are unacceptable to his own family for some reason or another, likewise the girl's parents might refuse to accept the proposal for a number of reasons, such as the would-be in-laws' reputation or on account of the indigence of the young man and his parents. The duty of the parents of the young woman is to ensure that their daughter and her offspring will be provided for and their fear is that if their daughter marries a totally destitute man, *labo-shaadle* (a man with only two shirts), a reference to silver-tongued destitute young men of urban centers who have no livestock, land, or stable employment, then they will be obliged to take her back later.

Romanticism and inexperience are thought to mislead the young and parents want to ensure that human reproduction occurs only in an acceptable fashion. Thus Somali society developed long ago mechanisms aimed at curbing impulsive population regeneration in an arid environment where life is precarious. The tradition of a young man or his parents displaying their wealth by holding the required ceremonies and paying the bride price are part of these societal mechanisms, with the focus being to ensure a safe and stable human regeneration. The payment of a bridal price and gifts by the family of the young man is not aimed at enriching the parents of the girl by selling her off to a groom, as has been erroneously reported by some Western writers during the colonial era. In fact, the payments are reciprocative and sometimes the balance that remains to the girl's parents is minuscule. Over the years, a daughter whose own nuclear family has not been successful will get a lot of assistance from her parents and siblings, exceeding any gifts they had received at her marriage.

It happens sometimes that the young man's financial state or that of his family might not be adequate to meet the expenses a formal demand in marriage might entail. In other cases, the young woman's family might be known to not be favorable to accepting a demand for the hand of their daughter from the members of a particular family or even to have an ongoing project to marry off their daughter to someone else. The option used to circumvent such restrictions, so the heart will have its way, is elopement.

Elopement (*la-tagis*) is all the more difficult and exhilarating when it happens in the countryside, as it involves elements of physical danger from other men in pursuit of the eloping party, from hunger, thirst, and cold, and from wild beasts, especially in the past. Somali folktales are full of young women who cleverly overcame the verbal as well as the physical constraints placed on them by their families and eloped with the man of their heart. A well-known tale is that of a young woman whose father uttered the divorce-oath upon her mother if she ever married without his consent. This meant that if she went against his word, her mother would be automatically divorced. Naturally, no daughter wants to become the cause of divorce of her mother and this put much stress on her to come up with a solution so she could marry the man of her choice. One night, she started to sing:

> Oh what a starry night, what a starry night
> Oh Father Ali
> What a fine night to elope with a man (Author's translation)

The father, who did not know there was an actual project afoot, pleased with the lyrics of his daughter's song, laconically replied in chorus, "Oh daughter, you may." And she did just that in the dead of the night.

But elopement is not just seen as an exhilarating experience, it has always been associated with an aura of righteous defiance and pure romanticism in Somali society, and contemporary prose writers have added to its appeal by adopting it as one of their favorite subjects.[2] In the cities, elopement involves going secretly to a judge in a nearby town to get married. The reason for traveling is to have the physical distance required under Islamic law between the location of the parents and those wanting to get married when the parents of the girl are not present at the ceremony.

Arranged Marriages

There is a difference between traditional marriages, in which the partners have chosen each other but opt to go through the various traditional ceremonies, and arranged marriages, in which the partners do not know each other well or had little *hasaawe* (conversation). Most marriages are not arranged.

Arranged marriages happen under some specific circumstances. For example, a young man or woman might not have succeeded in attracting a mate at all. A man might stay around as a bachelor until well into his thirties before his relatives start worrying about his lack of progeny, but for a woman the time when she might be asked, either in jest or in earnest, if she is going to find her own man is usually after she enters her late twenties. Relatives then act as go-betweens to find a mate for the concerned and usually persist until that person is married off. Often in such cases, a woman in her thirties or late twenties might have to marry a man who is in his fifties. Friends other than close relatives sometimes hook up an individual with someone else with such expression as "I know a good woman [or man] whom you would like."

After the concerned man and woman accept each other with regard to marriage, the traditional ceremonies and customs might still be observed in full or in reduced form or not at all, except for the indispensable religious part of it. Widows or widowers might find a mate also in similar ways through their friends or relatives.

Forced Marriages

There is another type of arranged marriage in which the will of the young woman counts little; this might be properly called forced marriage. Today, there are fortunately fewer such marriages. To compel a young woman to say yes before the *qadi* (judge) or *wadaad* (priest), mental coercion rather than physical threat is most often used and the threat of parental curse and banishment from the family are often enough to produce the desired effect. One might ask why such forced marriages might occur when the Somali ideal is for the partners to freely choose each other before coming before the qadi or wadaad. One reason is the financial position of the family. The parents of the young woman might believe that marrying off their daughter into a well-to-do family would be in her own best interest in the long run; the parents think they know better or they might have an eye on how their own family could profit from the situation either immediately or in the future.

Sometimes forced marriages have nothing to do with the finances of the marrying family or the poverty of the family who is forcing their daughter into marriage. This is the case, for example, when an old wadaad asks a family for the hand of their daughter. Traditionally, in the countryside, people were afraid they would incur the wrath or worse, the curse, of a wadaad, and they would even agree to allow their daughter to marry an itinerant wadaad who would leave the locality in a few years. Other cases involve an older man who may have achieved prestige as an elder and who wants to take a second wife; it happens also that such older men are, in the countryside, well-to-do in livestock or agricultural lands. But the heart of the young woman might have belonged to the young and poor poet of her locality and, in such cases, she has to be dragged to the marriage house. Some forced marriages later develop into a stable household, while others end in the flight of the young woman from the household into a different locality, usually a town far from her own people and into an uncertain future. However, even in a forced marriage, the husband is still accountable to both Islamic and Somali traditional laws that protect women; and therefore cases of serious injury are usually unheard of as a result of such marriages.

Child betrothals are not known among the majority of the people; however, among the Rahanwein of southern Somalia, a little girl may be promised in marriage, when she comes of age, to an older teenager or man. Such girls wear a headband to mark their status. This custom is, however, a dying one. No marriage can, of course, occur unless the wadaad or qadi is convinced that the person is mature enough.

POLYGAMY, SUCCESSION, AND DIVORCE

Polygamy (multiple marriage partners) is one of the exotic aspects associated with Muslim societies such as Somalis in the Western media. It is true that in theory under Islamic law the permissible limit of wives for a man is four. But that is only theory; what most non-Muslims, especially Westerners, are not aware of are the conditions demanded to be filled by the qadi or wadaad. First, there is a financial stipulation of being able to meet the needs of two households, and secondly, it is stipulated that a man should be able to treat equally, not only financially but emotionally, all the wives and their offspring. The latter stipulation is, according to some Muslims, impossible to meet, and therefore the question whether polygamy is allowed is not a closed one neither among Somalis nor among Muslim peoples. Most educated and urban Somalis frown upon polygamy. In fact, traditionally, it was not the ordinary man who married a second wife, but patriarchs relatively wealthy in livestock or cultivated land.

Dumaal (succession) is a Somali tradition that is dying out. At the death of a husband, if the widow is willing, she gets married to her husband's oldest surviving brother or if he is unavailable to one of his brothers, or eventually to a paternal cousin, if, for some reason, no brother of the deceased is available. Even in the past, this practice was not a popular one, as the proverb attests to: "a bashful man will not beget children from the widow of a relative." Somali culture teaches utmost respect and deference between in-laws, and it is understandable that any man would feel uneasy at the prospect of upholding this tradition, which was meant as a solution to a societal problem, namely that of finding a father for the children of the deceased and a husband for the widow.

Another tradition that is moribund today is known as *higsiisan* (succession). According to this tradition, if a young married woman dies, her sister, upon her own agreement, as this was a tradition in which not much pressure could be applied by the parents, would marry the young widower. This was thought to be for the good of the children as their own aunt would be also their step-mother; additionally, this was a way to keep alive the relationship between the two families.

In the case of a divorce, *furis/furniin*, the husband vocalizes the divorce formula in front of a qadi or a wadaad in the presence of witnesses. In most cases, much reconciliation effort either by the qadi or wadaad and close relatives precedes any dissolution of marriage. Women may sue for divorce by going to a qadi's court in towns; in the countryside, divorce is sought by a woman usually after she leaves the conjugal home for that of her parents or relatives, who would then, in case of irreconcilable differences or cruelty, demand the husband pronounce the divorce formula. In case of the husband's refusal to do so, the woman and her relatives would petition for divorce before a qadi's court. The rate of divorce is not known statistically but it can be said to be low. Being divorced does not carry any social stigma for either party, and both parties usually remarry. Nevertheless, in the past, for economic reasons divorce was a difficult option for a woman; however, now, with increased possibilities of employment and self-employment available to women, divorce is not seen as a dreaded situation anymore.

After a divorce is pronounced, the general norm is to divide the children according to age and gender; very young children almost always go to the mother and older girls stay with the mother and boys with the father. Usually divisions of children or furniture are solved through a consensus rather than through a qadi's court—real estate, vehicles, herds of livestock, or property of value belong to the party to whom it is registered or belongs and are never divided up, although use of them might be accorded amicably to the other party. Alimony is always paid by the husband and only when the ex-wife has custody of some of the children. No alimony is paid to a man who marries a wealthy woman and gets divorced from her. Upon divorce also the wife may demand from the husband the payment of the *meher* (marriage security), an amount in kind or in monetary denominations agreed upon by the bride and groom on the day of their marriage to be paid then and there or later to the wife in case of divorce. Actual payment is usually contingent on the finances of the husband and the size of the meher—some brides pick large amounts in the beginning to keep up with the meher of the neighbor's girl and realistically do not expect to get payment in the case of divorce.

CIRCUMCISION AND INFIBULATION

Circumcision, *halaadays* or *gudniin,* is an old tradition. It is a ritual that is seen as a purification, as attested by the word halaalays (making pure) from the Arabic *halaal* (pure). It is performed on children of both genders usually between the ages of five and eight.

Circumcision, in the case of boys, is not different from the way it is done around the world. When it is done in the countryside, it is done without any local anesthetic, and involves the removal of the prepuce, which is disposed of immediately by burial. Freshly circumcised boys are told not to reveal the circumcised organ to females, except the mother; they are told if they don't obey, they might not heal properly. The object of such a tale is evidently to give the young boy a lesson in societal morals now that he is no longer a little boy.

Among Somalis, women also get circumcised, as is the norm in some other societies. Lately female circumcision (FC) has attracted much attention in the West where it is known as female genital mutilation (FGM). There is no single form of FC and it is not peculiar to Africa. Geographically, the practice straddles Africa and Asia. In Asia, it is confined to Muslim Asia. However, in Africa, it is not confined to Muslims. FC is an ancient tradition that spans several millennia and was in existence before Judaism, Christianity, and Islam, though ordinary Somalis are likely to think that this practice is stipulated by Islam. There are two procedures of FC found among Somalis and elsewhere.

The first form is the more severe form and it is known as infibulation; it is also called the pharaonic type of circumcision, because of its use in ancient Egypt. This type of procedure entails the ablation of much of the labia and the suturing of the sides of the vulva, leaving a small orifice the size of a bean for the discharge of menstrual blood and urine. This type of circumcision is practiced in a cultural belt that runs roughly along the sides of the Red Sea on the African side, where perhaps its origin lies. This is the most prevalent among Somalis of pastoralist origin. This form of surgical intervention is waning in favor of the milder form, although it still continues unabated in rural areas.

The milder form of FC is known as *sunna.* This type involves the ablation of the clitoral prepuce and a partial clitoridectomy. Sunna is the most widespread form of FC in the world and it is found in Muslim Asia from Arabia to Indonesia, the largest Muslim population in the world.

The origins of FC are not as simple as is often depicted. Many theories have been put forward to explicate its beginnings, some of them controversial. The only thing known for sure is that FC had existed for several millennia and was known to the ancient Egyptians. It is likely that the pharaonic type of infibulation is the older practice and it had its roots in an ancient religion in which priestesses who had undergone this kind of procedure served as the guardians of temples and shrines. Gradually it became a popular practice in the belief that there was some prestige attached with being a circumcised woman. Additionally, among pastoralist populations such as Somalis, the practice became part of the population regeneration mores, even if that is not evident to the common people anymore, as it resolutely hinders or minimizes impregnation until such a time when it is socially permissible.

NOTES

1. Isak Dinesen (1954). *Out of Africa*. London: Penguin Books, 156.
2. B.W. Andrzejewski (1984). "Somali Prose Fiction Writing 1967–81," in Thomas Labahn, ed., *Proceedings of the Second International Congress of Somali Studies—Volume 1: Linguistics and Literature*. Hamburg: Helmut Buske, pp. 379–410.

SUGGESTED READING

Ahmed, Christine Choi. 1995. "Finely Etched Chattel: The Invention of a Somali Woman." In Ali Ahmed Jimale, ed., *The Invention of Somalia*. Lawrenceville, N.J.: Red Sea Press, pp. 155–89.

Aden, Amina H. 1989. "Somalia: Women and Words." *Ufahamu* 10, no. 3: 115–42.

Dinesen, Isak (Karen Blixen). 1954. *Out of Africa*. London: Penguin Books. See pages 155–64 on Somali women.

Kapteijns, Lidwien. 1991. "Women and the Somali Pastoral Tradition: The Corporate Kinship and Capitalist Transformation in Northern Somali." *Working Papers in African Studies* No. 153. Boston: African Studies Center.

———. 1995. "Gender Relations and the Transformation of the Northern Somali Pastoral Tradition." *International Journal of African Historical Studies* 28: 241–59.

7

Social Customs and Lifestyle

AN EGALITARIANISM CUSTOM OF GOVERNANCE

SOMALIS have, perhaps too often, been described by Western writers, as an egalitarian people of nomads, or as an acephalous nation of bards, in other words as anarchists who value personal freedom and oral skills such as poetry. Indeed, to some visitors, Somali society might seem to have traversed the ages without much change in lifestyles or customs—nomads draped in flowing robes and tending sheep evoke a bucolic image right out of the Bible in most Western minds. Another recurring image of Somalis is that they are divided into independent clans headed by traditional patriarchs—again biblical imagery for Westerners. For sure, there are a lot of nomads in flowing robes tending sheep and camels; but not all Somalis tend herds of livestock, neither are stock-raising and other economic activities mutually exclusive. For example, the transport entrepreneur who owns his or her bus or the restaurant owner or even the airport official who stamps your passport might have been a former livestock owner or herder and may still keep a few sheep or camels in the country to supplement his or her income.

Somali values of egalitarianism are embedded in both Islam and in Somali pastoral culture, which is itself grounded in pastoral Cushitic culture. Somalis tend to think that humans are equal before Allah, the creator, and will be rewarded or punished for their deeds. The ruler is not thought of as superior to the average individual and Somalis have never known the rule of divine kings or divine priests nor have they had slavery or institutionalized inequity of humans from birth. Somalis have never known a culture in which feudal subserviency and strong political and religious hierarchies were the norm. Even the nation-state is a new concept to the Somalis and other peoples in the Horn, the prior political history of the Horn being about loose empires, sultanates, and city-states. The nation-state is also a relatively recent concept, in comparison to the multiethnic empire-state. The prior history of Somalis is more about independent pastoral clans, sultanates, and city-states whose leaders were never absolute potentates and where there were no estates or classes of people such as nobility or commoners, but only professional classes such as religious men, blacksmiths, pastoralists, merchants, and so forth.

Consensual rather than coercive governance is more appealing to Somalis, and Somalis expect their leaders to be persons capable of persuasion by having the oral skills required for "disputation, litigation, negotiation, agreement, and consensus."[1] Somali egalitarianism is therefore about basic rights; it does not mean equality of capital or riches, for there have always been poor and rich Somalis, whether the riches were camels or another form of wealth. Indeed, as far as capital accumulation and entrepreneurship are concerned, Somalis have always been traders, merchants, and entrepreneurs. Somali entrepreneurs and merchants are even important in the economies of East African countries such as Kenya, Tanzania, and Uganda, and to a lesser extent in several other African countries. Somali refugees who have recently immigrated to South Africa typically started street vending enterprises to support themselves as a first step toward larger enterprises. Somalis immigrating to Western countries such as the United States have opened restaurants and markets. Entrepreneurial dynamism and adaptation are therefore elements of Somali culture.

But is that enough to depict Somalis as rugged individualists who shun authority and control of any kind—in other words, as anarchists? Or are Somalis people who developed democratic norms respectful of human dignity and rights when other peoples were under feudal lords? Unfortunately, too many analysts and writers tended to see "anarchy" in Somali culture and then went on to attribute the present total collapse of the central authority as the product of the anarchistic and individualistic nature of Somalis of pastoral culture. For instance, I. M. Lewis, the best known anthropologist on Somalis, who described Somali society as a "pastoral democracy," wrote: "The first thing to understand about the Somalis is that they are not as other men. Richard Burton, the famous Arabist and explorer who trekked across their lands in the 1850s, called the Islamic Somali nomads a 'fierce and turbulent race of republicans.' More pungently, a Ugandan sergeant with the British forces fighting the Mad Mullah went on record as telling his officer: 'Somalis, Bwana, they no good: each man his own sultan.' "[2]

The two above statements within this quote appear in many texts about Somalis and are used as anecdotes illustrating the chaotic and anarchistic cosmos of Somalis. They have become stereotypes that serve to illustrate and perpetuate a generalization that has little sociological significance. The difference between such exotic anecdotes and the tall tales of early travelers and geographers is one of time.

First, Burton's depictions in the above quote of Somalis as a "race of republicans" rather than as subjects of a king was a correct observation—Somalis never had a monarch or any rigid central government prior to the nineteenth century. But Somali republicanism is not the equivalent of anarchism—to the Somalis, anarchy is as much abhorrent as absolute totalitarianism. Somalis, as Muslims, concede authority to their representative authorities as the Koran (4:60) tells them: "O ye who believe! Obey ALLAH, and obey His Messenger and those who are in authority among you." Additionally, Somali oral literature itself teaches in adages and proverbs the importance of leadership. One example of such proverbs gives the following wisdom: "No one can live in a country or city without a ruler or government" (*Balad aan boqor lahayn laguma galo*).

As for the Ugandan colonial sergeant quoted above, it is essential to put his words in the context of his own culture. The sergeant was from the Buganda kingdom of what is now Uganda, a society in which the Kabaka, the king, held life and death authority over his subjects, and where the death of a king called for the sacrifice of a large number of commoners. Even the chiefs of the Buganda would have looked like tyrants to the Somalis that the sergeant met, for Somali clan chiefs, unlike the traditional chiefs in other places, were and are mere ceremonial heads of committees. Decisions are made by a committee (*guddi*) or by selected representatives (*guurti*), the pastoral parliament. No doubt then that the Ugandan sergeant was greatly astonished at the egalitarianism of Somalis who had fealty neither for kings nor for men of religion, although they had a healthy respect for just authority and pious men of religion.

The Somali clan is itself a product of the pastoral democracy of Somalis. The clan, in its essence, is a minimalist association in which members agree to adopt a common social pact (*heer*) for dealing with community problems and for helping each other; for example, when a family loses its animals to a drought, the clan members pitch in with donated animals, or when rustlers steal a family's animals, the clan members take action to seek restitution first by negotiation. In urban areas, the clan, as an extended family, provides a social net, and sums of money are collected for an indigent person (*qaadhaan*). The concept of who might appeal for help is very flexible; for example, if five Somalis from five different clans are in a foreign city and one of them needs help, the others are morally bound to act as the kith and kin of the fifth and come to his or her aid; however, if there are many Somalis, then one is supposed to seek material help first from those nearest to him or her in clan genealogy. This is a general schema and there are other venues of appeal for charity such as alms at a mosque.

Against this background of Somali governance system and social solidarity, based on the principles of guurti (commission, committee, or parliament) and heer (common law), colonial rule, first imposed on Somalis in the nineteenth century, ran against the ideal of consensual governance. To the colonial power, the centralization of all powers under one governor was the most efficient way of running the colony. Centralization was therefore essential to the colonial regimes instituted among Somalis. While both the British and the Italian colonial regimes were centralized regimes, British rule in the north was more benign and allowed some leeway for consultation with the population. In the north, district and regional governors typically consulted with the traditional leaders (akil) on important matters and with the qadi on points of law. Not so with the Italians, like the ancient Romans of what is now Italy, who were bent on imposing their laws through direct imposition on the Somalis—the objective being nothing less than the latinization of the Somali culture. Their system of governance was not only centralized to the extreme but was dictatorial with input always coming from the top. Additionally, the south experienced the period of Italian fascism in the 1930s when everything of Somali origin was to be replaced with Italian norms, which were thought to be superior. Colonialism, therefore, undermined the role of traditional leadership and the republican mode of governance. Somali modes of consensus building and democratization through consultations were deemed outmoded and tribal, and a system of colonial appointees and official ordinances from the top were the new norm of rule.

Despite the fact that the alien norm of top-to-bottom governance was clearly a violation of Somali culture and ethos, after independence and the formation of the Somali republic, the same political system of centralized regime was kept, with the government appointing district governors. The colonial educated elites continued to function and rule in the old colonial type of administration (used largely by the Italians to govern the south as an Italian colony) with all its centralization, rigidity, and one-way communication. The government and its political appointees had all the power and the local populations had almost none. There was a parliament during the first nine civilian years, but the parliament did not initiate steps for the devolution of decision-making powers to the regions and districts, in short to the people. No provisions were made for the government to consult with the people in the regions. As can only be expected in such a situation, the central government began administering the regions just as the colonial administration did—by dictating to them through directives. It sent to every region a new governor to replace the colonial governor and a new district commissioner to replace the colonial one. The new governor and the new district commissioner, most often unacquainted with the region or district they were sent to rule, put themselves up in the residences of their colonial predecessors and even retained, in most cases, the services of their European predecessors' "boys" and maids.[3]

When Siad Barre came into power, he inherited the existing system of governance that was extremely centralized; it suited his dictatorial temperament and his only additions to the governance system were more governors and government appointees for his loyal friends and more instruments of repression. Siad Barre himself was a product of the fascist era and his knowledge of repressive methods of governance was largely obtained during the years of fascism.

The breakdown of law and order in Somalia cannot be attributed to the existence of pastoral clans, Somali republican values, or to an inborn anarchist trait of Somalis; on the contrary, today's turbulence is the result of the widespread use of violence by the Barre regime and the destruction of Somali humanitarian and republican values under the colonial regimes that had preceded it. Under Barre's two decades of brutal governance, a whole new generation of urban Somalis was born who had no benefit of the humanism, egalitarianism, and republicanism of the culture of their forefathers. Their personas took shape in an era in which experiential input came from Barre's violent state security services, and from an array of new entertainment modes such as the theaters showing films in which violence was supreme. As a result many of the youngsters that man the "technicals," a type of battle wagon bristling with machines, display bravado behavior and recklessness totally inconsistent with Somali pastoral culture. They pose for the camera in that now famous "Rambo" pose known around the world through the movie of that name starring the American actor Sylvester Stallone. (Somali nomads have no access to films at all but urban children do, and when that particular film was in theaters in 1986 in Mogadishu, police officers had to be called in to stop youngsters from breaking into already tightly packed theaters.)

The Somali culture has, however, the basic elements for renewal and reconciliation. Its elements of heer (contract, common law) and guurti (assembly, parliament) are the foundations for universal democracy and with little modification they have been shown to be the means to renewal and transformation into a modern democratic society. Today, while some areas of the former Somalia are still reeling from a continuing civil war, consensual democracy through Somali values is already at work in some areas. In the Republic of Somaliland, for example, comprising the northern regions of the old Somalia, the restoration of peace and governance has largely been achieved by rekindling and institutionalizing the guurti system. The same process has also produced good results and the return of law and order in the region that now calls itself the Puntland State of Somalia and whose capital is at Garowe.

SOCIAL ORGANIZATION AND DIVISION OF THE SECULAR AND THE SPIRITUAL

The basic unit of the Somali society is the *reer*, the nuclear family (the parents and the children). The same word can also be used to refer to a community or a clan (*qolo* or *qabiil*). Somali clans have developed social and penal codes to solve problems between individuals as well as between clans. This is known as heer (written in Somali as *xeer*). Heer is a set of laws, seldom written, that members of a clan or neighboring clans decide to respect. Heer also means precedence; thus if someone says to someone else *waa inoo xeer*, it means "you have set a new precedent and you will be subject to it in turn." Rural communes have therefore always avoided setting bad precedents and have respected the existing heer. Infractions to the heer are to be brought before a selected assembly (guurti) or a committee of *heerbeegti* (law experts) who will hand down a verdict. The guurti is therefore a kind of tribunal for judging infractions as well as a parliament that makes political decisions.

Somali traditional law (heer) always coexisted with the *sharia* (Islamic law), since the two met each other over a millennium ago. The two legal systems became complementary in many respects. For example, while homicide and rape were usually treated under the heer law, family affairs such as divorce were treated under the sharia. Traditional law has also coexisted and still coexists with statutory or state laws introduced by the colonial regimes.

The division of spheres between heer and sharia followed closely the division of secular and religious domains (i.e., state and church) in Somali life. The secular world was that of politics and governance, while the religious domain was concerned with spiritual matters. The secular world belonged to the *waranle* (the spearman), while the religious domain belonged to the wadaad (the priest). This separation of church and state had, therefore, happened long before the arrival of Islam among Somalis and has continued to exist despite attempts to erase this division by foreign-inspired wadaads. Of course, among Somalis, a political leader could be a wadaad in the first place; but to become a politician or a leader is to become a waranle (a secular). Historically, Somali wadaads kept closely to the religious domain and in return enjoyed immunity from the feuds of the waranle. However, during the past decade, a period in which vast areas of the south had fallen under the sway of warlords, a new breed of wadaad who wields political and military power has emerged. These latter-day wadaads have been appropriately called wadaad waranle (literally priest with a spear), a paradoxical term, for in the minds of Somalis a spear (waran) signifies violence, an image not usually associated with holy men. Whether the age-old separation of the secular from the spiritual continues in the tradition of Somalis or whether that division will be erased, as a minority wants an emulation of what has happened in some Muslim countries such as Afghanistan or Iran, is something yet to be seen.

THE RITES OF PASSAGE

Birth Ceremony

At the birth of a child, Somalis usually hold a ceremony on the seventh day after the birth. This ceremony, *wanqal* (literally the slaughter of a ram), marks the addition of the child into the family and fulfills several social purposes. The first objective of the wanqal is evidently an expression of thanks to the almighty, a second objective is to give the child a name, and a third objective is a social gathering of relatives to celebrate the occasion. As is evident from its very name in Somali, a ram is slaughtered to feed the guests of the family including the wadaad, without whose presence the ceremony cannot proceed. On the occasion, the father asks the wadaad to choose a name for the child, which he does by suggesting names from a list of Muslim names, all Arabic in origin. Sometimes the father might just tell everybody what name the child is going to have and the wadaad would agree with him unless the name is socially inappropriate.

The wanqal ceremony is sometimes held after the usual seven days, but sometimes, especially in towns, a poor family might have no ceremony at all. However, among pastoralists, with many rams to spare, this tradition is observed at the birth of every child. Sometimes two rams are slaughtered for the birth of a boy and one ram for a girl. In some families, only the birth of a boy might occasion the slaughter of a ram or two while some families uphold this ceremony for babies of both genders; the latter is largely true of today's well-to-do urbanites.

In the past, and to some extent today, the bones of the ram or rams that had been sacrificed for the occasion were collected after the feast, and particular attention was taken beforehand that no bone was broken by the family members or the guests. The collected bones were then tied up in a bundle and hung from the boughs of a majestic tall tree. Some such trees still laden with a bundle of bones are occasionally seen in old-growth woods.

The birth of a son, among pastoralists, is also the occasion to start an investment fund of sorts for the future head of a family. This means giving a young she-camel to the baby son. The offspring from that she-camel will be his when he grows up. To solemnize this tradition, some hair is cut off from the designated she-camel and tied around the umbilical cord of the baby before the cord is buried. This tradition is known as *hudun-hidh*, from *hudun* "umbilical cord" and *hidh* "to tie up" (written as *xudun-xidh* in Somali).

After childbirth, the new mother traditionally enters a period of homebound seclusion that lasts for forty days. Among pastoralists this tradition is much observed, but in urban centers the necessities of daily life make it a difficult tradition to observe. No intimacy between the couple is allowed during this period. At the end of the forty days, a ceremony known as *afartanbah* (the exit from the quarantine) takes place. This is a ceremony held for women only and attended only by women. This tradition is still observed in both town and country.

At the end of a year, another ceremony, *gardaadis* or *kalaqaad* in some areas, is held. During this ceremony, the child, who in the old traditions was not taken outside the home for a period of one year, is taken to the outside. The child symbolically crosses the threshold or the doorstep of the home on his or her way to the outside world. For this ceremony, the maternal uncle, in the case of a boy, or the maternal aunt, in the case of a girl, takes up the child on his or her shoulders and crosses the threshold or doorstep with the child perched on his or her shoulder. The uncle or the aunt then walks around the perimeter of the settlement, in the case of a pastoral family, or around the courtyard, in the case of an urban family, with the child still on his or her shoulders. It is supposed that the child will pick up the character of the uncle or aunt who introduced him or her to the outside world. If in later life the child develops into an individual not sharp of mind, people would jokingly blame the uncle or aunt, by saying "look, what a fine young man [or woman] you introduced into the world."

Marriage Ceremony

In a traditional setting, the marriage request is handled by the older relatives of the man. As soon as the would-be groom advises them of his wish, they establish a formal contract with their counterparts among the woman's relatives. This happens at a meeting in which one of the elders from the man's side, usually the most eloquent or best known among them, formally announces the request for the hand of the daughter. Acceptance of the request is formalized with a handshake and is followed by the payment of an engagement gift (*gabaati*) paid by the family of the suitor. This customary gift could be in kind or in cash, although in modern times it is mostly in cash. The cost of the meeting such as food or *qat* leaves, a mild stimulant drug that today has a wide use among Somali men, is borne by the man and his family.

The next stage is the full payment of the bride price (*yarad*). Bride price was traditional among pastoralists in the form of camels, which was augmented by wealthy pastoral families, in the past, with a horse and even a rifle. Camels are still given in the countryside, but people give less camels than they used to before—in the nineteenth century, thirty or more camels were usual whereas today six or eight is normal in most places and even two or three are sometimes given. Among southern agriculturists a cow or two and a few sheep replace the camels. In towns, a sum of money paid at the first meeting is usually the amount paid, and about half of that is immediately returned to the giving family, while the rest is divided among the family of the daughter and the elders of the extended family. In urban towns, there are many cases when no bride price ritual is observed, and in modernist circles it is considered an anachronism.

After all the traditional ceremonies had been dispensed with either by observing them or ignoring them, as might well happen in urban centers, the legal and religious part of the marriage takes places. This is the performance of the marriage act. The couple is wed formally by a wadaad or a qadi (muslim judge) after obtaining mutual consent in the presence of at least two witnesses. The officiating man of religion then asks the lady how much her marriage surety (*meher*) is going to be—an amount to be paid by the husband in the case of divorce. This could be either in kind or in cash depending upon where one is. The ritual is concluded by the wadaad or the qadi with a recital of the Fatiha, a short chapter in the Koran. From that point, the couple are legally man and wife. In conformance with Muslim ideals no exuberance or requests of "kiss the bride," as is common in the Western culture, is shown at this stage—osculation between the genders is itself a taboo in public. Joyous celebrants have to wait for the night of the wedding.

The wedding celebration may take place immediately after the pronunciation of the marriage act or it might take place months later. When it does not take place immediately, the man and his family use the interregnum to prepare for the cost of the ceremony. However, in the countryside, the celebration takes place usually immediately after the marriage act.

The night of the *aroos* (the wedding ceremony) is a time of celebration and exuberance. The ceremony ideally takes place in the new home of the couple whether that is a bridal aqal (Somali portable home) or a townhome, but in today's urban centers it may take place at a hotel reception room or at the home of a relative that is deemed spacious or appropriately dignified. Whatever the venue, much feasting and dancing are done on this occasion. Traditionally, the bride and the bridegroom arrive separately at the wedding home, escorted by their respective genders from close relatives and friends. In addition, one best man (*minhiis*) accompanies the groom while one bride's maid (*minhiisad*) comes with the bride. The best man sits or stands next to the groom for the duration of the reception while the bride's maid does the same beside the bride.

Traditional dances and singing take place during the wedding. However, only the young and the unwed dance or sing. This is an occasion for them to rate each other with the aim of selecting a mate. It is also at this time that a budding poet might compose a few lines of verse in honor of the newlyweds. The wedding ceremony lasts for seven days and each night is the occasion for dancing and singing by the young people. On the seventh night, the *todobo-bah* (end of seven) takes place and marks the end of the wedding period. In towns, often one night of ceremonies might take place to minimize costs. Some townspeople also observe the todobo-bah ceremony to close the wedding period.

On the night of the todobo-bah, for those who practice it, the opening of the *heedho* container is undertaken. This is a gift container dressed in the image of a bride. The heedho is at its core a wicker container just like any traditional milk vessel with two parts, the cover and the base. A dish of *muqumad* or *oodkac*, as it is known in some areas, is placed in the interior of the base. Muqumad is a dish made of meat; it is prepared from jerked meat (i.e., meat that has been cut into long strips and dried in the sun and boiled in ghee, which when taken care of properly, by not touching it with the fingers, can remain unspoiled for several months). Traditionally, this was the food of the traveler, caravaneer, and warrior. Muqumad was and remains the part of the wedding gift offered by the mother at the wedding of her daughter.

The gift of muqumad has been part of the Somali tradition for a long time. As a ready-made dish, muqumad is convenient, like fast-food, for new-lyweds, and it is also given to the guests of the wedding as a snack. While that might always have been the case, it is unknown when people started dressing up the muqumad container as a symbolic bride, for that is what the container represents when it is bedecked with the full array of dresses and embellishments. The container itself is decorated with cowrie shells on strands of leather before being clothed and embellished. First after the mu-qumad dish has been inserted inside the base container, the cover is placed on top. Then the container is clothed in a dress from top to bottom; the next step is the most delicate one and it is the one most cherished by the ladies who do it. This step involves tying the now clothed container with an embroidered string, which is tied in such a way to form a veritable enigma when it is time to untie it. The last end of the string, which allows the unraveling of the tangle, is placed in a spot where it is difficult to detect. On the night of the presentation of the heedho, the male relatives of the groom are invited to do the honors and untie the strings around the container, since the container symbolically represents the bride, her male relatives have no right to try to untie its string as that would symbolically constitute incest, whereas a male from the groom's side runs no such interdiction since he symbolically represents the groom himself.

The untying of the string and the opening of the container follow strict procedural rules by the man who tries to open the container. The first step is to salute the symbolic bride then the decorative items on the clothing of the container. Only then would one try to find the end of the string. Any false step brings a sanction from the guardian of the container, a lady from the bride's side; a false step such as lingering too long on one step may also disqualify one from continuing. The man who succeeds in unraveling the enigmatic tangle has the pleasure of being the first to taste the Somali am-brosia. Variations on the theme of the heedho today include a separate gift container or containers for women and other food items such as desserts and sweets in the container rather than the traditional muqumad.

In large towns, some Western influences have crept into Somali weddings of the well-to-do. These recent influences include dressing the bride in a white Western-style bridal dress complete with a tiara and the groom in a Western-style tuxedo. Additional Western influences include the cutting of the bridal cake and Western-style dances with pop music. The opposite trend

Heedho: bridal containers are opened on the seventh night of the wedding.

of dressing in traditional Somali clothes and drinking camel milk together in lieu of tasting the wedding cake have also been observed, partly as a return to tradition and partly as a reaction to the Westernization of Somali culture.

Death Rites

Somali death rites are essentially Islamic in procedure and not much has survived from the pre-Islamic death rites or mourning customs. When someone dies among Somalis, there are no laying-in-state or vigils and the deceased must be promptly interred, as is customary among Muslims. First the body is washed and then placed in a white shroud (*kafan*) which is tied around the extremities and in the middle of the corpse. The body is then placed in a casket (*nahash*) without a cover. The casket is only used for transporting the body and will be used again—such caskets are the property of mosques. In villages or in the countryside, mats replace the caskets.

The burial itself is simple and brief. First the wadaad leads a short prayer in which the name of the deceased is called by his or her first name followed by those of his or her mother and grandmother, for the time since birth, unlike during the lifetime of the deceased when the person was known by his or her first name followed by those of the father and grandfather. This is therefore a moment to evoke the name of the mother that gave birth to the person. Finally, the body is taken out of the casket or mat and lowered by several men to the grave. Once inside the grave, the body is placed in a niche dug into the side of the grave. Before the niche is closed, the men inside the grave take the shroud away from the sides of the body so that the body touches the dust, as a symbol of the final destination of humans and the end of the cycle of life itself. It states in the Koran that "HE created him out of dust, then he said to him, 'Be,' and he was." The niche is closed with stones or wood. Finally, the grave is filled with sand and at this stage it is customary for all adult males present to help and, if not holding the shovel, to symbolically throw a handful of sand into the grave. While the filling of the grave is taking place everyone chants *Al-mowtu xaqu Laahi* (Arabic for: Death is Allah's law). Women and children always stay at a distance from the actual burial. But women come afterward to sprinkle water on the grave, a tradition that has the practical value of keeping the sand from being blown away but is probably pre-Islamic and might have symbolized a libation of some sort in the past.

After the body has been buried, everyone leaves the grave immediately and no lingering and wailing is allowed. Somalis, as Muslims, are taught to accept death and life as Allah's law. This does not mean there is no mourning and wailing. The female relatives often engage in ritual wailing and tears may follow freely, but as always, men, socialized to hold back tears, do not wail in public. The presentation of condolences to the grieving family is always preceded by the ritualistic sentence in Somali *Ilaahay samir iyo iimaan ha inaga siiyo* (May Allah, by this incident, fortify our faith and patience). Anyone hearing this is supposed to respond with *aamiin* (may it be so).

After the burial has been concluded, Somalis may observe traditions that are their own rather than Islamic. These are funeral feasts or rather meals, for they are just that. Generally, the first funeral feast, known as *ahan* (*axan* in Somali letters) among northern Somalis, is held on the day of the burial itself. Depending on the wealth of the family of the deceased, some sheep, an ox or a camel, are slaughtered and food is prepared. The grave-diggers, the wadaad who presided over the burial rites, and everyone else who is present or is a neighbor partake of the food that is consumed communally. There is strictly no festivity and the ceremony has a religious function of healing as the wadaad reads chapters from the Koran. This is also a time when people evoke the history and the deeds of the deceased in their conversations. In about a year, another feast (*fide*) might be held, although this is less often the case today. Additionally, some families may from time to time hold a remembrance feast (*hus; xus* in Somali), for a departed father or mother.

After the death of a husband, a wife traditionally wears the *hangal* or *asay* mourning attire. This consists, in its most formal practice, of a white dress and a white head scarf and at its simplest of only a white head scarf. The widow also abstains from the use of any cosmetics or creams on her body for the duration of the mourning period, which lasts four months. She also may not remarry during that period to prevent any doubts about the parentage of any children born after her husband's death. In the past the widow of a slain man used to shave her hair, but nowadays the wearing of the mourning attire is more rigorously observed in rural areas than in urban areas.

As for the tomb itself, it might be said its upper structure underwent considerable changes over the centuries. Now the visible part of the grave is a simple earth mound or a square structure of mortared bricks. Over the centuries, the structure has become more simple and less labor intensive. In fact, the labor spent in erecting a traditional grave was considerable in the past and this occasioned a large funeral feast to feed the diggers and the constructors of the tomb. Older graves are large cairns or tumuluses with upright slabs of stones all around. Two taller slabs mark the head and the foot of the grave while the middle of the structure consists of a pile of stones or a mound of sand with sloping sides. Very ancient graves of remarkable construction are known as *taalo* (monument) and are still found mostly in the northern areas, the original homeland of the Somalis. The construction of these elaborate graves of the taalo type ceased a long time ago, maybe after Islam, and people started referring to them as *gaalo* graves (i.e., the graves of the non-Muslims). Glorification of graves is not allowed under Muslim tradition and that may explain the gradual decline of monumental graves. Sometimes when stones are lacking, wood from huge tree trunks were used instead of stones to surround the grave. Some of these graves are surrounded by a stockade of tree trunks and grown over with trees and underbrush and are known as *hawaal* (grave), an archaic word that gave rise to the modern habaal (grave). In the 1970s, many such graves were robbed of their protective wooden stockades by charcoal makers, so today such graves are indeed a rarity.

There are some Somali myths related to death that predate Islam. One of them concerns the Tree of Life on the Moon. In Somali mythology, the face of the moon has a tree on it—the Tree of Life. When a new leaf grows on the tree, a baby is born; when that leaf becomes pale, the person becomes sick, and if it falls, the person dies. Today's Somalis say, figuratively speaking,

ʿalaantiisiiba ʿadaatay (literally his leaf has become pale) when someone is very sick or is in great danger. Another myth of death concerns the arrival of the *huur* (marabou stork); it is thought to be a harbinger of death and to be able to see the angel of death coming to take a person's life.

COUNTRY LIFE

Socially, *gu* (long rains) is the season of good times and when most marriages occur in the countryside. It is also the season when people from the city visit their relatives in the countryside literally to drink plenty of camel milk and breathe the fresh country air. This is also the breeding time for livestock. Unluckily, it also corresponds to the period when idle young men are wont to wander far and wide from their nomadic settlements in search of camels to rustle and ladies to woo. In the course of these events, clashes are bound to occur between bands of young men that would take months for the clan patriarchs to solve and compensate aggrieved parties from either perceived smears on family honor or from rustled camels.

The daily activities of a person in the countryside depend upon whether that person is a pastoralist, a farmer, or agropastoralist, practicing both livestock raising and cultivating a plot of land, or whether one is a shopkeeper in a small rural village. Whatever one's economic activities, rural life is a lot of hard work.

In a pastoral family, everyone is up early in the morning. The milch camels or cows as well as ewes and goats are milked. The adults usually drink tea in the morning while the children drink milk. No cooked food is eaten in the morning—cooked meals are for lunch and supper. Then the animals are let out of the pens and everyone hastens to his or her assigned task of the day. The midday meal might just be milk or a cereal-based meal such as rice, sorghum, or corn. As evening falls they lead the animals back into the pens. The second milking is done in the evening, and after all the evening tasks are done and the evening meal has been consumed, the time of rest and storytelling starts. The routine of the agriculturist is similar in many ways, the major difference being fieldwork.

Among one of the most interesting activities at a pastoral settlement is the cleaning of the milk vessels. In a land where water is precious, people came up with a method of sterilization that does not use water. Milk-drinking vessels, which are made either from wood or from wicker, are scoured with burning pieces of wood (*ʿulid*) that come from a special tree whose soot is not very acrid. Large milk-holding vessels are fumigated (*hogays*) over a fire-oven dug in the ground. The oven has two openings: one that draws draft,

Nomadic father milks his milch camels.

and the other that acts as a flue and fumigates a vessel placed on its top. The scouring with burning wood and fumigation destroy bacteria; they also leave behind a soot that inhibits bacterial growth. After a milk-vessel has been cleaned in this way, no touching with the hand or fingers is allowed to avoid contamination. Constant cleaning of this type makes the milk vessels start to have a black and shiny color in the inside.[4]

CITY LIFE

Most towns are small and life is very provincial. Towns depend on country produce for food; thus as points of commerce, their employment is dependent on the country folk. Many towns of the interior started as garrison towns in the colonial days. Most of the oldest towns are along the coasts, and today as before, Somali and foreign ships load and unload goods at these port cities.

In most of the small towns, employment means either government employment as police or clerk of some government agency or private employment as a storeowner or shop employee. In larger towns, employment opportunities are more varied with people engaged in a wider variety of service and manufacturing jobs.

In towns, a favorite place for leisuretime socializing for adult men is at the tea shop. Women do not come to tea shops or bars, although they used to

Young girl helps her older sister to milk a ewe.

work as waitresses there in the south; however, this is no longer the case as a result of a conservative trend since the civil war. Another favorite pastime activity in towns is the habit of chewing *qat* leaves. Qat, scientifically *Catha edulis*, is a shrub whose leaves contain a stimulant drug. The amount of stimulant in the leaves is not much so one would have to chew a large bundle of leaves before getting a high (*mirqaan*) from it. Although use of this plant as a stimulant was known for a long time in the Horn of Africa, qat chewing became popular in the 1950s among song artists, musicians, and truck drivers. Before that time, there was little use of qat among Somalis. But today the use of qat is a national problem since most urban men chew it. Qat use itself is not limited to Somalis; it is also widely consumed in Yemen, the only other place where the proportion of qat users is as high as that among Somalis. Qat is also chewed in Ethiopia, Kenya, and in other places in the world where migrant Yemenis and Somalis are found.

Qat itself does not grow in Somali areas; therefore, most of the qat consumed by Somalis is imported from either neighboring Kenya or Ethiopia, which contributes greatly to the economies of these countries while depleting the incomes of Somali families. Various attempts to curb the use of qat have produced little success. The British tried to stop it in the 1950s when they governed the north. However, the Somalis saw it as an injustice and a double standard since the British were drinking whisky and alcoholic beverages. Qat

Dry-goods store owner in his well-stocked shop.

was again banned in 1983 by the government of dictator Mohamed Siad Barre. Unluckily, this last attempt was a half-hearted step by the government aimed more at depriving Somali guerrillas based in Ethiopia from hitching rides on qat trucks, and commerce in qat continued under the hands of the supporters of the regime. The Barre government publicly permitted qat use in its last days in 1989. Since 1991, qat use has increased greatly among unemployed youth and militia members.

MEANS OF LIVELIHOOD

Traditionally, the peoples of the Somali peninsula have been mostly herders and farmers in the countryside where the bulk of the people lived. In the towns, concentrated mostly on the seaboard, they were mostly traders and crafts people making shoes and other items for use by the majority rural population on which the town folk depended. Despite the fact that the Somali peninsula has one of the longest coastlines in Africa, fishing was not and is not a widespread economic activity, although it is gaining ground. Perhaps, because of the easy availability of mutton, fish production had never been a competitive economic activity. This is probably the only explanation for the dislike of fish that is attributed to the majority population with Somali roots.

Before the nineteenth century, the economy of the Somali peninsula was well integrated with those of the Horn and the rim of the Indian Ocean, Red Sea, and the Gulf. The principal export was without doubt incense (frankincense and myrrh) in ancient times; other produce included ghee (clarified butter), ostrich feathers, turtle shells, and fabrics, the latter mainly from the Benadir region in the south, where the allendi fabric that rivals that of West Africa was and is still manufactured by traditional weavers. Dhows, both foreign and Somali, used to sail and come with the monsoons in an ancient trading network connecting northeastern Africa, Arabia, India, and the Malayo-Indonesian littoral. Today's trade is more diversified in content, but the main economic links are still with the countries of the Horn, and those on the rim of the Indian Ocean, Red Sea, and the Gulf.

Livestock

It is said that God did not create a land without resources—that would be unjust to the inhabitants whose lot fell on that land. In Somali-inhabited areas of the Horn, there are neither verdant tropical areas nor mines of gold; so Somalis adopted livestock raising, an economic activity best suited to their dry land. It is therefore livestock, such as sheep, goats, and camels raised by pastoralist families, concentrated mostly in the northern and central regions, which continues to be the principal economic activity, providing jobs and livelihoods to at least 60 percent of the population. Livestock exports earned 77 percent of export earnings in 1980, 86 percent in 1981, and 81 percent in 1982.[5] Even today, if there are no official statistics, it can be assumed the situation has not changed.

By any estimates, Somalis own a lot of livestock, having the world's highest camel production, the only other record being frankincense production. According to the last census, taken in a particularly harsh drought year when millions of animals died, there were in the Somalia of 1975, a livestock population of 33.7 million consisting of 24.7 million sheep and goats, 3.7 million bovines, and 5.3 million camels.[6] However, despite the lack of hard statistics, it can be said that the herds number at around 40 million, of which about 2 million are culled for export in a good year.

With all these milk-producing animals, the land of the Somalis is deservedly the land of milk, for Somalis drink a lot of milk and eat a lot of mutton. The nomadic families, who rear the milk-producing herds, are hardy and healthy folks. They may not have the benefits of modern schools and tap water; but out with the herds in the countryside, they lead simple, healthy, and happy lives, free from the abject poverty, pollution, and diseases so characteristic of overpopulated Third World metropolises; they are also free from the exploitation and drudgery suffered by the landless peasantry in many countries. Their major concerns are the rains and the price of livestock in the nearest town. However, the distribution of the herds is not uniform across the land and therefore the availability of protein-rich foods such as milk and meat is not uniform.

Agriculture

Agriculture is practiced wherever soil and water permit. Therefore, it is possible to find a good green patch of vegetables being cultivated in an otherwise dry zone. Traditionally there are, however, two zones that have stood out as agricultural zones: the southwest in the hinterland of the Benadir coastal region and the extreme corner of the northwest, now in the separate state of Somaliland.

In the southwest, the Rahanwein and Bantu villagers essentially practice subsistence agriculture of the rain-fed type. This interriverine region, usually defined as the area between the two rivers of Juba and Shebelle, is sometimes described as the Mesopotamia of Somalia. This is the sorghum belt; it produces the most grain in the form of corn and sorghum. The variety of sorghum cultivated here is a form known as Baidoa; its grains are reddish in color and are smaller than the variety cultivated in the northwest. Paradoxically the southwest, the granary of Somalia, has traditionally been the poorest region in Somalia and its peasant-herders hardly enjoy incomes equal to those of the livestock-raising pastoralists of the central and northern regions. The reasons why the agropastoralists of the southwest fare less well than the relatively well-off pastoralists in the central and northern regions are manifold.[7] The main reason is that the farmers in the riverine region have always been subsistence farmers; they till the soil but do not produce much extra grain for sale, and even when they have a surplus, their tradition is to bury it in underground silos (*bakaar*) for use in lean years. On the other hand, livestock breeding is a highly monetized activity (i.e., a market-oriented activity), and through exports to Arabian countries it is part of the wider regional economy. Thus, the bulk of the export earnings comes from livestock exports, and instead of the farmer supporting the pastoralist, it has always been the pastoralist, through taxation at the market, supporting the farmer. The methods and implements used in the interriverine region are of a type to permit only subsistence levels—the main agricultural tool is the hand-held hoe (*yaambo*), which is used for digging and weeding. The word yaambo has been borrowed, as well as the techniques of agriculture used in the area, from Bantu-speaking peoples who used to inhabit the southern regions before the arrival of the Cushites such as Oromos and Somalis.

While most farming is of the rain-fed type in the the southwest, irrigation-fed agriculture is practiced along the two rivers. To the local people, this wet area is known as *Dhoobooy* (the muddy), named after the rich alluvial deposits left behind after the flooding of the rivers. Riverside agriculture had existed for centuries and was practiced by the riverine Bantu peoples of southern Somalia. However, in the early years of the twentieth century, Italian colonialists got concessions on the best arable land and started huge plantations, under the active encouragement of the fascist regime, for the exploitation of sugar, bananas, and cotton. On these colonial farms, called *asendo*, after the haciendas of the Spanish conquistadores, there was a huge mansion in the middle. The Italians also installed a regime of forced labor and worker concentration by creating villages adjacent to the plantations, a practice that usually targeted the riverine agricultural communities, from whom the land was originally taken.

The establishment of huge plantations for cash crops such as sugar and bananas created a class of seasonal workers, some of whom were landless and some of whom cultivated some fields in the drier rain-fed areas. These are the *jibaal* people (jibaal is a local unit of land measure); the workers are paid per the number of jibaal or tracts cleared of weeds or worked otherwise. Over the years, going to Dhoobooy to work several jibaals became part of the culture of the seasonal workers in a pattern no less socially disturbing than that described by John Steinbeck in his novel about the California migrant workers, *The Grapes of Wrath*.[8] Poor farmers in the *Dooy* (dry rain-fed areas) dream each year or after a bad harvest of going to work in the banana fields and of getting literally their beards wet by standing below the banana branches laden with fruit. But the wages are generally so low that the workers have little or nothing left even after several days' work.

After independence, the first minister of agriculture tried to introduce a wage reform. The minister was from the northern regions that had just united with the ex-Italian colony and was unaware of the collusion between southern Somali politicians and the big farmers, who were mostly Italians at the time. He was quickly relieved of his post.[9] Gradually, Somalis with means or with the right political connections replaced the Italian farmers and created more plantations. The frenzy to possess arable land in the river basin was at its highest during the later years of the Siad Barre regime, when those with close clan connections to the president were forcefully grabbing land. In July 1983, for example, kinsmen of the president dispossessed forty-three families of 150 hectares in the village of Hufey in the upper Juba valley; the families were left to cultivate a mere nine hectares in the vicinity.[10]

In the agricultural region of the northwest, in Somaliland, rain-fed farming is practiced; small-scale irrigation, using wells and ponds, is also employed mainly in orchard plantations. The northwestern farmers around the town of Gabiley and Borame use the traditional Somali plow (*irfi*) and plow-oxen, or, if they can afford, tractors. As a result, farmers in the northwest have always had better incomes than those of the southwest. A type of sorghum grown there is *elmi jaama,* named presumably after the farmer that introduced it into the area; its grains are larger than the variety known in the south. However, its growing time is longer than that of the southern variety. Additionally, in the north fruit and vegetable farming is very important and some valleys have been completely turned into fruit and vegetable orchards to supply the increasing demand of cities.

Manufacturing and Other Industries

While livestock and agriculture dominate the economy, other sectors include manufacturing and fishing. Manufacturing has always been geared toward satisfying domestic consumption through import substitutes. Today most of the heavy industries, almost all public owned, have become decrepit or ruined by the civil war. Among these are the sugar mills at Jowhar and Marereey, the textile manufacturing facility at Balad, the cement plant at Berbera, the oil refinery at Mogadishu, and various other plants concentrated mostly in the south and around the capital city Mogadishu. Private industries have always tended to be much smaller in scale and have included soap and detergent plants, soft-drink bottling, and shoemaking. It can be said that the manufacturing sector is the one that has suffered the most from the war. At this time, manufacturing has returned to the most basic industry of all: small workshops for fixtures and furniture. Investors are afraid to put a lot of money in a huge undertaking such as plants as long as the political situation is unstable.

Fishing has perhaps been the smallest sector of the Somali economy. Various government programs have tried to encourage growth in this sector through the establishment of fishing cooperatives and government-financed fishing boats. Fish canning plants were also established. However, after the collapse of the state, and in the absence of stifling bureaucracy, enterprising Somalis have found that they can get good prices for lobster, shrimp, and shark fins. Because of a lack of protection for Somali coastal waters, foreign fishing trawlers, using much more sophisticated but environmentally dangerous equipment such as dragnets, have also found how lucrative fishing in undefended Somali waters can be. Day and night these foreign "pirate fleets" plunder the marine resources of Somali waters, which includes the Exclusive Economic Zone (EEZ) two hundred nautical miles from the shore; through the use of illegal methods including explosives and gill nets, they damage the coastline and deplete marine resources.[11]

Today, thousands of tons of marine produce are caught illegally by fishing ships from several nations such as Japan, Taiwan, Korea, Italy, as well as other countries. In some cases, the fishing nets of Somalis have even been deliberately torn up by the crews of these ships. To defend their livelihoods and their natural resources from extinction, Somalis have resorted to forceful means such as detaining fishing ships and crews, which is usually reported as Somali piracy, but which amounts to a minor defense from the Somalis against predatory fishing concerns from bigger economies who take advantage of the current plight of Somalis.[12] Sometimes the defending Somali "Davids" in small boats have even lost their own lives in these skirmishes with the "Goliath" boats.

Quantification of the Somali Economy

Even at the best of times, when there was a functioning bureaucracy and a ministry of planning, the quantification of the Somali economy was far from correct. Conventional economists are report-compilers and paper-chasers; but most Somalis work and deal in a paperless economy in which business transactions and money transfers worth thousands of dollars are enacted with words. No wonder then that on a balance sheet, Somalia had always appeared as a chronic deficit country and as one of the lowest income countries. On paper, Somalia appears to be one of the poorest countries in the world with incomes as low as $150 in per capita income. However, the Ugandan economist Vali Jamal has shown how incorrect conventional economic data-gathering was in Somalia.[13] He demonstrated that rural incomes and workers' remittances miss the official statistics. Jamal's alternate data on milk production alone, from the official 451.4 million liters to his estimated 2.92 billion liters, would make Somalia not the eighth poorest country but a middle-income country with a per capita income of more than $400.[14] Figures would matter here because they influence, for example, foreign investments and international loans.

There are no official current records; but the old records show that livestock has always dominated exports.[15] In the years from 1979 to 1983, livestock exports earned an average of 78.10 percent of all officially recorded export earnings; on average the total earnings for livestock and meat, including fish, were 81.77 percent of export earnings. In the same period, the main crop, bananas, earned only 6.94 percent, a figure that was not much better than the 4.2 percent average officially earned from frankincense exports during the same period (frankincense earnings were probably higher than this figure suggests since there was much smuggling of this commodity to Arabian markets from the northern coasts).

These brief statistics suggest that Somalia could have capitalized on meat, fish, and livestock exports to the Middle East by investing in better livestock and rangeland management and through more manufacturing of meat and fish products to feed the increasingly wealthy populations in the Gulf countries. Instead, the government earmarked most agricultural expenses for crop production in the small area that supports banana and other crops along the river banks.[16] But by 1983, frankincense exports, a crop that received a zero investment from the government planners, eclipsed banana exports by officially earning 8.9 percent of total earnings as opposed to the 7.9 percent from bananas, a crop that swallowed a lot of investment either through crop investments or structural investments such as roads and canals. Typically, in 1983, the planned investment in crop production stood at 68.89 percent of planned agricultural investments while the figure for livestock, the big earner, was only 28.06 percent of the total. Economic planning implied, therefore, that increased public investment in the sectors with less potential was catering to the land appetites of the ruling class who had invested much in the riverside plantations. From these statistics, it is clear that the hardy stock-breeder was not receiving any tangible benefits in the form of services, while producing most of the export earnings.

If Somalia's economy was difficult to quantify in the years of a national government, it was even more so from 1990 to 2000, the stateless years. However, in the absence of asphyxiating bureaucracy and profiting from a lack of a taxation system, private enterprise is flourishing everywhere. Of course, lack of a government does not, however, afflict all areas; the north, or Somaliland, which now considers itself independent and outside of Somalia, is politically stable, and livestock exports are again finding their way to their traditional markets. An example would be that during the months of January to March 2000, 1.3 million head of animals were exported through the northern ports, mostly through Berbera.[17] Fueled by revenues from livestock exports and the workers' remittances, the northern economy has since 1995 witnessed an unprecedented boom. In turn construction has started in earnest, attracting workers from the south and Ethiopia. Banana exports have also restarted in the south through the involvement of the U.S. firm Dole in a sector dominated by Italian concerns. Fishing and marine product exports are up as well. Overall, as before, workers' remittances, previously mostly from the Gulf oil states but now from Europe and North America, still form a sizeable portion of the economy.

Most people in the West who saw the horrible pictures of the famine in Somalia's southwestern region would think that there is no functioning economy in Somalia. Virtually without international investments, Somalis are restarting destroyed businesses, setting up enterprises whose activities straddle the ethnic divisions that tore up the country in the first place. As journalist Michael Maren, who is more intimately familiar with the situation in Somalia than journalists on a one-time mission, wrote: "The progress that has been made in Somalia is substantial. Somalis themselves possess most of the resources they need to rebuild their own country. Sometimes this is difficult for Westerners to accept. We want to believe they need us. The truth is that they don't. Without foreign intervention Somalis will rebuild their economy. Then they will rebuild their political systems."[18]

EDUCATION

Traditional education among Somalis is dispensed in private Koranic schools as has been the case for centuries. In these schools, the educational fare consists of learning to read and write, usually on long wooden slates, the characters of the Arabic language. The aim of this kind of education is primarily to read the Koran, the Muslim holy book. Nowadays, some Koranic schools in urban areas also teach secular subjects as well.

Modern secular education started in the early part of the twentieth century. At first Somalis were apprehensive of the education dispensed in the first modern schools, as these were run either by Christian missionaries or by the colonial governments. Somalis feared that their children would be turned into Christians, especially since the language of instruction in those schools was a European language. Eventually, due to the constant efforts of Somali teachers and oral artists, such as poets and composers, the image of modern schools as tools for modern development gained ground. In this regard, the role of oral artists, who themselves had little or no schooling in their childhood, was critical. Through songs and verses that became popular catchy tunes, they drilled in the minds of Somalis the importance of a good modern education. One of the most popular tunes, and the signature music of Radio Mogadishu for many years, was composed by the poet, composer, and musician Abdillahi Qarshe.[19] Among its lines:

Aqoon la'aani waa iftiin laa'ane (Lack of education is a lack of
   light)
Waa aqal iyo ilays laa'aane (It is homelessness and darkness)
Ogaada, ogaada dugsiyada ogaada (Be attentive to schools)
Oo gaada, oo ogadaa (Be attentive)
Walaalayaal oo adaa (Brothers and sisters go to schools)
   [Author's translation]

Gradually the number of students enrolled in modern schools increased.
However, such schools were limited to urban centers. By the 1970s and
1980s, however, it could be said that modern schools were getting closer to
rural areas as elementary schools were being opened in villages.

Literacy campaigns, after the official adoption of a Latin writing script for
Somali, increased literacy rates to double-digit percentages. In the rural literacy campaign of 1974–75, all senior and junior secondary schools were
closed for a year and all the students and their teachers were sent to the
countryside to teach basic literacy skills to the rural population of pastoralists
and agriculturists. Literacy campaigns were also launched in urban centers
with secondary school students, teachers, and civil servants as the teachers.
The message of such campaigns was captured in a now famous motto: *ama
bar ama baro* (either learn or be the teacher). Such mass literacy campaigns
were, of course, made possible by the use of Somali language rather than the
previous foreign but official languages such as English and Italian.

Still, education in Somalia was hampered by problems inherent in the
management of the education sector. First, as inherited from the colonial
governments, the modern educational sector remained a centralized public
sector. No private educational institutions, except for Koranic schools, were
allowed and whatever existed was taken over by the Ministry of Education
when the military junta came into power in 1969. Evidently, the intent of
the military regime was to control the content of the education dispensed in
schools. Centralization also had the perverse effect of concentrating all the
major higher educational institutions in Mogadishu.

During the struggle that led to the toppling of the Barre regime and the
ensuing civil war, most schools and educational facilities were destroyed. The
recovery might be said to be ongoing but it is hampered by continued in-
stability in some areas. In the yet unrecognized but de facto state of Somaliland in the north, schools are functioning again and higher education
institutions have sprung up including two universities, the University of Hargeisa and the University of Amoud.

FESTIVALS AND COMMEMORATIVE DAYS

Excessive public exuberance and displays are not part of Somali custom; this is due partly to the ascetic nature of Somali pastoralist culture and partly to the Islamic teachings of sobriety and piety. Public revelry is therefore unknown and the Somali night is one of silence, as one European expatriate opined. However, Somalis are not without joyous celebrations and commemorative days. These can be divided into ancient pre-Islamic, Islamic, and state-related celebrations.

Only one pre-Islamic celebration of importance exists—the *dabshid* (the lighting of the fire), which marks the beginning of the Somali solar calendar. The calculation of the start of the solar year is made by weather and stellar experts and has a practical value for stock-breeders and farmers.[20] During the dabshid a small bonfire is lit in the evening and everyone is supposed to try to jump over it. Burning sticks from the bonfire are also thrown into the sky. The dabshid also has been referred to as *neyruus*, a Persian word for the Persian new year (*nairuz*), due to the use of fire in dabshid, which early Muslims probably took as a fire worship as was the case among pre-Islamic Persians. There is no other evidence of a relationship between the dabshid and the Persian nairuz. The solar calendar, whose reckoning was aided by lunar and stellar observations, has been known among Cushitic groups such as Somalis and the Oromo for millennia. Somalis also take notice of the Arabic lunar calendar year, which is in use among Muslims, but they do not celebrate its start.

Properly Muslim celebrations include the birth of Mohamed the prophet, *mawliid*, and the *'iid-al-fitar*, marking the end of the annual fasting period. The prophet's birthday occasions the reading of hymns and a feast in Somali homes. Publicly, except for extra colored lights in urban centers, there are no celebrations or festivities on this occasion. The most publicly celebrated of Muslim holidays is the *'iid-al-fitar*, which comes at the end of Ramadan, the holy month of fasting. For that day, families who can afford to buy a sheep or goat and prepare a large feast. People dress in their best and children receive gifts from parents and relatives. Small children in bright new clothes can be seen crossing the streets bound for a relative's home where they would be received with a gift, food, and cookies. Streets, given beforehand an extra cleaning, shine with colored lights.

Nationalist holidays include June 26 for the independence of the north (Somaliland) from Great Britain in 1960. Somaliland, now a de facto state with a government and a parliament, has also been celebrating May 18 for the past ten years as the Somaliland Day, in commemoration of May 18,

Young men play an impromptu game of soccer in the street.

1991, when the union with the south (Somalia) was abrogated. In the south, July 1 is a holiday marking independence from Italy in 1960.

SPORTS AND GAMES

Modern sports such as soccer and tennis have become popular among Somalis; soccer or football is especially popular, and youngsters kicking balls can be seen in urban open spaces. The British introduced field hockey and cricket in the north. Cricket did not catch on but field hockey did to a certain extent and there were field hockey teams in the north until the 1960s. Basketball was introduced in the 1960s by American expatriates and caught on well in the 1970s. However, by far the most popular sport is soccer.

Amateur and semiprofessional teams have played tournaments since the 1960s, at first with the encouragement of private sponsors; however, later during the Barre era most teams were state-sponsored with ministries and state-owned companies owning a particular team. The players were thus professionals and received salaries from the owning agency. Amateur sport was left to regional and scholastic teams for which tournaments were held yearly. Of all the tournaments, the one that drew the most crowds was the interregional tournament, as this drew on the regional loyalties of the fans. This was a series of games in several sports, of which the most notable was soccer. The finalists from the regional groups would come to the capital city where the winners of the year would emerge.

The last interregional tournament was held in 1989 in a year when the northern regions were engulfed in terrible fighting and government planes and artillery had flattened the majors cities of Hargeisa and Burao. But the tournament was still held to mask the realities at hand and to dispel from the minds of the southern public, especially those of Mogadishu, any doubts as to whether the regime was losing its grip. But with no teams from the northern regions coming—the indigenous population of these regions having fled into Ethiopia—the government came up with fictitious teams sporting the colors of these regions. As the anecdote of the time has it, a member of the Benadiri people of Mogadishu asked the minister of sports whether it was true that there were indeed qualifying games going on in the northern regions, as the national radio was stating. The minister is said to have responded in the affirmative upon which the Benadiri man retorted prophetically: *Alore, finaalka Xamar lee la imaanaayaanoo* (Well then, the finals will be played out in Mogadishu). The finals of the war game was, of course, played out in January 1991 when Gen. Siad Barre's regime was chased out of Mogadishu and out of power.

Since 1991, sports teams have been reestablished in some areas with the help of private sponsors. As before, in all communities, soccer remains the favorite and impromptu games between adolescents or more organized teams can be seen taking place.

Games and Sports of Old

Somalis had some indigenous games before the introduction of modern sports. Among these was a little known ball game called *go'oso*. This is somewhat similar to rugby but nowadays it is rare to see it being played. Traditional board games have, however, survived and are still popular. Although there is no formal interdiction, traditional games, except childhood games, are played only by men. Perhaps the most popular board game is *shah* (written in Somali as *shax*), known in the central regions as *jar*; if one sees a group of people watching a board game in a village, town, or out in the countryside, it is probably shah and no other game. Shah is a strategy game played on a board with twenty-four points, *guryo* (houses); the board design results from three rectangles, an inner rectangle engulfed by a larger one, itself surrounded by the exterior one; straight lines drawn from the four sides of the inner rectangles to the sides of the exterior rectangle result in twenty-four points for placing the pieces. The board format can be drawn on the sand while the pieces, twelve for each player, can be almost anything such as pebbles, glass, camel-dung, or as has been observed during the past decades, the caps from soft-drink bottles. The facility one may equip himself or herself with necessary for a shah probably accounts for the popularity and the survival of this game over the centuries.[21]

Unlike chess in which the positions are predefined, in shah one player positions a first piece followed by the second player; the person who succeeds in positioning three pieces in a straight line has the privilege of first moving one of the pieces of the opponent. Strategy is therefore important from the outset and thereafter consists of maneuvering to align three pieces in a straight line. In the countryside, it is played mostly by older men, and every village has a champion or two known to all.

Another popular game played with the same materials is the *shantarah*, also known as *korkabood*. The board is formed by five horizontal and five vertical lines that intersect; thus there are twenty-five points. Unlike shah, when starting to play a turn, each player places two pieces at a time. The player who plays last is then invited to move a piece from the adversary's set, which he does with an eye to furthering his own strategy for winning. The person who is able to move his piece into an empty point or home while jumping over an adjacent piece from the adversary's set has the right to move a piece belonging to the adversary from the board and the game continues until there is a clear winner.

In large towns, imported board games have made inroads and one may see Somalis calmly playing a game of dominoes, known as *dumnad*, or chess (*jees*) on the terrace of a tea shop. Card games, also a cultural import, are known; but playing for money is frowned upon and gambling is illegal.

NOTES

1. Michael E. Meeker (1989). *The Pastoral Son and the Spirit of Patriarchy.* Madison: University of Wisconsin Press, 145.

2. I.M. Lewis (1992). "In the Land of the Living Dead," *Sunday Times.* 30 August.

3. Colonial masters used to call their male servant "boy" even when the servant in question was older than the master.

4. Oval-shaped vessels that remarkably look like those of Somalis (i.e., dark on the rims and the inside, doubtless from scouring with burning wood or fumigation), have been found buried with "Ginger," a predynastic Egyptian mummy from c. 3200 B.C. See: Carol Andrews (1984). *Egyptian Mummies.* Cambridge: Harvard University Press, 4.

5. IMF (International Monetary Fund) (1984). *Somalia: Recent Economic Developments*, April 4, (SM/84/72), 2.

6. Ibid.

7. Gunnar Haaland and Willem Keddeman (1984). "Poverty Analysis: The Case of Rural Somalia." *Economic Development and Cultural Change* 32 (July):843–60.

8. John Steinbeck (1939). *The Grapes of Wrath.* New York: Viking Penguin.

9. Conversation with a former Somali diplomat, Mowlid Mohamed Diriye, January 2000.

10. Alex De Waal (1993). "The Shadow Economy." *Africa Report* 38, no. 2: 24–25.

11. UN Integrated Regional Information Network (IRIN), "Somalia Revisited—Irin Special Report on Mogadishu," April 28, 1999.

12. See: Reuters, *Taiwanese Ship Fined for Illegal Somalia Fishing,* February 20, 1998; see also: Reuters, *Somalis Fine Italian Boat for Illegal Fishing,* December 26, 1988.

13. Vali Jamal, "Somalia: Understanding an Unconventional Economy," *Development and Change* 19, no. 2 (April 1988) 203–65. See also: Vali Jamal, "Nomads and Farmers: Income and Poverty in Rural Somalia," in D. Ghai and S. Radwan (1983). eds., *Agrarian Policies and Rural Poverty in Africa.* Geneva: International Labor Organization, 281–311.

14. A simple calculation confirms Jamal's estimates. Let us suppose that there are 40 million livestock (sheep, goats, cattle, and camels) in Somalia, a reasonable figure, of which 30 percent is under lactation. Since Somalis milk sheep, goats, camels, and cows, animals with differing milkouts—sheep give the least milk—let us round the production per animal to only 1 liter for only 200 days of the year, a reasonable figure again. The total milk production per day and liter would then stand at 2.4 billion liters. This is a conservative estimate, and in a good year, milk becomes so plentiful that pastoralists, unable to sell it, dump it.

15. IMF (1984), 73.

16. Ibid., 32.

17. USAID, FEWS (Famine Early Warning System) Bulletin, February 26, 1998.

18. Michael Maren, *Progress in Somalia Is Endangered by Foreign Presence.* Not dated. Available on Nomadnet: http://www.interport.net/~mmaren.

19. The first line of this song is now a proverb.

20. Lewis, I.M. (1958), 62.

21. Jama Muse Jama, November 11, 1999. Shax and Other East African Board Games. Somaliland Forum (somaliland@yoyo.cc.monash.edu.au).

SUGGESTED READING

Lewis, I.M. 1961. *Pastoral Democracy: A Study of Pastoralism Among the Northern Somali of the Horn of Africa.* London: Oxford University Press.

————. 1955. *The Peoples of the Horn of Africa: Somali, Afar and Saho.* London: International African Institute.

Loughran, John, Katheryne Loughran, John Johnson, and Said S. Samatar, eds. 1986. *Somalia in Word and Image.* Washington, D.C.: Foundation for Cross-Cultural Understanding.

8

Music and Dance

INSTRUMENTAL MUSIC is not a domain that Somalis cultivated much before the twentieth century; that does not mean, however, that Somalis have been in the past an arrhythmic people. The songs (*hees*) or verses sung at the traditional dances or at the spirit possession rites were accompanied by clapping and on occasion by percussion instruments. The different types of poetic genres have inherent melodies and can be accompanied by music. For example, the music of the *baar'ade* genre is light and swift while that of *geeraar* is slow. The work songs, lullabies, and children's songs are all accompanied by clapping, chorus lines, and vocal utterances with no meaning except to produce a vibrato.

Why did Somalis, open to commerce and to the outside world of their wider region, not use many instruments in their music? One easy answer, which has become a kind of stock answer for all writers short of insight into Somali culture, is that most Somalis were pastoralists and had to be light on the move, although not all the Somalis had to be on the move—certainly not the citizens of the ancient trading cities like Zeilah. A more plausible reason might lie in the lack of a court and a king—in most parts of the world, before commercialization of music and artistic productions (i.e., in the days when there was no music- and song-buying public), kings and feudal nobles, the patrons of the arts, were the sponsors and consumers of the works of musicians. But Somalis had neither king nor feudal lords and art without a patron and without a buyer had to be practiced in ways compatible with one's daily activities.

Some instruments were, nonetheless, in use before the twentieth century (i.e., the drum, a reed flute, and occasionally the lute). The drum is the traditional Somali drum; it is portable and may have a strap for the shoulder. Such drums are used for accompanying religious chanting and for some popular dances. The reed flute, now rare, is used by lonely young shepherds and is often fashioned by them. It should be pointed out that some of the southern populations have cultivated instrumental music much more than the majority population from an original Somali stock. This is notably the case of people with origins in ancient Bantu culture such as the Benadiris of the coastal Benadir region and the riverine Wagosha. Among them, native instruments include a wide variety of drums of larger sizes, and a string instrument, the lyre, known as *shareero*. This latter instrument, with its distinctive plaintive tunes, characterizes that brand of music that might today be truly characteristic of Benadiri music.

Today there is a lot of music coming from a wider variety of instruments among Somalis and the radio, whose introduction had tremendous impact on the production and the development of modern song and music. Somali music, a unique kind of music that might be mistaken at first for music from nearby countries such as Ethiopia, the Sudan, or even Arabia, can be recognized by its own tunes and styles. Still, traditional dances, with the exception of those of the Benadiri and the Wagosha, are mostly not accompanied by musical instruments. However, the *jiib* (chorus line), and *sa'ab iyo jaan* (clapping and beating of the feet) are used to keep the beat and woe to the person who makes an out-of-step measure for he or she will be scolded for having spoiled *dhabqi* (the beat) and might be asked to become just one of the spectators outside the circle of dancers.

Technically, Somali music has been identified as mainly pentatonic (i.e., using only the first five tones on a musical scale, instead of thirteen in the Western music).[1] Until the 1970s, there were no regular music schools and artists learned their craft by apprenticeship and by fiddling. In the 1970s, the Ministry of Education introduced the first musical training courses for eligible students in the junior high schools and one such school opened in the provincial town of Baidoa in 1975.

Although Somalis are aware of musical compositions without lyrical verses, music that is not accompanied by the human voice is not appreciated. Music therefore comes with songs and it is only after the lyrical verses, *midho* (literally grains), have been composed that the tune, *lahan*, is fashioned to suit the inherent musicality of the verses. To make sure that the music never overwhelms the voice of the singer, musicians lower the volume as soon as the singer starts singing. Metallic and heavy percussion sounds are alien to Somali ears, and Somalis consider loud music vexatious to the soul. Harmony and the notes of a single guitar or lute and the beat of a small drum, sometimes accompanied by notes from a wind instrument, are the staple of Somali music. Somalis therefore do not expect the music of songs to have a fast tempo nor do they expect the singer to jump up and down or add any entertaining antics to the vocal performance; usually the singer stands almost still and concentrates only on the song, occasionally making a flourish with the hands. In this regard, the Somali song show has the features of sobriety found in Western concert halls where people go to hear classical music or an opera singer.

Somali music is perfect for Somali folklore and songs but inadequate for the rapid movement and swivelling of Western pop dances—discotheque dancing is itself not known to most Somalis, and discotheques, which numbered less than five in the whole country before the war, are considered places of ill-repute, while any suggestive dancing is considered to be the equivalent of cavorting with the devil. Young intrepid Somalis who want to dance à la Western, therefore have to play Western pop music, usually in the privacy of a home. Of course, some Somali artists have tried to introduce into their repertoires the strong pulsating sounds and fast beats typical of Western pop music; foremost among these is a lady by the name of Maryan Mursal, to date the only artist to have released an album under a Western label. However, in general, Somali music remains loyal to its rather placid and bucolic tunes, intended as a soft accompaniment that would not deter the listener from savoring the sense of the verses of the song and the melodious voice of the singer (ʿodka).

A somali song is usually the product of the fruitful cooperation between three persons: the composer of the lyrics, *midho*, the composer of the music, *lahan*, and the singer, *ʿodka* (voice). Sometimes the composer of the lyrics and that of the music are the same; at other times, the composer of the lyrics is also the singer. The least numerous in the entertainment business, *maaweelo*, are probably the musical composers, for the majority of songs have been set to music by one of several composers such as the late Abdillahi Qarshe, nationalist, poet, and composer who excelled equally as a composer of lyrics and of music, earning him the title of *aabaha fanka Soomaaliyeed* (father of modern Somali music). The scarcity of professional musicians might, therefore, account for the stability of music styles in popular songs since the 1940s.

The beginnings of modern Somali music have been linked with the birth of the *balwo* and the *heello* lyrical verses (sung poetry), in the period after World War II.[2] The difference between the balwo, which came first, and the heello was in length: balwo was about four lines whereas the heello was much

longer. There is nothing new about the balwo or heello light verse compositions in themselves. What was new, however, was the musical accompaniment as well as the subject matter, which was overwhelmingly about love,
although other subjects such as nationalist themes were also the focus of the
heello songs. The balwo is said to have been introduced in 1944 by the verses
of Abdi Sinimoo, a truck driver from the town of Borame and his friends,
including a lady by the name of Khadija Balwo. The succeeding heello, much
longer and accompanied by its particular music from the *daf* (tambourine),
ʿuud (lute), and maybe some notes from a *foodhi* (a flute), were the hallmark
of composers such as Hussein Aw Farah, Mohamed Ismail "Balo-ʿas," and
many others in the 1950s. Today the balwo and the heello are no longer
being composed as far as musical styles are concerned; nowadays, Somalis
speak of *hees* "song" and the music that accompanies it is more eclectic than
ever.

One might well wonder what suddenly brought the flowering of romance
and liberty in an otherwise conservative society in the 1940s. First, this was
an era in which Somalis looked at impending changes as the hope that independence was becoming nearer and more tangible—the independence
movement was gaining momentum and poets and composers were at its
forefront as its spokespersons. Second, to understand the reason for the blos-
soming of the romantic genre in Somali poetry and song in the 1940s and
1950s, we have to look at the pre–World War II period. In that period, the
1930s, we find a poor baker and romantic poet, Elmi Boodhari, reciting his
compositions about his unrequited love for Hodan until he reportedly wasted
away and died.

Elmi Boodhari was not, by any means, the first poet to compose romantic
poetry, for Somali poets have been composing poems about love forever and
indeed the old bards used to compose a poem or two for the ladies of their
hearts. However, the old bards were remembered mostly for their verses about
clan politics, battles, hardships, and loot; whereas Elmi Boodhari was unique
among Somali poets as being the only one whose poetry was only about love.
As he said in his own verses, he felt he had to sing only about love:

        Waa laygu eemaray cishqiga inaan ku ooyaaye
        Allahayow afkaygiyo sideen aadmiga u eeday

        I have been compelled to weep for love's sake
        Oh God! How much has my mouth betrayed me
        And how people have been cruel to me! (Author's translation)

In the above lines, Boodhari is speaking of those who ridiculed him for having allowed himself to waste away from love, something seen hitherto as incompatible with the ethos of Somali manhood, for Somali men are trained to have control over their emotions. Boodhari's verses were not set to music but they became popular from one end of the Somali-speaking territory to the other, as they were recited in public. Boodhari of course, missed the popularity that would be his, as he died of grief in 1941, but today it can be said he had his revenge on Somalis, as his suffering sparked the flowering of modern Somali music and song.

The balwo and heello composers picked up the tunes and rhythms from recited verses. A look at some balwo and heello verses from the 1940s and 1950s shows how the composers set their verses in existing forms and tunes. Thus, for example, we have the following pairs of lines from a timeless traditional Somali verse in a story for children, "Dhagdheer" (The Long-eared).

Hohey bohalaha Xargagan
Nin xiimayay xidhaan

Oh, the ditches of Xargagan
They do block the flight of a man (Author's translation)

The balwo composer in turn composed the following lines:

Hohey Lacageey wax kala haadshaay[3]
Ninkii haya way u hadashaa

Oh, money, the one who categorizes
It does speak for he who has it (Author's translation)

Likewise the balwo lines below recall easily those of Boodhari:

Waxaanad helaynin
Ee aad handataa
Hahey! Hagardaamo weeyaan[4]

Something that you do not have
But you desire
Oh! Is a torment (Author's translation)

Elmi Boodhari verses circa 1930s:

Wax aanad haynin ood ku hammidaa hadimo weeyeene
Hohey iyo hohey maxaa hadimo la ii geystey

Something you desire but cannot have is a torment
Oh, how much I have been tormented (Author's translation)

The music and verses of the balwo and heello genres in the 1940s and 1950s did not sit well with the wadaads; the verses were licentious to them since they openly spoke about romantic desires or gave descriptions of female beauty that extended to the breasts and silhouettes of women. However, despite stiff opposition from the religious establishment, public singing and music became acceptable to everyone as the number of radios among Somalis increased. The presence of women singers also initially raised some brows among the religious community. The first women who braved initial public disapproval to play roles in Somali plays and sing in public were Khadija Abdullahi "Daaleys" in the south and Shamis Abukar "Guduudo-Carwo" in the north.

While the rudiments of the modern sung poetry such as balwo and the subsequent heello were certainly the forerunners of the modern Somali song and music, two cities have always stood out as its hearth. The first, and perhaps the older, is Hargeisa, the northern capital. There modern northern music or music with inspiration from pastoralist melodies and poetry prospered; and since the majority of Somalis could identify with it, whether they were in the south or in Kenya and other neighboring countries, it become easily the dominant music. The foremost composer of northern Somali music is without doubt the late Abdillahi Qarshe, who had much influence among the younger composers. Instrumentation in this kind of music was minimal and did not go much beyond the daf (tambourine), lute, and occasionally a violin or a flute—in short, instrumentation with traditional instruments already in use in the wider region of the Horn and Arabia. Purely northern music of this kind is the one that accompanies the balwo and heello poems set to music in the 1950s.

The other hearth of Somali music is Mogadishu in the Benadir; there a different kind of music, drawing its sources from Benadiri culture of Swahili or Bantu origins, used different instrumentation and tunes. A notable instrument was the shareero (lyre). Additionally, because the Benadiri society was more open to outside influences and more eclectic in its own ethnic composition, early modern Benadiri music adopted outside influences from Europe through the noticeable use of the piano and the electric guitar. Styles from American jazz and swing were also introduced into Benadiri music along with wind instruments such as the saxophone. Nightclubs with bands were introduced by the large Italian colonial community who enjoyed music and were much more open to the jazz and big band styles emanating from the United States in the 1920s and 1930s; in contrast, the music of the north in its beginning consisted purely of local elements, and Western influence in its composition was nonexistent. Other influences on Benadiri music would come from India through the medium of Indian films in which, like Somali plays, singing and acting scenes occur. Benadiri composers and actors were known to produce pastiches of Indian films including tunes and scenes for their own play (*riwaayad*) called in the Benadir *kunjeerto* (from Italian concerto).[5] This is the music of Benadiri composers such as Ahmed Naji, a famous playwright, composer, and singer.

However, sometime in the mid-1960s a mixture of these two kinds of music emerged from the fact that each influenced the other, although it can be said that the most noticeable change was to northern music rather than to Benadiri music. This is due in some ways to an increased instrumentation of northern productions and to a decreased number of musicians in the northern tradition in the style of Abdillahi Qarshe. Hargeisa and the north did not produce a sufficient number of musicians after the 1960s, and theatrical productions from the north had to rely sometimes entirely on Benadiri musicians to instrumentalize their productions. This was the case for most of the 1980s and later.

Most, although not all, popular songs today were composed as part of a play. Somalis love going to plays and are ready to pay high prices for a good play but they do not buy solo albums, the reason dating back to the Somali tradition of oral reciters (men and women who were able to recite poetry from memory for the enjoyment of all). No one paid to listen to a reciter; however, a strict unwritten copyright law stipulated that one must tell the audience the name of the composer and the circumstances surrounding the creation of the poem without which its meaning would be incomplete—the only exception to the rule being folksongs. Today the cassette recorder has made oral reciters obsolete and people listen to recordings of songs and poems and sometimes whole plays that are copied either at home or at stores with professional equipment. This makes it impossible for artists to become rich in monetary terms from their productions; artists, however, get respect and fame for their works just as the bards of old did for their compositions— poetry and music have been said to have been traditionally one and the same among the Somalis, and it seems that this is still true in many ways.[6]

Stars of the 1960s, still singing today.

FOLK DANCES

Somali folk dances are numerous. Some are known in one or two regions while others are widespread and might be found among all Somali groups. Probably the most widespread folk dances are the *dhaanto* and *batar*; other well-known regional dances include the graceful *gabley-shimbir* "bird's dance" and the *seyliᶜi*, named after the ancient city of Zeilah. However, the structure of all folk dances is basically the same.

The structure of dances consists of three parts: sung poetry, rhythmic clapping and beating of feet, and displays of dance steps by one or two persons. Before any dance can start, there must be a lead singer who is able to motivate the dance with his or her voice and skills in impromptu poetical compositions. Once the lead singer starts singing, the beat of the dance is established with clapping and beat of the feet—sometimes, a drum is used as an additional aide to keep the beat. A talented lead singer makes his or her compositions on the spot and entertains the crowd sometimes with a jibe at a person in the dance area or sometimes with praise directed at the young person of his or her liking. Singing at dances and composing light verse at dances serve as training grounds for young poets who, when they become older, will hopefully mature into the heavier styles of poetry. Both young

Folk dancers in traditional dress.

women and men sing and compose verse at dances. When the beat and the singing has raised the spirits of the dancers to a high point, a young dancer jumps into the arena formed by the participants and shows his or her skills in the formal steps of the particular dance. This ends a cycle of the dance but another one gets started as the lead singer intones fresh verses.

Occasions for folk dances are usually weddings or nowadays holidays such as independence day. In the countryside, among pastoralists, *gu*, the season of rains, is the time of weddings and dances. Young people of nomadic settlements also occasionally organize dances with the acquiescence of the parents; but such dances take place within sight of the parents who act as chaperons and prevent any individualized deviations either from the patterns of dance or its aftermath.

The Somali dance arena is a place of oral creativity and healthy exercise; it is also a place where young men and women become acquainted with one another with an eye to choosing a future mate. Because of that, young men and women who are relatives do not dance together in such dances. Dances are also expressions of joy and exuberance within the limits of the social mores of Somalis.

Not all folk dances are of Somali origin and there are dances that can be ethnic within the Somali context insofar as they are practiced by minority groups whose ancestors spoke a Bantu language such as Swahili, in the case of Benadiris, or some other language, in the case of the riverine Wagosha. Among these groups the folk dance steps are not as rigidly formal as those of the majority of Somalis, and the individual dancer can put more artistic expression into his or her own style of movements. Singing verses are replaced with instrumental music from percussion and string instruments; thus, unlike the Somali dance of pastoralist origins in which the focus is on the voice of the singer and his or her verses, the focus of the dance among southern groups shifts to the movements of the dancer, as happens in an identical way in a Western discotheque. People of pastoralist origins find such a shift abhorrent and a kind of culture clash has existed in the south ever since the great Somali migrations of the past.[7]

NOTES

1. John W. Johnson (1996). "Musico-moro-syllabic Relationships in the Scansion of Somali Poetry." In *Voice and Power, The Culture of Language in North-East Africa, Essay in Honour of B.W. Andrzejewski.* R.J. Hayward and I.M. Lewis, eds. London: SOAS, 77.
2. See John W. Johnson (1974). *Heellooy Heelleellooy: The Developments of the Genre Heello in Modern Somali Poetry.* Bloomington: Indiana University Press.
3. The Somali lines appear in Johnson (1974), 66.
4. The Somali lines appear in Johnson (1974), 64. They are said to have been composed by a certain Shey-Waal.
5. Hassan Sheikh Mumin (1974). *Leopard Among the Women.* Translated by B.W. Andrzejewski. London: Oxford University Press, 8.
6. Johnson (1996), 74.
7. See Francesca Declich (1995). "Identity, Dance and Islam Among People with Bantu Origins in Riverine Areas of Somalia," in Ali Jimale Ahmed, ed., *The Invention of Somalia.* Lawrenceville, N.J.: Red Sea Press, 189–221.

SUGGESTED READING

Andrzejewski, B.W., and Lewis, I.M. 1964. *Somali Poetry: An Introduction.* London: Clarendon Press.
Banti, Giorgio, and Francesco Giannattasio. 1996. "Music and Metre in Somali Poetry." In *Voice and Power, The Culture of Language in North-East Africa, Essay in Honour of B.W. Andrzejewski,* R.J. Hayward and I.M. Lewis, eds. London: SOAS, 83–128.
Declich, Francesca. 1995. "Identity, Dance and Islam Among People with Bantu

Origins in Riverine Areas of Somalia," in Ali Jimale Ahmed, ed., *The Invention of Somalia*. Lawrenceville: Red Sea Press, 189–221.

Johnson, John W. 1974. *Heellooy Heelleellooy: The Development of the Genre Heello in Modern Somali Poetry*. Bloomington: Indiana University Press.

———. 1996. "Musico-moro-syllabic Relationships in the Scansion of Somali Poetry." In *Voice and Power, The Culture of Language in North-East Africa, Essay in Honour of B.W. Andrzejewski*. R.J. Hayward and I.M. Lewis, eds. London: SOAS, 73–82.

Lewis, I.M., and M.H. Mukhtar. 1996. "Songs from the South." In *Voice and Power, The Culture of Language in North-East Africa, Essay in Honour of B.W. Andrzejewski*, R.J. Hayward and I.M. Lewis, eds. London: SOAS, 205–12.

Mumin, Hassan Sheikh. 1974. *Leopard Among the Women*. Translated by B.W. Andrzejewski. London: Oxford University Press.

Glossary

Balwo   The miniature music and song genre that was popular in the 1950s; the precursor of the heello genre. It had traditional instrumentation.

Barwaaqo   Prosperity; a season with plenty of water and grass; from bar "raindrops" and waaqo "God"

bashbash iyo barwaaqo   A traditional wish; "plenty of prosperity and splashing" (prosperity to you) from bashbash, an onomatopoeia for the sound made while splashing in water, and barwaaqo "god's raindrops."

Golis   The northern mountain chain.

Guban   The low-laying coastal northern areas; it means the "burnt" on accounts of its dryness.

Guurti   A committee of elected elders. A parliament.

Haud   Plateau country of mostly flat terrain of open or wooded spaces.

Heello   A music and song genre that succeeded the balwo genre and characterized by the music of Abdillahi Qarshe.

Punt   The name ancient Egyptians gave to the northern Somali coasts.

Qadi   A judge who hears usually only cases of family or civil law among Somalis.

Samale   A mythical ancestor held by some Somalis as the "father of Somalis."

Tog   A dry rivulet with a strong current when it rains.

Waaq   God in the old Cushitic religion.

Wadaad   A Somali priest and ritual leader, clergy as opposed to lay person.

Waranle   A warrior, spearman; lay person as opposed to clergy; secular as opposed to religious.

Selected Bibliography

Adan, Alawi Ali. 1992. "General Review of Somali Arabic Literature." In Hussein M. Adam and Charles L. Geshekter, eds., *Proceedings of the First International Congress of Somali Studies* [Held in 1980]. Atlanta, Ga.: Scholars Press, pp. 299–314.

Aden, Amina H. 1989. "Somalia: Women and Words." *Ufahamu* 10, no. 3:115–42.

Afrah, Mohamed D. 1993/94. "A Nation of Poets or Art-loving People? The Role of Literature in the Present-day Somali." *Hal-Abuur* 2, no. 2 & 3: pp. 32–37.

Afrah, Mohamed Dahir. 1981. *Maana faay.* (A Somali Language Novel) Mogadishu.

Africa Watch. 1990. *Somalia: A Government at War with Its Own People.* New York: Africa Watch.

Ahmed, Christine Choi. 1995. "Finely Etched Chattel: The Invention of a Somali Woman." In Ali Ahmed Jimale, ed., *The Invention of Somalia.* Lawrenceville, N.J. Red Sea Press, pp. 155–189.

Alpers, Edward. 1992. "Toward a History of Nineteenth Century Mogadishu: A Report of Research in Progress." In Hussein M. Adam and Charles L. Geshekter, eds., *Proceedings of the First International Congress of Somali Studies* [Held in 1980]. Atlanta, Ga.: Scholars Press, pp. 125–44.

Andrzejewski, B.W. 1971. "The Role of Broadcasting in the Adaptation of the Somali Language to Modern Needs." In W.H. Whiteley, ed., *Language Use and Social Change: Problems of Multilingualism with Special Reference to Eastern Africa.* London: Oxford University Press for International African Institute, pp. 263–73.

Andrzejewski B.W., and Sheila Andrzejewski. 1993. *An Anthology of Somali Poetry.* Bloomington: Indiana University Press.

Andrzejewski B.W., and Musa H.I. Galaal. 1963. "A Somali Poetic Combat." *Journal of African Languages and Linguistics* 2, pt. 1 (pp. 15–28), pt. 2 (pp. 93–100), pt. 3 (pp. 190–205). East Lansing: Michigan State University, African Studies Center.

Andrzejewski, B.W., and I.M. Lewis. 1964. *Somali Poetry: An Introduction.* London: Clarendon Press.

Banti, Giorgio, and Francesco Giannattasio. 1996. "Music and Metre in Somali Poetry." In R.J. Hayward and I.M. Lewis, eds. *Voice and Power, The Culture of Language in North-East Africa, Essay in Honour of B.W. Andrzejewski.* London: SOAS, pp. 83–128.

Basset, M. R., trans. 1897. *Histoire de la conquête de l'Abyssinie (XVI siècle) par Chihab Eddin Ahmad Ben 'Abd El Oader.* Paris: Ernest Leroux.

Burton, Richard. 1987 [1856] *First Footsteps in East Africa.* New York: Dover Publications.

Campbell, Colin. 1988. "Libya, Mercenaries Aiding U.S.-Supported Somalia." *Atlanta Journal Constitution,* October 6.

Carroll, Anthony J., and B. Rajagopal. 1993. "The Case for the Independent Statehood of Somaliland." *Journal of International Law and Politics* 8:653.

Cassanelli, Lee V. 1975. "Migrations, Islam, and Politics in the Somali Benaadir, 1500–1843." In Harold Marcus, ed. *Proceedings of the First United States Conference on Ethiopian Studies, 1973.* East Lansing: Michigan State University African Studies Center, pp. 101–15.

———. 1982. *The Shaping of Somali Society: Reconstructing the History of a Pastoral People, 1600–1900.* Philadelphia: Pennsylvania University Press.

Casson, Lionel. 1989. *The Periplus Maris Erythraie.* Princeton: Princeton University Press.

Castagno, Margaret. 1975. *Historical Dictionary of Somalia.* Metuchen, N.J.: Scarecrow Press.

Declich, Francesca. 1994. "Multiple Oral Traditions and Ethno-historical Issues Among the Gosha—Three Examples." In Mohamed Mohamed Abdi, ed., *Anthropologie somalienne.* Paris: Annales Littéraires de l'Université de Bescançon, pp. 87–100.

———. 1995. "Identity, Dance and Islam Among People with Bantu Origins in Riverine Areas of Somalia." In Ali Jimale Ahmed, ed., *The Invention of Somalia.* Lawrenceville, N.J.: Red Sea Press, 1995, pp. 189–221.

Dinesen, Isak [Karen Blixen]. 1954. *Out of Africa.* London: Penguin Books.

Diriye Abdullahi, Mohamed 1995. *Fiasco in Somalia: US-UN Intervention.* Occasional paper no. 61. Pretoria: Africa Institute of South Africa.

———. 1996. *Parlons somali.* Paris: L'Harmattan.

Faarax, M.J. Cawl. 1974. *Aqoondarro Waa U Nacab Jacayl.* Mogadishu: Akademiyada Dhaqanka iyo Hidaha.

Freeman-Grenville, G.S.P. 1962. *The East African Coast: Select Documents from the First to the Earlier Nineteenth Century.* Oxford: Clarendon Press.

Galaal, Muuse Haaji Ismaa'iil. 1956. *Hikmad Soomaali.* London: Oxford University Press.

Galaydh, Ali K. 1990. "Notes on the State of the Somali State." *Horn of Africa Journal* 12, no. 1 & 2: 1–28.

Ghalib, Jama M. 1994. *The Cost of Dictatorship: The Somali Experience.* New York: Lilian Barber Press.

Greenfield, Richard. 1991. "Said's Sad Legacy." *Africa Report,* March–April.

Guleed, Abdillahi Derie. "Notes on Somali Poetics." In Hussein M. Adam and Charles L. Geshekter, eds., *Proceedings of the First International Congress of Somali Studies* [Held in 1980]. Atlanta, Ga.: Scholars Press, pp. 346–61.

Hersi, A. 1977. "The Arab Factor in Somali History." Doctoral dissertation, University of Los Angeles.

Huntingford, G.W.B. 1955. *The Galla of Ethiopia.* London: International African Institute.

IMF (International Monetary Fund). *Somalia: Recent Economic Developments,* April 4, 1984 (SM/84/72).

Jimale, Ali Ahmed, ed. 1995. *The Invention of Somalia.* Lawrenceville, N.J.: Red Sea Press.

Johnson, John W. 1974. *Heellooy Heelleellooy; The Development of the Genre Heello in Modern Somali Poetry.* Bloomington: Indiana University Press.

———. 1992. "The Influence of Radio Hargeisa on Modern Somali Oral Poetry." In Hussein M. Adam and Charles L. Geshekter, eds. *Proceedings of the First International Congress of Somali Studies* [Held in 1980]. Atlanta, Ga.: Scholars Press, pp. 324–32.

———. 1996. "Musico-moro-syllabic Relationships in the Scansion of Somali Oral Poetry." In R.J. Hayward and I.M. Lewis, eds. *Voice and Power: The Culture of Language in North-East Africa—Essays in Honour of B.W. Andrzejewski,* London: SOAS (African languages and cultures, suppl. 3), pp. 73–82.

Kapteijns, Lidwien. 1991. "Women and the Somali Pastoral Tradition: The Corporate Kinship and Capitalist Transformation in Northern Somali." *Working Papers in African Studies No. 153.* Boston: African Studies Center.

———. 1995. "Gender Relations and the Transformation of the Northern Somali Pastoral Tradition." *International Journal of African Historical Studies* 28: 241–59.

Laitin, David D. 1977. *Politics, Language and Thought: The Somali Experience.* Chicago: University of Chicago Press.

Laurence, Margaret. 1954. *A Tree for Poverty: Somali Poetry and Prose.* Hamilton, Ont.: McMaster University Library Press and ECW Press.

Lewis, Herbert S. 1966. "The Origins of the Galla and Somali." *Journal of African History* 7, no. 1: 27–46.

Lewis, I.M. 1955. *The Peoples of the Horn of Africa: Somali, Afar and Saho.* London: International African Institute.

———. 1955–56. "Sufism in Somaliland: A Study in Tribal Islam." *Bulletin of the School of Oriental and African Studies* 17: 581–602; 18: 146–60.

———. 1960. "The Somali Conquest of the Horn of Africa." *Journal of African History* 1, no. 2:213–29.

———. 1961. *Pastoral Democracy: A Study of Pastoralism Among the Northern Somali of the Horn of Africa.* London: Oxford University Press.

———. 1966. "Conformity and Contrast in Somali Islam." In I.M. Lewis, ed. *Islam in Tropical Africa.* London: Oxford University Press, pp. 253–67.

———. 1969. "Spirit Possession in Northern Somaliland." In J. Beatrie and J. Middleton, eds. *Spirit Mediumship and Society in Africa.* London: Routledge, pp. 188–220.

———. 1990. "The Ogaden and the Fragility of Somali Segmented Nationalism." *Horn of Africa* 13, nos. 1 & 2 (January-March, and April-June).

———. 1994. *Blood and Bone: The Call of Kinship in Somali Society.* Lawrenceville, N.J.: Red Sea Press.

Lewis, I.M., and M.H. Mukhtar. 1996. "Songs from the South." In *Voice and Power, The Culture of Language in North-East Africa, Essay in Honour of B.W. Andrzejewski.* R.J. Hayward and I.M. Lewis, eds. London: SOAS, pp. 205–12.

Loughran, John, Katheryne Loughran, John Johnson, and Said S. Samatar, eds. 1986. *Somalia in Word and Image.* Washington, D.C.: Foundation for Cross-Cultural Understanding.

Mumin, Hassan Sheikh. 1974. *Leopard Among the Women: Shabeel Naagood, Somali Play.* Translated by B.W. Andrzejewski. London: School of Oriental and African Studies, Oxford University Press.

Nurse, Derek. 1992. "Shungwaya and the Bantu of Somalia: Some Linguistic Evidence." In Hussein M. Adam and Charles L. Geshekter, eds. *Proceedings of the First International Congress of Somali Studies* [Held in 1980]. Atlanta: Scholars Press, pp. 54–61.

Patwardhan, Dileef. 1981. "Imperialism by Proxy: Aden and Somaliland." *Indica* 18, no. 2: 105–20.

Prunier, G. 1992. "A Candid View of the Somali National Movement." *Horn of Africa* 13 & 14, nos. 3 & 4 and 1 & 2: 107–20.

Samatar, Said S. 1982. *Oral Poetry and Somali Nationalism.* Cambridge: Cambridge University Press.

———. 1992. "Sheikh Uways Maxamad of Baraawe (1847–1909): Mystic and Reformer in East Africa." In Hussein M. Adam and Charles L. Geshekter, eds., *Proceedings of the First International Congress of Somali Studies.* Atlanta: Scholars Press.

Samatar, Said S., and David Laitin. 1987. *Somalia: A Nation in Search of a State.* Boulder, Colo.: Westview Press.

Shabeelle, Rashiid Maxamed. 1975. *Ma Dhab Baa Jacayl Waa Loo Dhintaa?* (Is it true that people die of love?). Mogadishu: Wakaalada Madbacada Qaranka.

Swayne, H.G.C. 1895. *Seventeen Trips through Somaliland.* London: Rowland Ward, Ltd.

Touval, S. 1963. *Somali Nationalism.* Cambridge, Mass.: Harvard University Press.

Turton, E.R. 1975. "Bantu, Galla and Somali Migrations in the Horn of Africa: A Reassessment of the Jubba/Tana Area." *Journal of African History* 16:519–37.

Whiteway, R.W., trans. and ed. 1902. *The Portuguese Expedition to Abyssinia in 1541–1543 as Narrated by Castanhaso with Some Contemporary Letters; the Short Account of Bermudes, and Certain Extracts from Correa.* London: Hakluyt Society.

Index

Guulwadayaal, 32
Guurti, 139–142

Hadrawi (Mohamed Ibrahim), 83, 84, 86
Hamitic, 11
Harar, 19
Hargeisa: architecture, 105–107; butcher of, 43; destruction, 165; festival, 63; music, 174, 175; newspapers, 91; radio, 89; repression, 36; SNM capture, 37; weather, 5
Hassan. *See* Mohamed Abdulle Hassan
Hatshepsut, 7, 14
Haud, 1–3, 6, 26
Hawiye (clan confederation) 8, 28, 35, 38–40
Heedho, 97, 146–148
Heello, 171–174
Heer (traditional law), 125, 139–142
Heerbeegti, 142
Herodotus, 7, 14
Highlanders, 16, 22
Hijab, 118
Hintire (clan), 23
Homogeneity, 7, 36
Horses, 80
Horus, 15
Howe, Admiral Jonathan, 44–46
Hunter-gatherers, 10, 11
Hunting, 11, 111
Huseen Aw-Farah, 89

Ifat, 16
Incense, 7, 64, 68, 98, 99, 155
Independence: holidays, 163, 164, 177; movements, 25, 172; Somaliland, 26
Indonesia, 118, 155
Infibulation, 134
Inheritances, 59
Instrument, musical, 96, 169, 170, 174, 175, 178
Interriverine region, 40, 42, 156
Intervention (international), 43, 47

Invasions (Galla), 17
Irredentism, 26
Isaaq (clan confederation), 8, 35, 36, 38, 64
Ishaaq (Sheikh), 64
Isis, 66
Islam: arrival, 8, 13; art, 96, 102; existence with para-religion, 66; expansion by Somalis, 15; Kenya, 22; law, 132, 142; meaning and principles, 55–58; orthodox, 62; revivialism, 118; saints, 63, 64
Ismail Ahmed (Hadhuudh), 89
Ismail Ali Abokar, 29, 35
Ismail Jabarti, 64
Issa (clan), 40, 101
Italy: colonial agriculture, 157, 161; establishment of the colony, 23–24; forced labor, 157; governance methods, 140; influences from, 102, 106, 109, 110, 112, 114, 116, 175; support for the Barre regime, 38

Jazz, 175
Jiilaal, 3–5, 77, 78
Juba, 3, 5, 6, 10, 40, 68, 85, 158
Jubaland, 24
Judaism, 56, 134
Jurisprudence, 55, 57, 58
Justice, 30, 47, 59, 80, 81, 85, 114

Kenya: Bajunis in, 11; Bantu groups, 13; involvement in Somali affairs, 41, 47; Somali businesses, 138; Somali migrations, 15–16, 18, 22, 26, 123
Khaawe (Captain), 29
Khadija Abdullahi (Laaleys), 88, 174
Khedive (of Egypt), 18
Kingdom: Amhara-Tigrean, 17–19; Buganda, 139; Shungwaya, 10
Kismayu, 3, 11, 44
Koran: amulets, 60; lecterns, 97;

About the Author

MOHAMED DIRIYE ABDULLAHI, formerly a journalist in Somalia, is now an independent language consultant and translator in Montreal. He specializes in the language, cultures, and history of the peoples of the Horn of Africa. He has previously published *Parlons Somali*, a book on the Somali language and culture.